PAKISTAN
NATIONAL HUMAN
DEVELOPMENT
REPORT 2003

POVERTY, GROWTH AND GOVERNANCE

Akmal Hussain
With inputs from
A.R. Kemal, A.I. Hamid, Imran Ali, Khawar Mumtaz, Ayub Qutub

UNDP
Pakistan

© United Nations Development Programme 2003

All rights reserved. No part of this publication may be reproduced,
stored in a retrieval system, or transmitted, in any form or by any means,
electronic, mechanical, photocopying, recording or otherwise,
without the prior permission of UNDP.

ISBN 969 8736 00X

The analysis and policy recommendations of the Report do not necessarily reflect the views of the United Nations Development Programme, its Executive Board or its Member States. The Report is an independent publication commissioned by UNDP and authored by
Dr Akmal Hussain who deserves all the moral rights to this publication.

Typeset in Times
Printed in Pakistan by
New Sketch Graphics, Karachi.
Produced by
Oxford University Press
Plot No. 38, Sector 15, Korangi Industrial Area,
Karachi-74900, Pakistan.

Foreword

The National Human Development Report (NHDR) for Pakistan argues that poverty can only be overcome through the empowerment of the poor, especially poor women. The Report recommends a multi-dimensional strategy for poverty alleviation, including alternative economic growth strategies and governance reforms. The Report highlights the need for an integrated, national strategy of public policy and action.

The NHDR presents the first application of the Human Development Index (HDI) at the provincial and district levels. The HDI is a composite of living standard, longevity and education variables, and provides a baseline against which to measure the future trend in poverty, in Pakistan. This may be complemented by the baseline of social audits under way that additionally include subjective variables, including levels of citizen satisfaction, on devolution, health, education, police, justice, and water.

The Report recommends the formation of autonomous organizations of the poor, and further maintains that empowerment of the poor requires establishing institutional links between autonomous organizations of the poor and various tiers of local government. In this connection, the Report can be discussed in the context of the Local Government Ordinance 2001 that provides for the organization of independent Citizen's Community Boards equipped to access local council development funds for their community development projects to monitor the services that are essential for the poor. This concept has the potential to bring a breakthrough on autonomous organization for the poor, participatory development, state-citizen relations at the local level, and community empowerment.

I wish to congratulate the Principal Author for two years of hard work with great dedication. It is hoped that the first National Human Development Report will contribute in a constructive fashion to the ongoing public discourse on the reduction of poverty and the advancement of the Millennium Development Goals which Pakistan has endorsed.

Islamabad in March 2003

Onder Yucer
UN Resident Coordinator
UNDP Resident Representative

Acknowledgements

The poor in Pakistan in their songs and dances, as much as in the cadences of their speech celebrate their tradition that synthesizes Love and Reason. They affirm their humanity by giving of themselves to their families and friends: 'Burn the blood of your heart for your friends', runs a Sufi song. It is in this spirit that I undertook a two-year labour of love in writing this report.

To start with thanks are due to Mr Onder Yucer who set me off on this long and often painful journey. His trust and affection inspired me to give of myself for the research and writing of this report.

Special thanks are due to Dr Hafiz Pasha for his incisive comments and invaluable suggestions on my preliminary analysis of the survey data. His encouragement at a critical moment in the NHDR work were a great source of strength. Thanks are also due to him and his staff at UNDP Headquarters for their helpful comments on the first draft.

A profound debt of gratitude is owed to Mr Omar Noman whose diligent reading of the first draft and detailed suggestions were invaluable in improving the quality of the final version of the report. Thanks are due to Dr Socorro L. Reyes for her comments and written input which led to a more detailed analysis and policy suggestions on the gender issue in the final version of the report. I must also thank Ms Lena Lindberg, Dr Inayatullah, Mr Naeem Ahmad and the other staff members of the UNDP in Islamabad for their encouragement and comments on an earlier draft.

I am grateful to Dr A.R. Kemal and his team for the NHDR/PIDE Survey on the basis of which I was able to present the analysis in chapter 3. Thanks are also due to Mr A.I. Hamid for doing the Impact Assessment Spot Survey on the basis of which I was able to write sections II, III and IV of chapter 4. I am grateful to Professor Imran Ali for his analysis of the Pakistan area in the eighteenth and nineteenth centuries which is embodied in two boxes at the end of chapter 2 of the report. I am grateful to Ms Khawar Mumtaz for her paper on the gender perspective which was helpful for me in bringing the women's dimension as a vital element in the policy section III of chapter 5 of the report. Thanks are also due to Mr Ayub Qutub for his work on the environment which enabled me to write two paragraphs in sub-section V.11 at the end of chapter 5.

I would also like to thank Mr Umar Zafar (who gave of his time voluntarily) and Mr Wasay Majid for their assistance in estimating Human Development Indices. Particular thanks are due to Syed Khalid Ali who gave of his time and energy on a voluntary basis to help compile newspaper based reports on suicides.

Thanks are also due to Mr Muhammad Azeem for his indefatigable efforts in typing out successive drafts of each chapter. I am grateful to Mr Ijaz Ali Qureshi for the long hours of voluntary labour and imagination that he deployed in developing the formatting design of the report. Thanks are due to Savail Hussain for his helpful suggestions before the start of the research and for reading through the final version. I shall always remember with gratefulness, the commitment and hard work of the staff of Sayyed Engineers who kept the company running and thereby allowed me to take time off for two years, to research and write this report.

Finally thanks are due to my wife Rafia and the children, Savail, Jalal and Abbas for their patience, love and understanding.

Akmal Hussain

Contents

FOREWORD   iii

ACKNOWLEDGEMENTS   iv

OVERVIEW   vii

INTRODUCTION   xv

CHAPTER 1
The Multifaceted Crisis of Economy and Society   **1**
The Financial Crisis   3
The Economic Crisis   5
The Crisis of the Human Condition   10
Conclusions   32

CHAPTER 2
Economic Policy, Economic Structure and Poverty   **35**
Introduction   37
The Ayub Regime 1958-69: Economic Growth, Inequality and the Roots of Financial
   Dependence   37
The Bhutto Regime 1973-77: Investment, Growth and the Budget Deficit   41
The Zia Regime 1977-89: Economic Growth and the Prelude to Recession   43
The Deepening Crisis 1989-99: Economic Growth, Employment and Poverty
   in the Decade of the 1990s   45
Conclusions   47

CHAPTER 3
The Structure of Poverty and the Process of Poverty Generation   **51**
Introduction: A Conceptual and Empirical Perspective on Poverty   53
Poverty and Modes of Financing Consumption   54
Poverty Alleviation and Number of Earners in the Household   57
Local Power Structures, Markets and Poverty   60
Disputes and the Economic Cost of Seeking Resolution   68
Poverty and Illness   69
Micro-Enterprises and Poverty Alleviation   71
Credit for the Poor: Where Does It Come From, Where Does It Go?   72
Conclusions   75

CHAPTER 4
Poverty Alleviation through NGOs   **81**
Types of NGOs and the Participatory Development Approach   83
Selected Issues in Micro-Credit   85
Profiles of Participatory NGOs   89
Comparative Impact Assessment of NGOs   92
Strategic Issues of Up-scaling   94
Enabling Apex Structure for Poverty Alleviation with NGOs   98
Conclusions   100

CHAPTER 5
A Strategy of Economic Growth and Empowering the Poor   103
Introduction   105
Structural Factors in Slow Growth and Rising Poverty   105
Restructuring Growth for Faster Poverty Reduction   107
Direct Attack on Poverty   111
The Government's Policy Measures   116
Summary Policy Proposals   122
Conclusions   125

REFERENCES   129

ANNEXURES
Chapter 1   131
Chapter 2   149
Chapter 3   155
Chapter 5   177

Overview

I. THE SCOPE AND PRIMARY PROPOSITIONS

1. Pakistan is at a conjunctural moment in its history as it confronts a multifaceted crisis of the human condition. At the end of the decade of the 1990s the government faced financial bankruptcy, the real economy was in deep recession, poverty had reached alarming levels and the institutions of governance had eroded to a critical point. The National Human Development Report shows how each of these facets is dynamically interlinked, to suggest that an integrated and comprehensive strategy of public action needs to be pursued to overcome the crisis.

2. The Report traces the emergence of an economic structure characterized by a tendency for increasing loan dependence, slow GDP growth and growing poverty. This is done through a historical analysis of the pattern of economic growth, fiscal deficits and the process of poverty creation in the context of the economic policy of various regimes.

The patron-client model of governance practiced first during the British Raj and later in independent Pakistan involved winning political support through the transfer of state resources in the form of rents to a dependent economic elite. In a situation where government resources after independence were quite limited, such a form of governance may have been an important factor in growing fiscal deficits, restricting the international competitiveness of manufacturing industry and increasing poverty. Thus the failure to establish and deepen democracy in the past may have been a factor in deepening poverty.

3. The Report for the first time presents estimates of Human Development Indices (HDI) at the district and provincial levels in Pakistan. The variations in HDI between provinces and districts are indicative of regional disparities in both the level of economic growth as well as in terms of health, education and quality of life.

4. The Report locates the problem of poverty in Pakistan in the practice of governance on the one hand and the structure of the economy on the other. In this context the Report proposes that at one level the challenge of overcoming poverty is to change the structure of the economy so as to achieve both a higher economic growth as well as an enhanced capacity of GDP growth for poverty reduction. At another level the challenge is better governance such that the poor particularly poor women, are empowered to actualize their potential for a sustainable increase in incomes and a greater voice in various tiers of government.

5. The Report represents a paradigmatic change in the understanding of poverty and policies for overcoming it. The poor in Pakistan cannot simply be seen as free individuals with certain adverse 'resource endowments' making choices in more or less 'free markets'. By contrast we argue that poverty occurs when the individual household in a fragmented community is locked into a nexus of power that systematically perpetuates poverty. The Report for the first time shows how the poor face markets, state institutions and local structures of power that discriminate against the poor and deprive them of a large proportion of their actual and potential incomes. Therefore overcoming poverty is not simply a question of allocating more public funds, nor of addressing their vulnerability through 'risk management' or providing micro credit in a fragmented way, nor even of correcting 'market distortions' associated with macroeconomic policy. Overcoming poverty means empowering the poor to acquire greater control over their *use* of productive resources including their own labour, and keeping their incomes and savings in their own hands. It means enabling the poor to get organized and have institutionalized access over local

government, and participation in decisions regarding the allocation of government resources at the local level, and the design and implementation of local government projects for the poor. Overcoming poverty means shifting the location of the poor in the local power structures from being victims to active subjects in achieving equitable access over markets, and over institutions providing credit, health and education services.

6. Most studies on poverty in Pakistan have examined the problem simply in terms of measuring the number of people below certain poverty lines. However if poverty is to be overcome what is required is to understand the processes of poverty creation and to identify the points of intervention in the poverty process through which the poor can be enabled to overcome poverty on a sustainable basis. In the pursuit of this objective the NHDR study for the first time undertook to establish a new data set to be able to conduct an analysis of the processes through which poverty is perpetuated and the possible routes out of it.

Our survey data suggests that not only is there a high prevalence of disease amongst the poor but also that disease is a major trigger that pushes households into poverty. The survey data also show that one of the key factors which determines the ability of a poor household to pull out of poverty is whether or not the family has a second earner and the level of her/his education.

7. The NHDR quantitative data set is new simply because the underlying questions have not been asked before. Some of the questions raised are: How do distorted markets for inputs and outputs of goods and services result in the loss of the actual or potential income of the poor? If this is indeed the case then what is the magnitude of the income loss? How do local structures of power with respect to landlords, local administrative officials, and institutions for the provision of health, credit and dispute resolution deprive the poor of their income, assets and the fruits of their labour?

8. In exploring a strategy for overcoming poverty the issue of the NGO sector as a form of public action for community based poverty alleviation initiatives was examined. The question investigated was whether these alternative institutional forms of public action for overcoming poverty, can achieve sufficient coverage of the poor population and cost effectiveness, for a significant impact on the overall poverty problem in the country. In addressing this question the Report examines the institutional dynamics and management issues involved in achieving rapid coverage and efficacy of NGOs. A small sample spot survey was also conducted to investigate the impact of various types of NGOs on their beneficiaries with respect to nutrition, health and sustainable income increases.

9. On the basis of an analysis of the processes of poverty and the structure of the national economy, the Report articulates the outline of a three dimensional strategy for overcoming poverty: (i) The first dimension would consist of a major development programme that can provide health, education and basic services to the people together with employment opportunities. (ii) The second dimension indicates an economic growth strategy that can achieve both faster growth and an enhanced capacity of GDP growth to reduce poverty. It would consist of providing institutional support to small scale export based industries in the manufacturing sector, high value added export products such as milk, marine fisheries, fruits and vegetables in the agriculture sector, and software exports in the services sector. (iii) The third dimension presents the approach for a direct attack on poverty through participatory development at the local level. This is a process of building autonomous community based organizations through which the poor participate at the village/mohallah level to build their human, natural and economic resource base for breaking out of the poverty nexus. It specifically aims at achieving a localized capital accumulation process. This is based on the progressive development of group identity, skill development, local resource generation, increased productivity, incomes, savings and investment.

The Report examines the challenge and opportunity of local government institutions and the pitfalls of implementing decentralization reforms. It is proposed that formal decentralization of administrative functions does not necessarily help the poor. Empowerment of the poor in this context requires establishing institutionalized links between autonomous organizations of the poor and various tiers of local government.

II. CHAPTER OUTLINES

Chapter 1: This chapter gives a brief snap shot picture of the multifaceted crisis of finance, economy and society. There has been an unprecedented increase in the number of people in poverty and unemployment during the 1990s. The acuteness of the economic condition of the poor households is reinforced by extremely inadequate coverage and quality of basic services such as primary education and health, particularly for women. We have indicated some of the structural features in both the fiscal crisis as well as the crisis in the real economy. Unless these structural and institutional problems are addressed, growth is likely to remain slow and unstable, leading to still greater poverty in the future.

The impact of the crisis of poverty is particularly acute on the most vulnerable sections of society: Women and children. The suffering of women is intensified as they face social discrimination, gender inequality in the access over basic services, employment and income. The data presented in this chapter show that a disturbing proportion of poor children face mal nutrition and consequently increased susceptibility to disease. At the same time growing numbers of them instead of going to school are going to work in hazardous occupations where they are subjected to increased risk of disease and physical injury due to the work environment.

Poor households faced with hunger, frequent illness and seeing their children being physically and mentally mutilated, are confronted with the added distress of violence, kidnapping and theft due to the poor law and order situation.

It is clear therefore that in facing this multifaceted crisis of the human condition, the inter related dimensions of the economy, institutions and governance would have to be simultaneously addressed in an integrated national strategy of public action.

Chapter 2: This chapter presents a dynamic picture of the multifaceted crisis through a historical analysis of economy, society and State over the last four decades. The analysis examines the interplay between economic policy, the changing structure of the economy, and the poverty process. These processes accelerated during the 1990s and began to be manifested in terms of acute poverty, sharp slow down in the GDP growth, unsustainable fiscal deficits and intense pressures on governance.

The analysis shows how during the Ayub regime the mechanisms of rural poverty observable today, were rooted in the increased peasant dependence on the landlord and asymmetric markets for inputs and outputs that resulted from a particular structure of agricultural growth. The analysis also shows how the tendency for the economy's loan dependence so manifest today, may have originated in the economic policies adopted during this period. The government by providing State subsidies locked the economy into an industrial structure which was dominated by low value added industries incapable of generating foreign exchange for the country.

The structural constraints to fiscal space were exacerbated as successive governments engaged in financial profligacy, and allocating State resources based on considerations of political patronage rather than economic efficiency. Nationalization of industries and the growing losses of nationalized units laid the basis of subsequent fiscal haemorrhaging of the government. During the Zia regime, State funds were directed to attempting the establishment of a theocracy instead of urgently needed investment in economic infrastructure, and provision of health and education. Consequently when the cushion of foreign financial assistance was withdrawn after the Afghan war, investment and growth declined, budget deficits increased sharply and poverty intensified.

The decade of the 1990s was marked by a rapid deterioration in the institutions of governance and a worsening law and order situation. This resulted in an adverse environment for private sector investment and a lower level, and reduced efficiency of, public sector expenditure. Consequently during the decade of the 1990s the structure of GDP growth underwent further adverse changes as both capital and labour productivity fell sharply together with declining employment elasticities. A reduction in capital productivity led to slower growth, while reduction in labour productivity led to falling real wages. As both GDP growth and real wages fell, poverty tended to increase. This tendency was reinforced by declining employment elasticities. Thus deteriorating institutions of governance and associated adverse changes in the structure of the economy in this period laid the basis for a rapid increase in poverty and unemployment.

Chapter 3: In this chapter we have examined essentially three questions on the basis of our survey data: (i) Who are the poor? (ii) What pushes them into poverty? and (iii) What are the mechanisms which keep them poor? For the first time the processes of poverty generation are analyzed on the basis of quantitative data. The analysis shows how asymmetric access of the poor to local markets and the functioning of local power structures deprives the poor of a large proportion of their actual and potential income. We have also identified some of the major economic and social features of the poor population. This is with respect to the sources of income of the poor, the sources of their loans and level of indebtedness, their major occupations, their health status, the types and costs of health facilities they use and finally the types of disputes they face and the costs of resolution. Some of the major conclusions that emerge from our empirical analysis are as follows:

(i) Poverty and Modes of Financing Consumption: The total annual household income of the extremely poor is substantially less than the minimum food consumption requirement. Consequently they are obliged to borrow money for food consumption. Since availability of loans to the poor is extremely limited they suffer from acute nutritional deficiencies. Various forms of charity and remittances provide a significant source for financing consumption requirements of poor households with private sector charity being three times as large as that of the public sector.

(ii) Moving into and Out of Poverty: The data show that the income level of the second earner of a poor household is the key determinant of the probability of moving out or falling into deeper poverty. A predominant proportion of major earners in poor households are unskilled workers engaged in low productivity and low income occupations.

(iii) Local Power Structures and the Poverty Process:

- Due to the landlords power the extremely poor tenant farmers are obliged to pay as crop share a larger proportion of their farm produce compared to non poor tenant farmers. Consequently the extremely poor tenant households are likely to run out of their household stock of food grain and are obliged to purchase grain in the market at the end of the production cycle when market prices are high. Such households have to borrow for food consumption or face starvation.

- Given their food budget deficit many poor tenants are obliged to supplement their incomes by working part-time on the landlord's owner cultivated piece of the landholding. Given their superior power position, the landlords are able to pay a lower than market wage rate to their dependent tenants. (The wage rates of the poor are almost half the wage rates at which the non poor work for the same job).

- Due to inadequate access of the poor over institutionalized credit the extremely poor households borrow from the landlords. The resultant increase in leverage of the landlord, obliges many poor households to work for the landlord without any wage at all (57.4 per cent of extremely poor households worked for the landlord without wages).

- The tenancy arrangements of the poor during the last decade have worsened. Since the majority of the extremely poor are tenants (52.5 per cent), any deterioration in tenancy arrangements would therefore increase poverty.

(iv) Income Loss Resulting from Unequal Access over Input Markets: As many as 28.2 per cent of the extremely poor peasants have to buy their inputs from the landlord. The data show that on average the poor have to pay 11.8 per cent more than the actual amount which they would have to pay in case

these inputs were procured from least cost sources.

(v) *Income Loss Resulting from Unequal Access over Output Markets:* An overwhelming proportion of output sold by the poor farmers in the case of rice, cotton and wheat, is sold to traders and landlords who constitute an important element in the local power structure in many areas.

If the income loss resulting from market distortions in the input and output markets are taken into account together with regular monthly/annual bribe payments to local administration officials, then the total income loss is as much as one-third of the household income of the poor peasant.

(vi) *Poverty and Illness:* Frequency of illness and often its protracted nature with resultant high cost of treatment, is an important factor pushing marginal households into poverty and poor households into deeper poverty. On average 62 per cent of the poor in our sample were ill at the time of the survey. These findings are supported by the National Health Survey of Pakistan data, which show that amongst low income persons of 45 years and above, 45 per cent suffer from poor health, and 80 per cent suffer from poor to fair health. Our data also show that most of the ill respondents have been suffering for a protracted period. As many as 54 per cent go to private medical practitioners, 49.4 per cent travel on average more than six kilometers for their medical consultation. The average medical cost on the current illness was as much as Rs.1,885.

(vii) *Disputes and Poverty:* 48.7 per cent of reported disputes occur in poor households with the average cost of mediation being Rs.18,333 which is higher than the average annual household income of the extremely poor. Yet inspite of bearing this crippling burden (usually financed by borrowing money or selling livestock) the percentage of successful resolution of disputes is only 38.5 per cent.

Chapter 4: In this chapter we have examined the issue of NGOs emerging as an institutional basis, (alongside the government), for contributing to poverty alleviation. The total coverage of NGOs currently, is relatively insignificant compared to the magnitude of the poor population. The NHDR/PIDE 2001 survey for example shows that of the total loans received by all categories of the sample population, the percentage of loans received from NGOs was only 0.8 per cent in the rural areas and 1 per cent in the urban areas.

We have examined the issue of the increase in coverage of NGOs and the effectiveness of their impact on the poor. This was done in the context of examining different types of NGOs, the comparative effectiveness of their impact on the poor, and key organizational and management issues involved in up scaling. We also identified the elements of an enabling institutional structure at the national level, which could accelerate the growth and enhance the effectiveness of NGOs.

The NHDR Spot Survey showed that there was considerable variation with respect to the effectiveness of targeting of the poor between various NGOs. There was also considerable variation with respect to the impact of NGO intervention on incomes, nutrition and health of the poor. This has implications for organizational forms and work procedures.

Under the devolution programme a new structure of local governments at the district level is emerging, within which elected representatives will be expected to undertake (amongst other functions) poverty alleviation at different tiers of local government (district, tehsil, union council and village levels). Within this structure NGOs that enable the formation of autonomous organizations of the poor could play an important role in creating a systematic relationship between local governance and poor communities. Such a relationship would enable the poor to participate in identification and implementation of development projects as well as decisions related with access over markets and local power structures. It could also help broaden the social base of power, authority and the allocation and use of public resources.

If NGOs are to play this role they would need to function at the district level rather than across districts. This would be necessary if only to prevent centralized trans district and un-elected organizations to impinge upon an elected decentralized system. Equally important, the emphasis perhaps may need to shift from building centralized NGOs in a large number of districts with low intensity of coverage (and high overheads) in each, towards district specific NGOs which achieve full coverage of the poor population in the villages, union councils and tehsils of that district. The question therefore becomes how small NGOs operating at the village or union council level can grow rapidly and cost effectively to achieve full coverage of the poor population of that district. A related issue is how can organizations of the poor be enabled to become genuinely autonomous on the one hand and link up with local governments on the other. We have discussed some of the organizational and management issues that would need to be addressed in this context.

Chapter 5: In this chapter we have presented an outline of an economic strategy to achieve growth with greater poverty alleviation. It has two broad thrusts: (1) A restructured economic growth process that would not only enable a faster GDP growth but enhanced poverty alleviation for given GDP growth rates. (2) A direct attack on poverty which would empower the poor by enabling them to organize themselves at the local level, to increase their productivity, incomes, savings and investment. Thus the poor could achieve not only a sustainable increase in their incomes but in so doing also contribute to a faster and more equitable GDP growth rate.

The strategy of a faster and restructured growth is a four pronged one which addresses the main structural features of the economy. These features have been identified in our analysis in chapters 1, 2 and 3 as being the major factors underlying both the slow down in GDP growth during the 1990s as well as its reduced ability to alleviate poverty. Therefore the growth strategy would aim to: (a) change the composition of investment so as to generate faster GDP growth for given levels of investment. (b) Change the composition of GDP so as to increase the employment elasticity with respect to output and thereby enhance the employment generation capability of economic growth. (c) Accelerate the growth rate of exports and (d) Enable a shift of the labour force from low skill, low productivity sectors to higher skilled and higher productivity sectors in order to achieve a faster increase in incomes of the lower income groups. In consideration of these strategic parameters the proposed four-pronged growth strategy focuses on:

(1) Rehabilitation of the canal irrigation system so as to reduce transportation losses of irrigation water and provide more water at the root zone of the crops. This would not only generate faster employment but also help farmers to increase their yield per acre.
(2) Develop the ability to produce and export milk, marine fisheries and high value added agriculture products such as fruits, vegetables and flowers. Increased production and export of these products would not only put more income into the hands of the small agricultural producers and fishermen, but also accelerate export growth.
(3) Develop infrastructure such as dams (for both increased reservoir capacity and cheap energy production), ports, national highways, railways, farm to market roads, and cheaper coal based rather than furnace oil based energy production. This would not only create a facilitating environment for private sector investment but also generate employment and stimulate aggregate demand.
(4) Accelerate the growth of small scale enterprises (SSEs) which generate both higher output, employment and exports for given levels of investment. This could be done by facilitating the establishment in the private sector of Industrial Support Centres (ISCs). These would constitute the institutional basis for providing unit specific support to SSEs, to enable them to shift to higher value added products and accelerate their growth.

The second broad thrust of the strategy is a direct attack on poverty. It is proposed to facilitate the growth of autonomous organizations of the poor, especially of women at the local level to enable the poor to achieve better access over input and output markets and increase their productivity and incomes on a sustainable basis. An essential aspect of the emergence of autonomous organizations of the poor, particularly of women is to enable an institutionalized relationship of the poor with different tiers of local government. To the extent that this is achieved, it would not only enhance the ability of local governments to work for the poor but also broaden the basis of power and decisions related to resource allocation and resource use.

III. OVERCOMING THE NATIONAL CRISIS: KEY POLICY AIMS

- Emergence of a modern, tolerant, democratic polity as envisaged by the Quaid-i-Azam Muhammad Ali Jinnah. This would be the enabling political framework for overcoming the crisis of poverty, growth and governance.
- Re-establishing the writ of the State to control violent extremist tendencies. This is a necessary condition for investment and growth.
- Empowering women and removing the bias against them in law, public policy and social norms. This is necessary to unleash the creative potential of society to overcome the national crisis.
- Achieve a higher and restructured GDP growth that can enable faster employment and productivity growth of the poor.
- Change the structure of power at the local level in favour of the poor. This is necessary to reduce systematic income losses of the poor within distorted markets for inputs, outputs and in institutions for health, education, credit and dispute resolution.
- Facilitate the building of autonomous organizations of the poor, particularly poor women and establish institutionalized linkages with local governments. This is necessary to enable participation of the poor in decisions regarding local resource allocation, project identification and implementation.
- Provision of low cost and competent health care (especially preventive health care) to the poor. High frequency of disease, and high cost of medical treatment together constitute a major trigger that pushes marginal households into poverty, and poor households into deeper poverty.
- Improved quality and coverage of low cost health and family planning services to women. This is necessary to reduce fertility rates and improve health of mothers and children. This would help increase productivity and incomes of mothers as well as the children when the latter reach adulthood.
- It is important to achieve the government's target of stabilizing the population to a level of 204 million with a replacement fertility rate of 2.1 children per family by the year 2023. This is crucial for a faster increase in per capita incomes.
- Sharply increase the literacy rate and the coverage and quality of education. This can be an important factor in increasing the earnings not only of the main earner but also of the second earner, which (our survey shows) is crucial to pulling a household out of poverty.
- A large number of children from poor families are working in hazardous occupations which are causing repeated injuries, chronic diseases, physical and mental deformities and in some cases death. An administrative mechanism for ending child labour in hazardous industries urgently needs to be put in place.

Introduction

Pakistan is at a conjunctural moment in its history as it faces a multifaceted crisis. At the end of the decade of the 1990s, the government faced financial bankruptcy, the real economy was in deep recession, there was an unprecedented increase in poverty, and the institutions of governance had eroded to a point where the structure of the State was threatened. As a contribution to the on going effort to overcome this crisis of the human condition in Pakistan, The National Human Development Report (NHDR) aims to address three questions: (1) What is the nature of this crisis? (2) How did it reach this point? (3) How can it be overcome?

In examining the first question, we have identified the structural features of the economy which have given rise to narrowing fiscal space, slow GDP growth and rising poverty.

The second question is examined by analyzing in historical perspective the interplay between the deteriorating institutions of governance, the forms and practice of power, the structure of the economy, and the tendency for growing poverty.

In addressing the third question a new perspective on the nature and dynamics of poverty has been proposed and a detailed analysis conducted on the basis of a new data set. Most poverty studies in Pakistan have sought to estimate the magnitude of poverty in terms of the percentage of the population below variously defined poverty lines. However, if poverty is to be overcome what may now be important is to understand the processes of poverty creation and to identify the points of intervention in the process through which the poor can be enabled to break out of the nexus of poverty on a sustainable basis. The NHDR therefore investigates the processes through which the poor lose their actual and potential income. In this context the specific features of local power structures, and asymmetric markets for inputs and outputs are investigated by means of quantitative and qualitative data. On the basis of the analysis of the structure of the economy, the nature of governance and the dynamics of poverty, policies for overcoming the crisis are identified. These policies are located in a restructured economic growth process, reforms in the institutions of governance and autonomous organizations of the poor.

CHAPTER 1

THE MULTIFACETED CRISIS OF ECONOMY AND SOCIETY

Photograph by Zafar Ahmed

**The boatman stands to declare
That the ship is in the midst of a storm**

– SHAH HUSSAIN
17th Century Punjabi Sufi Poet (Translation)

CHAPTER 1

The Multifaceted Crisis of Economy and Society

Pakistan today stands at the cusp of history, between a crisis of the economy and society, and the possibility of overcoming it. In this section some of the major dimensions of this crisis will be briefly examined to indicate some of the broad areas in which action can be undertaken to address the problem.

Never before in Pakistan has there been such a deep and protracted economic recession, such a sharp increase in poverty and such a critical debt-servicing burden. For example:[1] (a) GDP growth declined from 6.1 per cent during the 1980s to 4.2 per cent during the 1990s; (b) growth of the large scale manufacturing sector declined from 8.2 per cent during the 1980s to 4.4 per cent during the 1990s; (c) the percentage of population below the poverty line increased from 18 per cent in 1987 to 34 per cent today; (d) debt servicing as a percentage of foreign exchange earnings has increased from 18 per cent in 1980 to about 40 per cent in the year 2000.

Let us examine in turn the financial, economic and human dimensions of the crisis in Pakistan.

I. THE FINANCIAL CRISIS

The financial crisis is a manifestation of the inter-play between problems of governance, the decay of institutions, and the adverse structure and slow growth, of GDP.

The essential feature of the problem in the context of economic revival, is that the government has severe fiscal constraints to undertaking major initiatives for stimulating the economy or directly attacking poverty. This is illustrated by the fact that in the year 2000,[2] 60.3 per cent of government revenue went into debt servicing. Successive governments had to finance an increasing percentage of current expenditure with loans. The key element in the financial crisis therefore is the problem of debt.

As the Report of the Government's Debt Management Committee points out, Pakistan has a serious debt-servicing problem in both external debt as well as overall public debt. External debt, obligations increased from US$10 billion in June 1980 to a peak of US$43 billion in May 1998. Debt servicing as a percentage of foreign exchange earnings rose even more sharply from 18.3 per cent in 1980 to 40 per cent in 1999.[3] The rapid increase in the debt servicing burden reflected the increasing weight of higher interest and short term loans in total debt, especially after the substantial high cost borrowing following the 1996 foreign exchange crisis. In 1998 a second foreign exchange crisis occurred after economic sanctions associated with Pakistan's underground nuclear tests. At this stage the government found it impossible to meet its debt servicing obligations in view of the fact that short-term debt could no longer be rolled over, and the foreign exchange reserve was extremely low. The government responded by freezing the foreign currency deposits held in Pakistan by individuals. Subsequently the government sought help from the Paris Club to reschedule debt payment. Nevertheless, Pakistan's external debt still stood at US$35 billion in the year 2000.[4]

External debt undoubtedly is the more pressing problem, yet the overall public debt represents an even more serious problem from a longer-term perspective. Total public debt (external plus domestic) increased from Rs.155 billion to Rs.3,196 billion, during the period 1980 to 2000 (see Table 1). The magnitude of this burden for the economy

The financial crisis is a manifestation of the inter-play between problems of governance, the decay of institutions, and the adverse structure and slow growth, of GDP

The essential feature of the problem in the context of economic revival, is that the government has severe fiscal constraints to undertaking major initiatives for stimulating the economy or directly attacking poverty

Table 1 Total Debt and Debt Servicing Burden (Rs. in Billion)

Debt Payable in Rupees	Mid 1980	Mid 1990	Mid 1996	Mid 1999	Mid 2000
Debt Payable in Rupees	59.8	373.6	903.9	1389.3	1571.6
Debt Payable in Foreign Exchange	95.6	428.5	992	1581.9	1624.5
Total Public Debt	155.4	802.1	1895.9	2971.2	3196.1
Public Debt Service as % of Revenue	19.6	35.7	46	61	60.3
External Debt Service as % of Foreign Exchange Earnings	18.3	23.3	31.0	40.2	39.5

Source: A Debt Burden Reduction and Management Strategy Report, Government of Pakistan, March 2001 (Various Tables).

Chart 1 Debt Servicing Burden

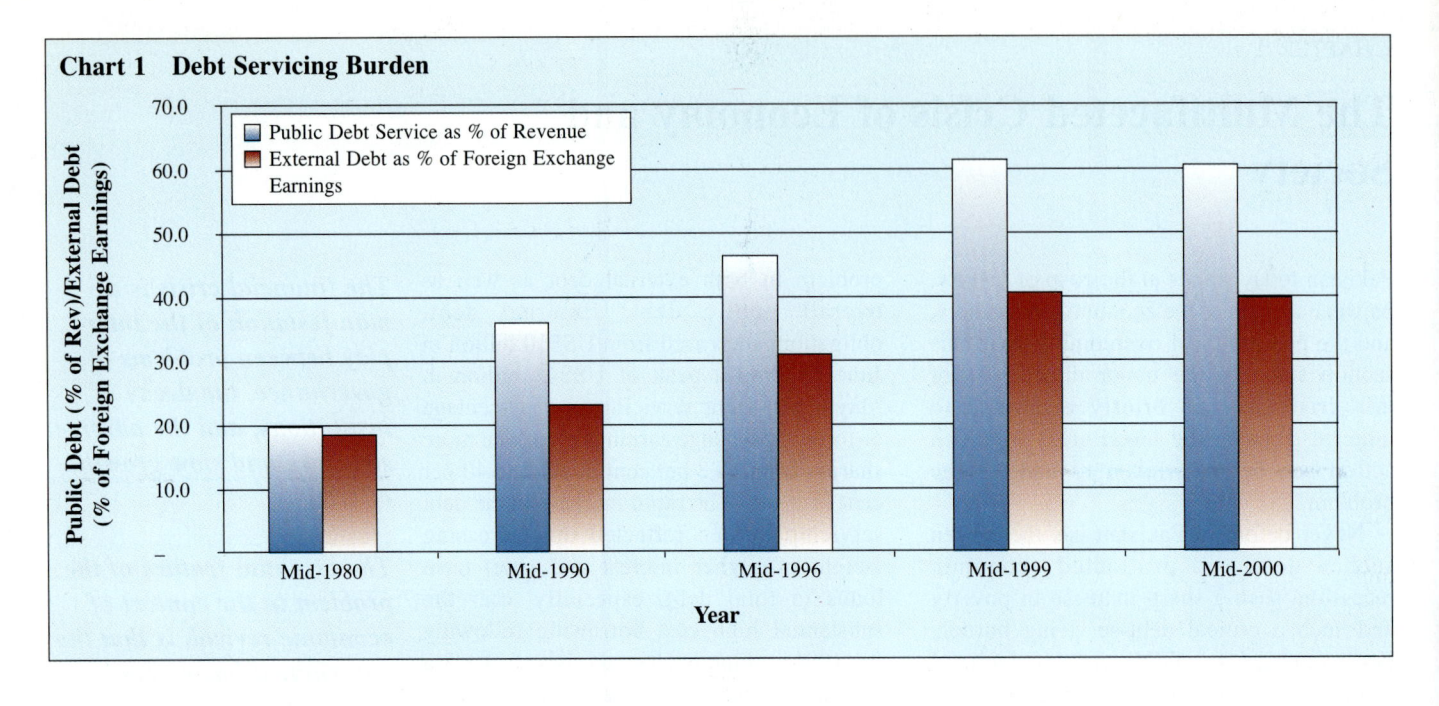

The debt-servicing burden of total public debt as a percentage of government revenue increased from 19.6 per cent in 1980 to 60.3 per cent in 2000

is indicated by the fact that public debt as a percentage of GDP increased from 66.3 per cent in 1980 to 100.7 per cent by the year 2000. The debt-servicing burden of total public debt as a percentage of government revenue increased from 19.6 per cent in 1980 to 60.3 per cent in 2000.[5]

Even though these figures of public debt and debt servicing represent a crushing burden, yet they understate government liabilities. The official public debt figures do not make any provision for contingent liabilities which might arise in the foreseeable future. These include guarantees to IPPs and other private and public bodies, unfunded losses of public corporations such as WAPDA, KESC and Pakistan Steel Mills, and the losses of public sector owned banks on account of bad loans.[6]

The rapid build up of debt, while it may be rooted in poor governance in Pakistan, has had significant adverse implications for GDP growth and poverty. Governments in the past had spent an increasing proportion of loans on non-development spending (current expenditure), to prop up their power base. The excess of current expenditure over government revenue increased dramatically in the last two decades. During 1980-85 the government revenue exceeded current expenditure by Rs.2.3 billion. By 1999-2000 current expenditure was in excess of government revenue by as much as Rs.96 billion.

Given the structure of governmental power, successive regimes when faced with fiscal pressures, chose to cut down development expenditure rather than expenditure on government itself. In fact current expenditure increased so sharply during 1980-1999 that despite of a huge reduction in development expenditure, fiscal deficits did not decline significantly.

Another feature of Pakistan's fiscal crisis, that is located in the problem of governance is that not only is the tax base narrow (tax revenue/GDP ratio was only 12.7 per cent in 1999-2000), but about 75.6 per cent of revenues come from indirect taxation[7] which is regressive with respect to income distribution. The persistent failure of governments to use tax revenues for the people combined with corruption in the tax collection system, has contributed to undermining the trust between the government and tax payers.

Chart 2 Total Debt Payable

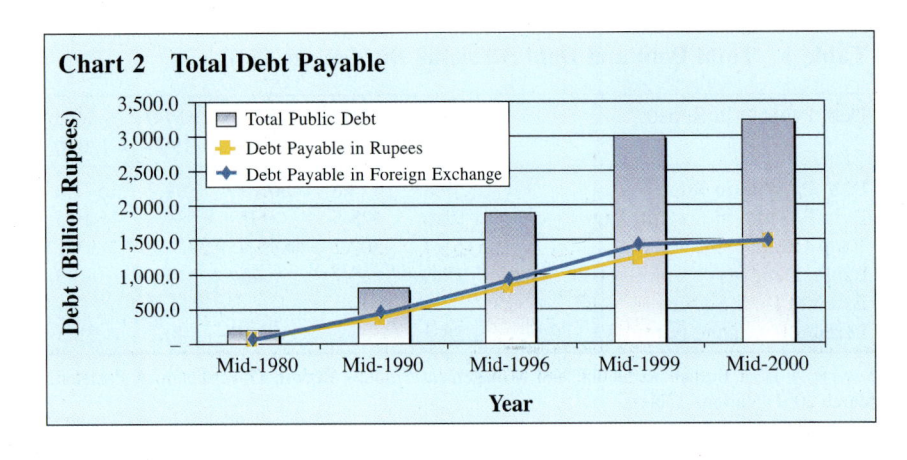

The institutional failure to broaden the base of direct taxes has meant that the governments have been under pressure to generate more revenues from indirect taxes such as regulatory duty and withholding tax. The impact of the recent sales tax and turnover tax is also essentially indirect since it is passed on to consumers. Indirect taxes impact the lower income groups more than the higher income groups. For example evidence on the increase in the incidence of taxation by income group over the period 1987-88 to 1990-91 shows that the increase in the tax burden as a percentage of income was highest at 6.8 per cent for the lowest income group (less than Rs.700 per month) and lowest at minus 4.3 per cent for the highest income group (over Rs.4,500 per month). Thus over time the tax burden on the poor has increased and on the rich has declined.[8]

II. THE ECONOMIC CRISIS

Underlying the financial crisis is a deepening crisis of the real economy. The growth rate of GDP has declined sharply falling from an average of 6.3 per cent in the 1980s to an average of 4.2 per cent in the 1990s. At the same time, poverty has increased at a pace unprecedented in Pakistan's history. This has contributed to sharpening social polarization and increasing the stress on institutions at a time when they have already been weakened by a historical process of institutional decay. (The interplay between the process of institutional decay, and the economic and political processes needs to be analyzed, but is outside the scope of this Report).

The declining trend in GDP growth has been accompanied by three adverse structural features of economic growth in the 1990s which may have not only accentuated poverty but also increased Pakistan's financial fragility with respect to the budget and balance of payments deficit: (i) Increased instability of GDP growth, fuelled primarily by a much greater amplitude of fluctuations in the output of the crop sector.[9] This has not only fuelled poverty but in a situation of slow overall growth of exports, unstable growth in agriculture exports has induced a fragility in the balance of payments. (ii) Declining employment elasticities of output in both industry and agriculture, thereby reducing the employment generation capability of the economy for given GDP growth rates.[10] (iii) Declining labour productivity in both agriculture and industry leading to the observed decline in real wages of casual workers, which is the predominant form of hired labour in Pakistan.[11]

Let us now briefly discuss the three major elements that underlie the slow down in GDP growth and the crisis in the real economy: (a) The crisis in agriculture (b) The water crisis. (c) The crisis in industry.

II.1 THE CRISIS IN AGRICULTURE

The pattern of growth in the crop sector during the 1990s is characterized by a slow down in the annual growth rate of major crops, a declining growth rate of factor productivity and an increased instability of output growth. For example the average annual growth rate of major crops declined from 3.34 per cent during the 1980s to 2.38 per cent during the 1990s (see Table 2). At the same time, the frequency of negative growth in some of the major crops during the last seventeen years has been significantly higher than in the preceding two decades. If we consider wheat, which is by far the largest crop (it accounts for over 30 per cent of value added in major crops), we find that the average annual growth rate has been steadily declining since the onset of the 'Green Revolution'.[12] (See Tables 2 and 3).

The slow down in the growth of yields per acre gives cause for concern in view of the fact that it has come at a time when the extensive margin in the crop sector has been reached and further growth will have to depend on increasing the efficiency of input use.

Under conditions in which higher input use per acre is required to maintain yields, subsistence farmers with few resources are likely to suffer a greater than average decline in yields compared to large farmers. At the same time due to lack of savings to fall back upon, poor farmers are relatively more vulnerable to bad harvests under conditions of unstable growth.[13] Consequently, slower and more unstable growth would be accompanied by a tendency for growing inequality in rural income distribution, together with increased poverty. The available evidence suggests that this is indeed the case in Pakistan.

Over time the tax burden on the poor has increased and on the rich has declined

The pattern of growth in the crop sector during the 1990s is characterized by a slow down in the annual growth rate of major crops, a declining growth rate of factor productivity and an increased instability of output growth

Table 2   Average Annual Growth Rates of Major Crops*: 1980-97

Period	1980-81 to 1989-90	1990-91 to 1996-97
Average Annual Growth (%)	3.34	2.38

Note: *At constant 1980-81 factor cost.
Source: Federal Bureau of Statistics, Government of Pakistan.

Table 3   Wheat Average Annual Growth Rate of Output and Yield/ Acre and the Frequency of Negative Yield Increase, 1960 to 1996

Period	Average Annual Growth Rate of Output (%)	Average Annual Growth Rate of Yield/Acre (%)	Frequency of Negative Yield Increase (Compared to Previous Year)
1960-61 to 1969-70	7.42	4.38	3
1970-71 to 1979-80	4.43	3.18	2
1980-81 to 1989-90	3.30	2.06	4
1990-91 to 1996-97	2.33	1.81	3

Source: Pakistan Economic Survey 1997-98, Government of Pakistan, Finance Division, Economic Advisor's Wing, Islamabad.

While the availability of irrigation water has been reduced, the requirement of water at the farm level has increased due to increased deposits of salts on the top soil and the consequent need for leaching

Table 7 (b) shows the Gini index (which is a measure of the degree of inequality) has increased from 26.85 in 1992-93 to 30.19 in 1998-99. At the same time, the percentage of population below the poverty line has increased from 17 per cent in 1986-87 to 26.3 per cent in 1996-97. (It increased further to 32.2 per cent by 1998-99).

Underlying the phenomenon of slow output growth of major crops together with increased instability of growth are five major institutional constraints:[14]

(a) Reduced water availability at the farm gate due to poor maintenance of the irrigation system and low irrigation efficiencies of about 37 per cent. (For a more detailed discussion, see Section II.2 of this chapter). While the availability of irrigation water has been reduced, the requirement of water at the farm level has increased due to increased deposits of salts on the top soil and the consequent need for leaching. For example, according to the government about 33 million tons of salts are annually brought into the Indus Basin Irrigation System, out of which 24 million tons are being retained.[15]

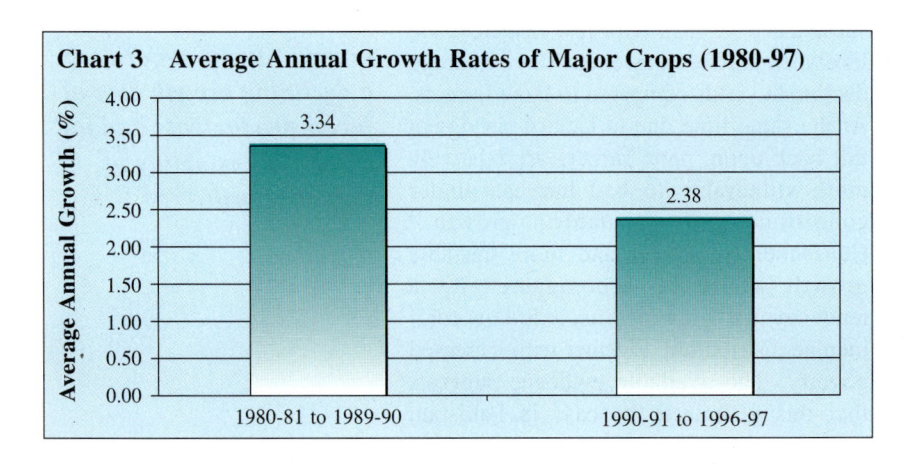

(b) What makes improved efficiency of irrigation even more important is that the extensive margin of irrigated acreage has been reached, so that future agricultural growth will have to rely on improving the efficiency of water use and other inputs. Thus the rehabilitation of Pakistan's irrigation system for improving irrigation efficiency has become a crucial policy challenge for sustainable agriculture growth.

(c) It is well known that high yielding varieties of seeds gradually lose their potency through re-use, changing micro structure of soils, and changing ecology of micro organisms in the top soil. Therefore, breeding of more vigorous seed varieties adapted to local environmental conditions and their diffusion amongst farmers through an effective research and extension programme is necessary. Yet there is no organized seed industry in Pakistan to meet the needs of farmers for the supply of vigorous varieties of seeds even in the major crops. In wheat, for example, the average age of seeds is 11 years compared to an average of 7 years for all developing countries. It has been shown that there was a sharp decline in growth of total factor productivity in Pakistan after 1975. Pakistan's lower factor productivity growth compared to India, can be attributed to the poorer level of research and extension in Pakistan compared to India.[16]

(d) A new dimension to the imperative of improving research capability in the crop sector is indicated by the possibility of declining yields per acre related with global warming. Given the sensitivity of wheat seed to temperature increase, even a 2-degree centigrade increase in average summer temperatures could mean an

Chart 3   Average Annual Growth Rates of Major Crops (1980-97)

absolute yield decline of between 10 to 16 per cent during the twenty-first century.[17] With a 2.8 per cent population growth, even a decline of 5 per cent in yield per acre associated with global warming, could mean serious food deficits for Pakistan. It is, therefore, necessary to develop heat resistant varieties of food grains.

The current ineffectiveness of agriculture research and poor diffusion amongst farmers is a cause for concern. This is particularly so in a situation where future agriculture growth and labour absorption will have to depend more on input efficiency than on enlargement of irrigated acreage and input intensification which were the major sources of agriculture growth in the past.

(e) One of the most important constraints to sustainable growth in the crop sector is the degradation of soils, resulting from improper agricultural practices such as: (i) lack of crop rotation and the resultant loss of humus in the top soil; (ii) stripping of top soil and resultant loss of fertility associated with over grazing; (iii) water erosion along hill sides and river banks due to cutting down of trees and depletion of natural vegetation. According to one estimate, over 11 million hectares have been affected by water erosion and 5 million hectares by wind erosion.[18]

II.2 THE WATER CRISIS

As Sandra Postel has argued[19] a key lesson of history is that while irrigation has been a powerful tool of human advancement for 7,500 years, yet improper management of water resources has caused most irrigation based civilizations, from Mohenjo-Daro to ancient Mesopotamia, to perish. As the people of Pakistan stand at the threshold of a new millennium, the question is: Shall our fate be any different? In this section we shall identify the key features of Pakistan's water crisis so that we may take the steps necessary to survive and prosper.

II.2.1 *Irrigation and Agriculture*: Perhaps even more than in the period of the Mohenjo-Daro civilization, irrigation today is vital to sustaining Pakistan's agricultural production and the economy as a whole. Irrigated land

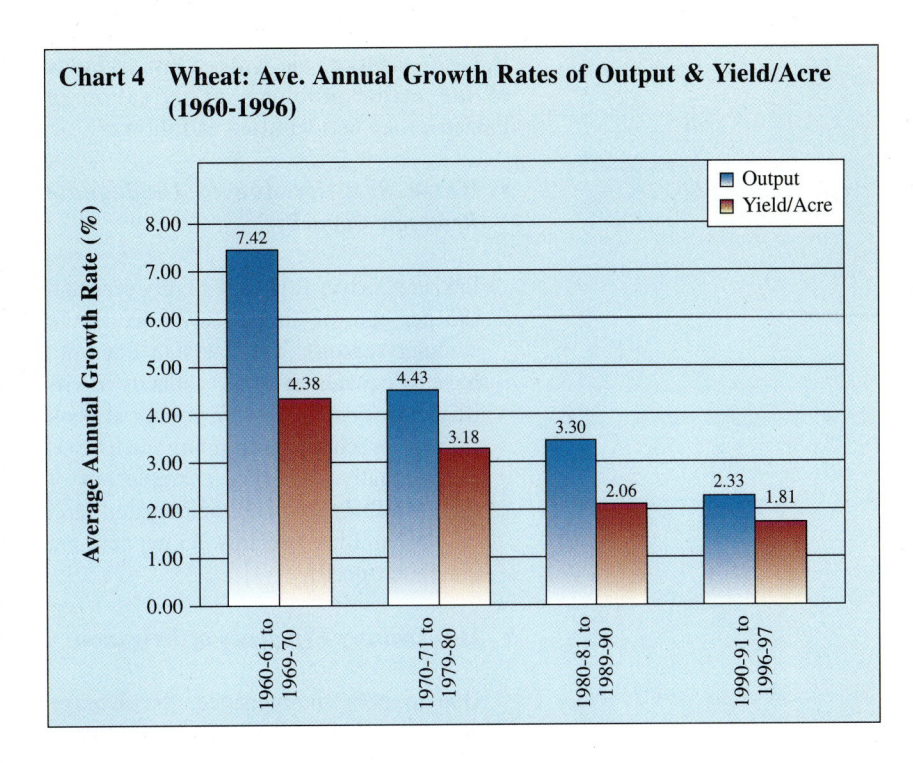

Chart 4 Wheat: Ave. Annual Growth Rates of Output & Yield/Acre (1960-1996)

Period	Output	Yield/Acre
1960-61 to 1969-70	7.42	4.38
1970-71 to 1979-80	4.43	3.18
1980-81 to 1989-90	3.30	2.06
1990-91 to 1996-97	2.33	1.81

supplies over 90 per cent of agricultural production, while agriculture in turn fulfills most of the country's food requirements, contributes 26 per cent of the GDP and employs 54 per cent of the labour force. Agriculture is also a source of raw materials for major domestic industries particularly cotton products which account for 80 per cent of the value of exports.

Even though irrigation is the life blood of Pakistan's agriculture and indeed its economy, yet successive governments in the past have allowed Pakistan's irrigation and drainage systems to deteriorate to a critical level.

Poor maintenance has resulted in the gradual deterioration in the canal irrigation system whose carrying capacity of water has been reduced due to lack of adequate de-silting and crumbling of canal banks. Delivery efficiency (from the canal head to the root zone of crops) is now as low as 35 to 40 per cent.[20] The annual diversion of water from the rivers into the surface irrigation system is about 93 million-acre feet out of which only about 37 million-acre feet actually reaches the root zone of crops. The remaining 56 million-acre feet is lost to canal seepage, spillage, breaches and watercourse losses.

Loss of such a large part of the surface water not only deprives farmers of water for crops but also contributes to water logging and salinity.

II.2.2 *Elements of the Water Crisis:*[21] Some of the major problems of irrigation in Pakistan may be identified as follows:

- ***Water Scarcity due to Inadequate Reservoir Capacity***

Pakistan's river flows are highly seasonal (85 per cent of annual flows are in the summer season). Yet Pakistan does not have adequate reservoir capacity in its irrigation system to store waters at peak flows. Consequently cropping intensity is exceptionally low. (For example out of the 16 million hectares of irrigated land only 5.7 million hectares, 35 per cent are double cropped).

- ***Low Delivery Efficiency of Irrigation***

Due to poor maintenance, the average delivery efficiency is only 35 to 40 per cent from the canal head to the root zone, with most of the losses occurring in the watercourses. This huge loss of surface water is a major factor in creating water logging and salinity. A significant proportion of the water lost through such seepage from the irrigation system flows into saline groundwater reservoirs thereby making it impossible for re-use by tubewell irrigation. Since Pakistan's agriculture depends almost completely on irrigation, in the face of increasing shortages of water in the future, improvement in the delivery efficiency of irrigation is crucial to sustaining agricultural production.

- ***Problem of Drainage, Water Logging and Salinity***

The surface drainage problem of the Indus Plain is inherent in its flat topography, and the associated lack of natural drainage channels and porous soils. This problem is compounded by construction of roads, railways and flood embankments without adequate provision in the design to facilitate natural drainage flows. Under these circumstances irrigation without adequate drainage leads to rising water tables and hence salinity and water logging. Therefore it is vital for sustainable agriculture to construct adequate drainage systems for the removal of excess water and salt from the soil. During the 1960s a number of Salinity Control and Reclamation Projects (SCARPs) were undertaken. Despite these efforts about 30 per cent of the Gross Commanded Area (GCA) is water logged and 14 per cent is salt affected.

- ***Inequitable Distribution of Irrigation Water***

Contrary to the assumption in the original design of the irrigation delivery system, in reality, water does not reach users at the tail end of the system. This is to a large extent due to reduced carrying capacity of canals resulting from inadequate maintenance. Illegal pumping from canals by big landlords who are able to bribe or pressurize the local irrigation department into silence, adds to the inequality of distribution.

- ***Inadequate Operation and Maintenance of the Irrigation System***

Pakistan's irrigation and drainage systems have been deteriorating because of inadequate maintenance. This is partly due to inadequate budgetary allocations for this purpose associated with financial mismanagement of successive governments since the 1990s. Perhaps equally important is the deterioration of institutions responsible for maintenance of the irrigation system. The gap between operations and maintenance (O&M) expenditure requirements and recoveries through water charges, has now reached 57 per cent for Pakistan as a whole, and over 80 per cent for NWFP and Balochistan.

II.3 THE CRISIS IN INDUSTRY

Pakistan's manufacturing sector has two structural weaknesses which constrain its long term growth and its capacity to generate adequate export earnings: (1) Since the last four decades the structure of the manufacturing sector has failed to achieve substantial diversification into non-traditional, high value added industries. Even in 1990-91, after three decades of industrial growth, textiles and food industries still contributed 40.4 per cent of value added in the manufacturing sector, compared to 48.5 per cent in 1959-60. (See chapter 2, Annexure Table 3). Lack of diversification is even more acute in exports. As Annexure Table 4, chapter 2 shows, textile and related exports constituted 50 per cent of total exports in the decade 1988-99, compared to 30 per cent in the earlier decade 1960-70. Furthermore, the textile industry itself is concentrated in the low value added end of the product spectrum, which has relatively low growth, and low export prospects in the global market. (2) The textile industry has since the 1960s suffered from inefficiency and a dependence on various forms of government protection. For example if value added in the manufacturing sector is measured at world prices its contribution to GDP is much smaller than appears to be the case in official statistics. Earlier in the 1960s, in terms of world prices the textile industry was estimated to have negative value added, even though textile manufacturers were earning large profits in rupee terms, due to various forms of protection and government subsidies.[22] However, even in 1990-91 when some of the market distortions had already been removed, more than 30 per cent of value added could still be ascribed to protection.[23]

The concentration of the manufacturing sector in the low value added end of textile industry has given Pakistan's exports a structural propensity for slow growth. It has also subjected exports to declining terms of trade on the one hand and induced a tendency for low industrial wage rates on the other.

The fact that the problem of low real wages of industrial workers as well as Pakistan's chronic balance of payments problem (hence dependence on foreign capital) are both rooted in the structure of industry, raises the following question: Why has Pakistan's manufacturing sector failed to diversify so far, into high value added and dynamic new industries? The answer perhaps lies in the nature of governance in Pakistan on the one hand and the historical nature of Pakistan's entrepreneurial elite on the other. These issues are explored in the ensuing chapter 2.

The current crisis in the large scale manufacturing sector, lies in the sharp slow down in growth: While historically it was growing at 8 per cent per annum, during the 1980s, it fell to 5.5 per cent in the 1990s and is now growing at less than 3 per cent.

The adverse effect on employment of the declining growth rate of output has been accompanied by a sharp decline in employment elasticity of manufacturing output from 0.17 in the decade of the 1980s to minus 0.10 in the 1990s. At the same time the efficiency of capital use in the manufacturing sector has declined (capital productivity declined from an index of 155.8 in the early 1990s to an index of 135.6 in the late 1990s). This implies that for given investment rates the growth rate of output would be lower than before. Consequently the adverse effect on output growth of the observed sharp decline of investment in the manufacturing sector would be accentuated. (Investment in manufacturing industries has declined from 4.7 per cent of the GDP, in the early 1990s, to 2.7 per cent of the GDP in the late 1990s.)[24]

Given the weaknesses in the structure of the manufacturing sector (indicated above), this decline has occurred due to two sets of factors that emerged in the 1990s:

(1) A changed international environment characterized by: (i) Reduced availability of cheap credit to local industrialists as concessionary foreign capital flows began to dry up. (ii) A changed pattern of global demand for industrial products with a shift to higher value added, and knowledge and skill intensive, products. Pakistan's industrial structure was not positioned to respond quickly to these changed market conditions.

(2) An erosion of the domestic framework within which investment and growth is sustained. The major factors in this regard are: (i) Sharply increased violence with the emergence of armed militant groups of religious extremists. There were frequent cases of professionals, traders and entrepreneurs being murdered and kidnapped for ransom during the 1990s. The resultant sense of insecurity of life and property was not conducive for investment. (ii) Political instability combined with frequent changes in the policy environment. (iii) Exceptionally high interest rates and shortage of credit to entrepreneurs due to high intermediation costs of banks and imprudent lending by nationalized banks on political grounds in the past.

The concentration of the manufacturing sector in the low value added end of textile industry has given Pakistan's exports a structural propensity for slow growth. It has also subjected exports to declining terms of trade on the one hand and induced a tendency for low industrial wage rates on the other

During the decade of the 1990s, there was an adverse policy environment in which the tariff structure and export incentives were distorted against entrepreneurs who were seeking to improve quality and productivity for export growth

(iv) Astronomical electricity tariffs, partly due to high distribution losses by WAPDA (estimated at 25 per cent) and partly due to an ill-advised shift into expensive thermal electricity generation units. (The per unit cost of thermal power generation in Pakistan is Rs.4.75 per unit, compared to only Rs.0.75 per unit for hydro electric power). (v) Lack of facilities for training skilled persons especially in the high skill sectors such as electronics and software development. (vi) An inadequate technological base through which industry can respond in a flexible way to changing patterns of demand. (vii) During the decade of the 1990s, there was an adverse policy environment in which the tariff structure and export incentives were distorted against entrepreneurs who were seeking to improve quality and productivity for export growth. (viii) In a number of cases low quality and cheap counterfeit copies of branded Pakistani manufactured products have been imported into the country. Failure to stop this illegal dumping has also had a significant adverse effect on Pakistan's manufacturing industry.

Slower growth in the large scale manufacturing sector in the 1990s was accompanied by slow growth in an export sector where there was continued concentration in the low value added sector, which suffers from declining terms of trade. Consequently there has been continued pressure on the balance of payments during the 1990s that was a constraint to the over all GDP growth.

III. THE CRISIS OF THE HUMAN CONDITION

In the three decades preceding the 1990s, while Pakistan's GDP growth rate and per capita income bore favourable comparison with low income countries as a whole, its social indicators did not. This suggests that both the content of GDP growth as well as of governance were lacking in human development. In the 1990s, the human condition in Pakistan deteriorated to an alarming level as the institutional structure of governance decayed rapidly. The GDP growth decline combined with adverse changes in the structure of GDP, to induce a sharp increase in poverty. In chapter 2 we will examine the inter play between economic policy, the deteriorating economic structure and the level of GDP growth and rising poverty. In this section of chapter 1, we will describe briefly the nature of the social crisis with respect to the provision of basic services. For this study, the disaggregated human development indices have been developed for the first time, for various provinces and districts of Pakistan. The provincial HDI will also be indicated in this section. The state of, and trends in education, health and population, will be briefly analyzed with special reference to women. We will then describe briefly the condition of women and children amongst the deprived sections of society. We will also indicate the risk to citizens of various kinds of crimes, to illustrate the multiple pressures faced by the underprivileged sections of society: The poverty pressure, the deprivation of basic services, and the sense of insecurity combine at the level of the family, to place acute emotional and psychological pressures on human beings.

III.1 HUMAN DEVELOPMENT INDICES: PROVINCES AND DISTRICTS

In this NHDR study for the first time in Pakistan, human development indices have been estimated for provinces and districts. The variation in HDI between provinces and districts are indicative of regional disparities in both the level of economic growth as well as in terms of health, education and the quality of life. (Only summary tables are provided in the text. For more detailed tables and method of calculation, see Annexure I). As table 4 shows, there is considerable variation across provinces with respect to literacy rates which vary from 51 per cent in the Sindh to 36 per cent in the Balochistan. Similarly the primary enrolment rate varies from 75 per cent in the Punjab, to 64 per cent in the Balochistan. As a consequence while the human development index for Pakistan, as a whole, is 0.541 the provincial HDI varies from the highest in the Punjab, at 0.557, to the lowest at 0.499 in Balochistan. Islamabad (a federally administered territory), is Pakistan's capital city, and has a greater weight of affluent citizens in its population with a far better social infrastructure than in

Table 4 Disaggregated Human Development Index for Pakistan (Province-wise, 1998)

Name	Literacy Ratio % 1998	Enrolment Ratio % 1998	Infant Survival Ratio %	Immunization Ratio % 1998	Real GDP per capita (PPP$) 1998	Educational Attainment Index	Health Index	Adjusted real GDP per capita (PPP$) Index	HDI
All Pakistan	45	71	95.5	49	1715	0.537	0.82	0.272	0.541
Punjab	46	75	95.4	55	1770	0.557	0.83	0.281	0.557
Sindh	51	64	94.9	38	1804	0.553	0.78	0.287	0.540
NWFP	37	70	96.3	54	1364	0.480	0.84	0.213	0.510
Balochistan	36	64	96.4	34	1677	0.453	0.78	0.265	0.499
Islamabad	72	58	95.9	72	1743	0.673	0.89	0.277	0.612

Note:
1. GDP per capita and Infant Survival Rates for Islamabad are calculated as an average of Punjab and Pakistan.
2. Enrolment rate is for primary level only.
3. Immunization refers to fully immunized children based on record and recall having received BCG, DPT1, DPT2, DPT3, Polio1, Polio2, Polio3, and Measles.

Source: (i) Estimation by Wasay Majid and Akmal Hussain. (ii) For data sources see Annexure 1.

any province of Pakistan. It is not surprising therefore that the human development index of Islamabad is 0.612 which is higher than that of any of the provinces in the country.

Provincial human development indices disaggregated by rural and urban areas are given in table 4 (a). In terms of HDI ranking the table shows that Sindh urban has the highest rank, with an HDI of 0.659 which is higher than for Pakistan as a whole (0.541). Punjab urban comes out second in the ranking with HDI of 0.657, NWFP urban third with an HDI of 0.627 and Balochistan urban fourth at 0.591. It is interesting that in terms of the rural/urban ranking of provinces while Sindh urban has the highest rank, Sindh rural has the lowest with an HDI of 0.456. This suggests a larger urban rural disparity in Sindh compared to any other province. Punjab rural has the highest HDI (0.517) compared to the rural areas of any other province.

Table 4 (b) presents district level HDI rankings of Pakistan. Jhelum has the highest HDI rank at 0.703 and Dera Bugti the lowest at 0.285. This table indicates the large disparities in terms of human development between the districts of Pakistan.

Table 4 (a) Ranking of Provinces by Urban/Rural and Overall Human Development Index

Name	HDI	HDI Rank
Sindh (urban)	0.659	1
Punjab (urban)	0.657	2
NWFP (urban)	0.627	3
Balochistan (urban)	0.591	4
Punjab (rural)	0.517	5
NWFP (rural)	0.489	6
Balochistan (rural)	0.486	7
Sindh (rural)	0.456	8
Punjab	0.557	1
Sindh	0.540	2
NWFP	0.510	3
Balochistan	0.499	4
Pakistan (Urban)	0.656	1
Pakistan	*0.541	2
Pakistan (Rural)	0.496	3

Source: (i) Estimation by Wasay Majid and Akmal Hussain.
(ii) For data sources see Annexure 1.

Note: The all Pakistan HDI differs slightly from the figure estimated by the UNDP Human Development Report 2002. This is because the district and provincial HDI estimates in the Pakistan NHDR use a proxy for life expectancy in the health index based on immunization rates and infant survival rates (in the absence of district and provincial level life expectancy figures). For details see Annexure 1 (b) Section V of this chapter.

Table 4 (b) Ranking of Districts of Pakistan by the Human Development Index

District	HDI	HDI Rank	District	HDI	HDI Rank	District	HDI	HDI Rank
Jhelum	0.703	1	Mardan	0.519	32	Khairpur	0.449	63
Ziarat	0.697	2	Lasbela	0.514	33	Thatta	0.447	64
Haripur	0.629	3	Khanewal	0.513	34	Lakki Marwat	0.444	65
Sheikhupura	0.621	4	Kech	0.512	35	Swat	0.442	66
Karachi	0.618	5	Vehari	0.508	36	Larkana	0.435	67
Abbottabad	0.598	6	Attock	0.507	37	Zhob	0.432	68
Bhakkar	0.581	7	Naushahro Feroze	0.506	38	Dera Ismail Khan	0.425	69
Kasur	0.577	8	Charsadda	0.506	39	Buner	0.423	70
Rawalpindi	0.576	9	Bahawalpur	0.501	40	Barkhan	0.420	71
Khusab	0.575	10	Pakpattan	0.498	41	Shikarpur	0.417	72
Mandi Bahauddin	0.568	11	Ghotki	0.496	42	Lower Dir	0.413	73
Lahore	0.558	12	Panjgur	0.496	43	Kalat	0.412	74
Loralai	0.556	13	Multan	0.494	44	Sibi	0.411	75
Sialkot	0.555	14	Nasirabad	0.492	45	Hangu	0.400	76
Chakwal	0.545	15	Hafizabad	0.486	46	Jacobabad	0.393	77
Gujrat	0.543	16	Sukkur	0.486	47	Gwadar	0.392	78
Sahiwal	0.541	17	Karak	0.484	48	Killa Abdullah	0.387	79
Rahim Yar Khan	0.541	18	Nawab Shah	0.481	49	Tank	0.384	80
Kohat	0.537	19	Chitral	0.479	50	Awaran	0.381	81
Mianwali	0.537	20	Lodhran	0.475	51	Upper Dir	0.369	82
Dadu	0.535	21	Narowal	0.472	52	Batgram	0.363	83
Sargodha	0.535	22	Dera Ghazi Khan	0.471	53	Bolan	0.360	84
Hyderabad	0.532	23	Chagai	0.468	54	Kohlu	0.348	85
Peshawar	0.531	24	Bannu	0.465	55	Kharan	0.346	86
Gujranwala	0.529	25	Sanghar	0.461	56	Jhalmagsi	0.345	87
Nowshera	0.529	26	Malakand	0.461	57	Tharparkar	0.343	88
Jhang	0.529	27	Mansehra	0.459	58	Kohistan	0.332	89
Mastung	0.528	28	Muzaffargarh	0.459	59	Shangla	0.332	90
Okara	0.528	29	Badin	0.459	60	Dera Bugti	0.285	91
Swabi	0.523	30	Killa Saifullah	0.455	61			
Mirpur Khas	0.522	31	Jaffarabad	0.454	62			

Source: (i) Estimation by Umar Zafar, Wasay Majid and Akmal Hussain.
(ii) For data sources, see Annexure 1 (b).

Chart 5 Province-wise Share in Top 31 Districts in Terms of HDI

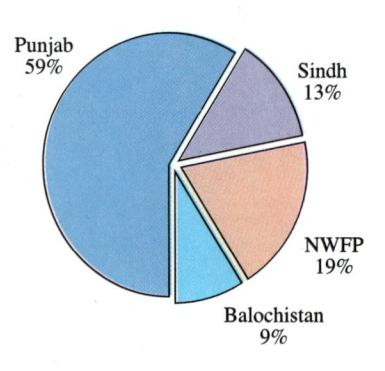

Punjab 59%
Sindh 13%
NWFP 19%
Balochistan 9%

There is also a wide variation in the human development indices within each province. [See table 2, in annexure 1 (a)]. For example in the Punjab, while Jhelum has the highest HDI (0.703), Muzzafargarh has the lowest (0.459). The size and overall development of a district also affects its HDI rank due to *intra* district variations in income and social infrastructure. Thus, for example Lahore has an HDI rank of 0.558 compared to 0.703 for Jhelum because of the much greater inequality of incomes and level of social infrastructure available to the poor and rich parts of Lahore district respectively.[25]

In the absence of intra district data, the average HDI for larger districts is pulled down somewhat due to the larger intra district variation in the level of human development, compared to small districts.

Again in Sindh there is a wide variation in the level of human development with Karachi HDI being highest, (0.618) and Tharparkar the lowest (0.343).

Significantly the intra provincial disparity in district HDI is greater in the provinces of NWFP and Balochistan where overall development is lower compared to the more developed provinces of Punjab and Sindh. Thus in NWFP, Haripur has the highest HDI (0.629), and Shangla the lowest (0.332), while in Balochistan the highest ranking district in terms of HDI is Ziarat (0.697) compared to the lowest ranked district of Dera Bugti (0.285). If we take the ratio of HDI between the highest and lowest ranked districts of each province as an indicator of intra provincial human development inequality, then the inter-district inequality ratio of Balochistan at 240 per cent is highest, followed by NWFP, at 189 per cent, Sindh at 180 per cent and Punjab at 153 per cent.

The inter provincial differences with respect to the human development index of

Chart 6   Pakistan: Province-wise HDIs

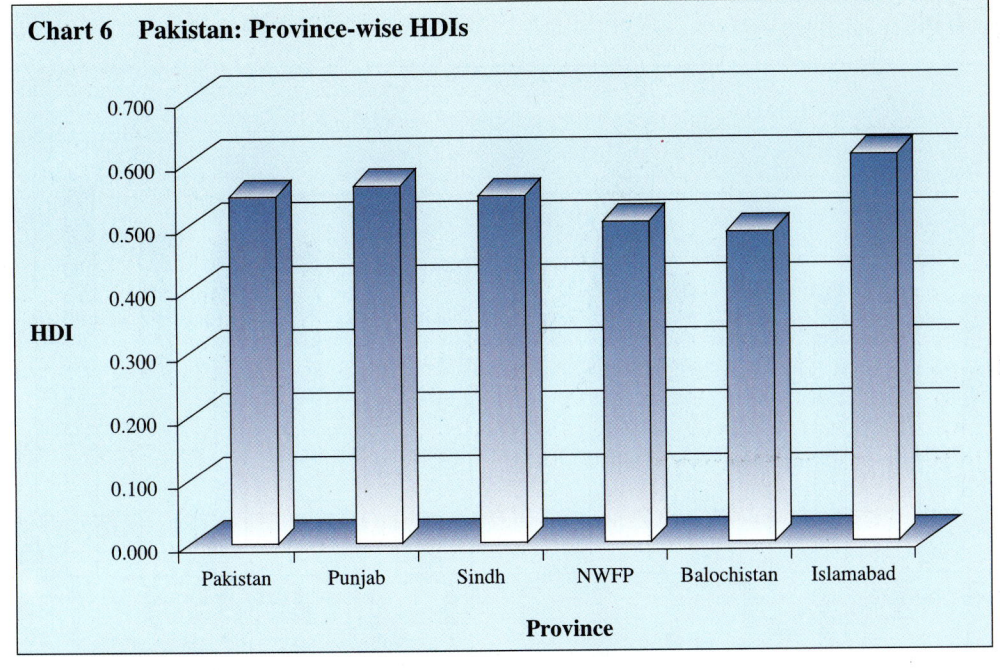

Province-wise Share in Middle 30 Districts in Terms of HDI

- Punjab 32%
- Sindh 29%
- NWFP 21%
- Balochistan 18%

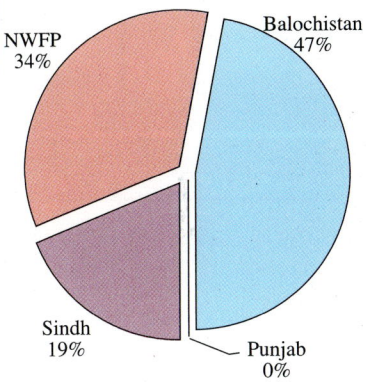

the districts within them, is illustrated by chart 5. It shows the province-wise share in the top, middle and bottom strata of districts in Pakistan with respect to HDI. In the group of top thirty-one districts of Pakistan in terms of their HDI, Punjab districts have by far the largest share at 59 per cent, with Sindh only 13 per cent, NWFP 19 per cent and Balochistan with the smallest share at 9 per cent. There is clearly a concentration of high ranking districts of Pakistan in the Punjab province (in terms of HDI). Conversely in the group of bottom thirty districts of Pakistan (in terms of HDI) Punjab has none, while Sindh has 19 per cent, Balochistan as much as 47 per cent and NWFP 34 per cent. In the group of middle thirty districts (in terms of HDI), both Punjab and Sindh have

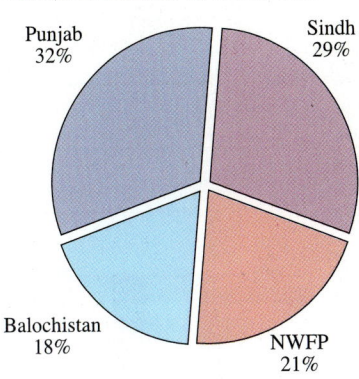

Province-wise Share in Bottom 30 Districts in Terms of HDI

- Balochistan 47%
- NWFP 34%
- Sindh 19%
- Punjab 0%

Chart 7 (a)   Punjab: District-wise HDIs

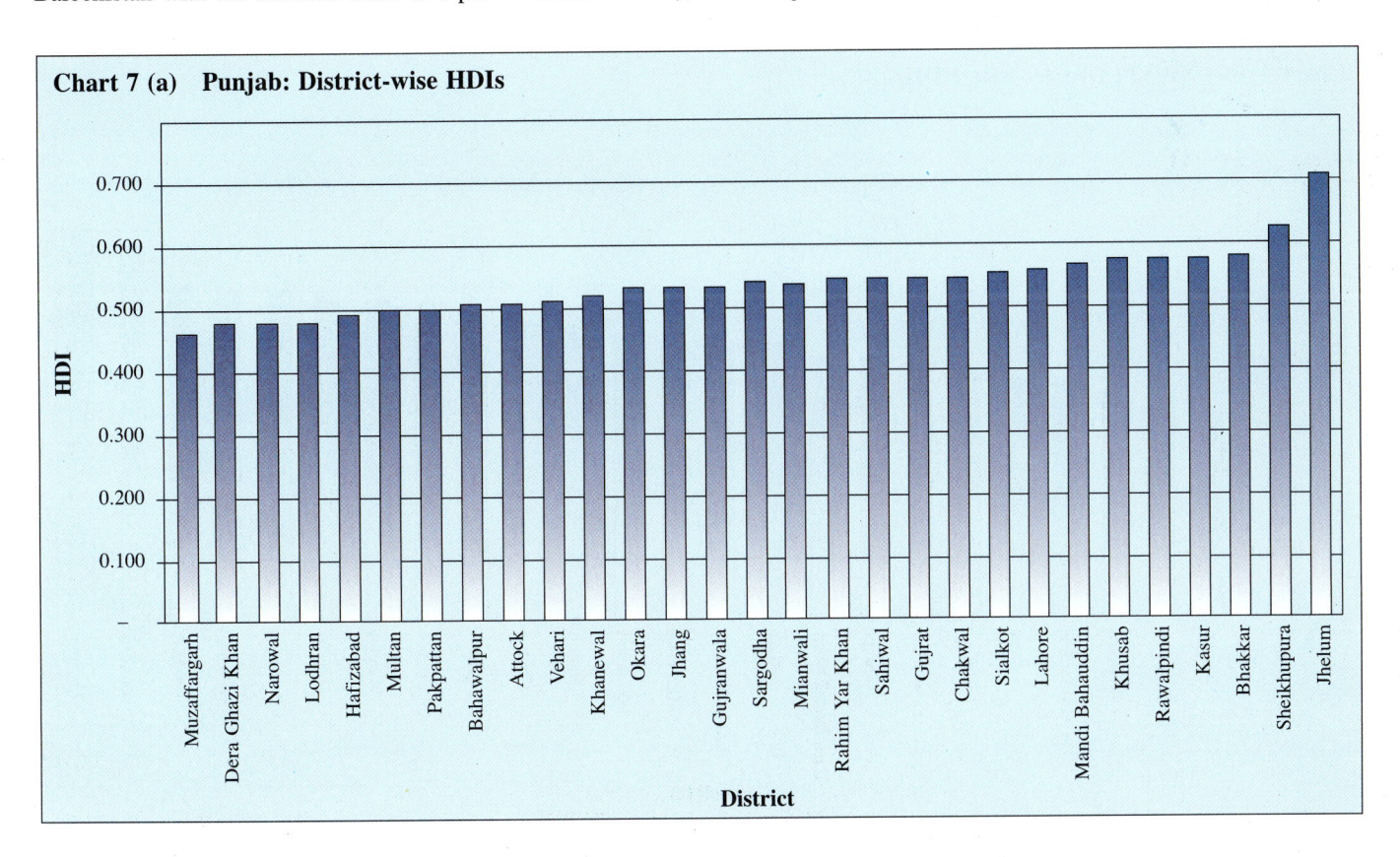

Districts (left to right): Muzaffargarh, Dera Ghazi Khan, Narowal, Lodhran, Hafizabad, Multan, Pakpattan, Bahawalpur, Attock, Vehari, Khanewal, Okara, Jhang, Gujranwala, Sargodha, Mianwali, Rahim Yar Khan, Sahiwal, Gujrat, Chakwal, Sialkot, Lahore, Mandi Bahauddin, Khusab, Rawalpindi, Kasur, Bhakkar, Sheikhupura, Jhelum

THE MULTIFACETED CRISIS OF ECONOMY AND SOCIETY

Chart 7 (b)   Sindh: District-wise HDIs

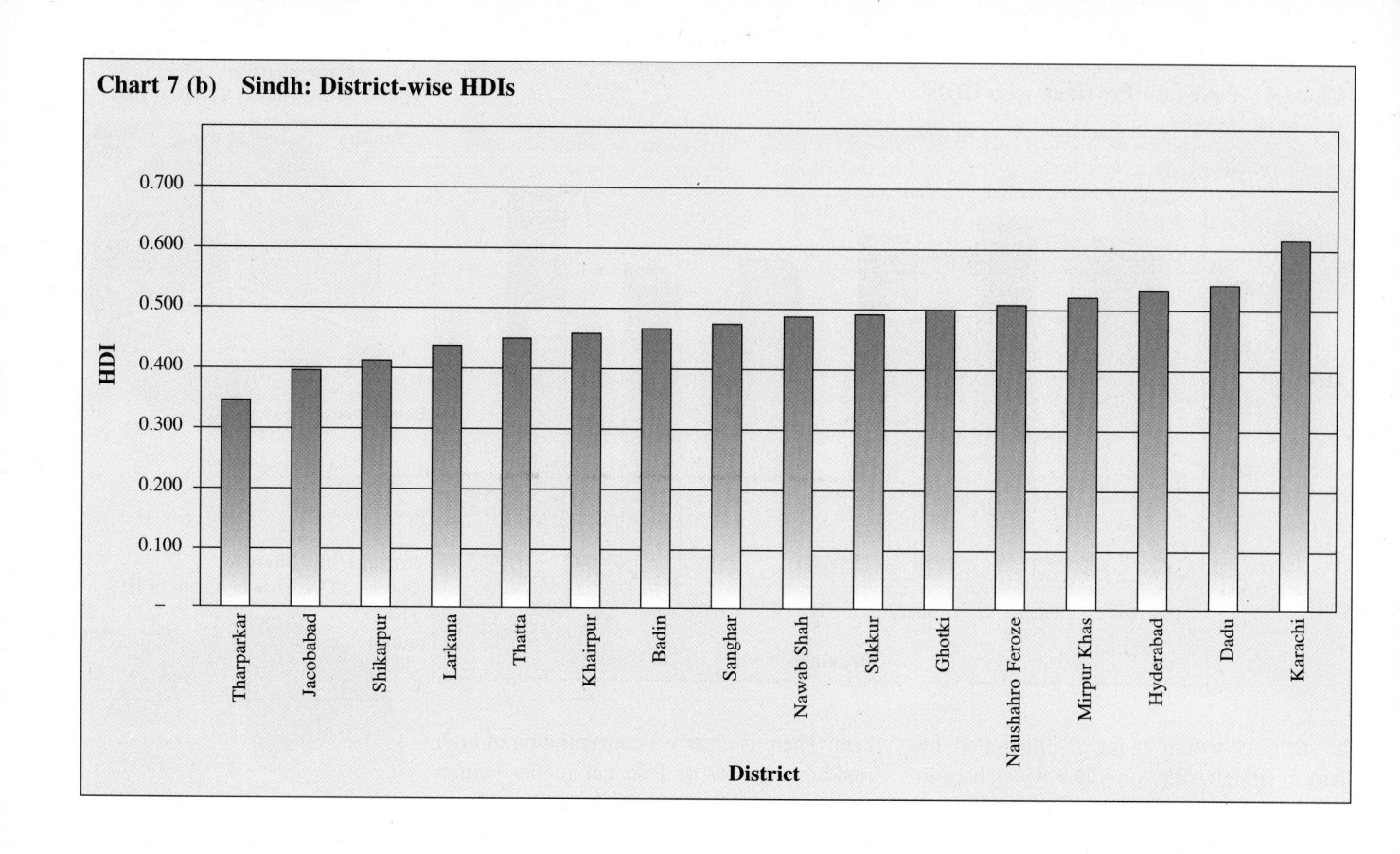

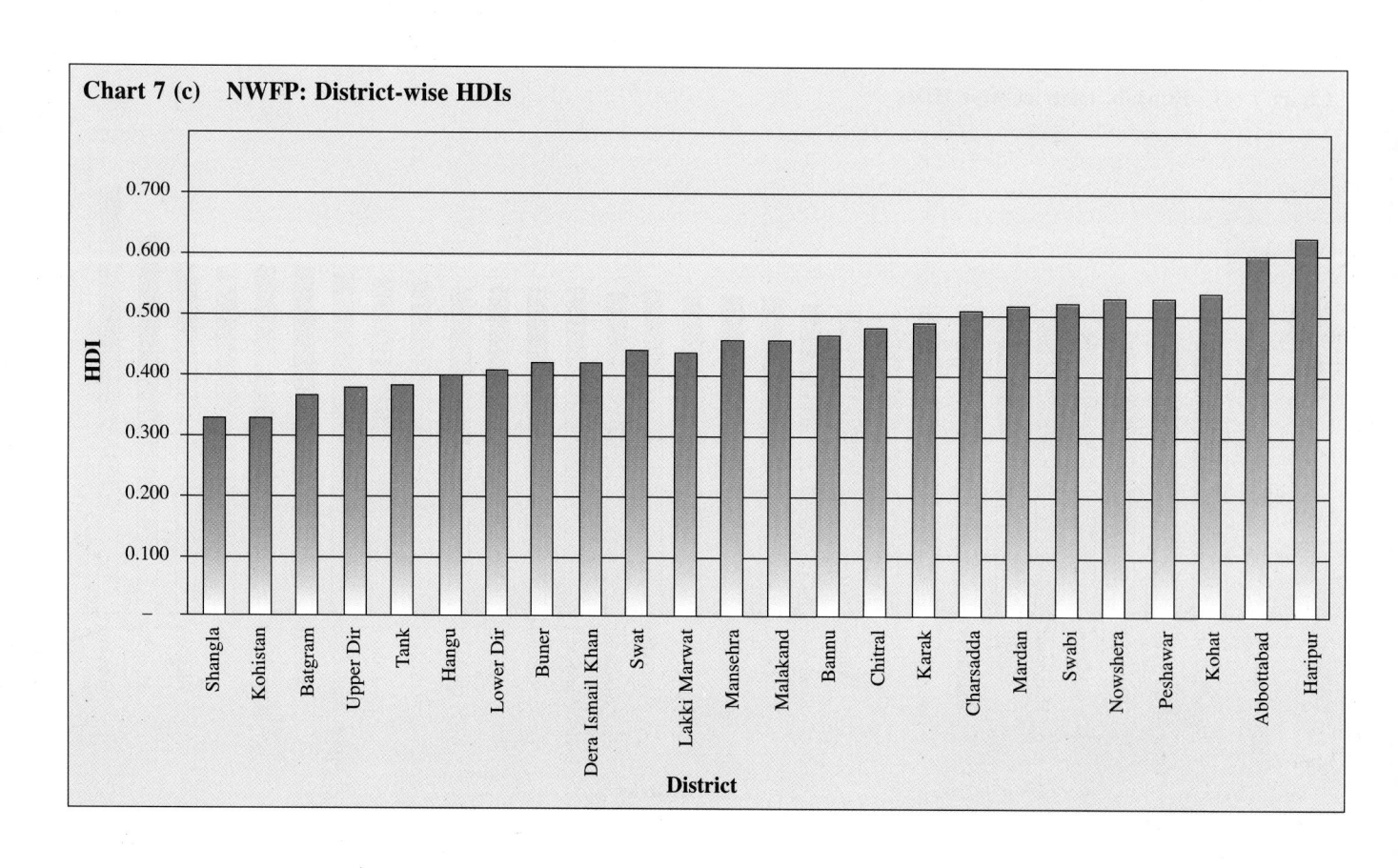

Chart 7 (c)   NWFP: District-wise HDIs

Chart 7 (d) Balochistan: District-wise HDIs

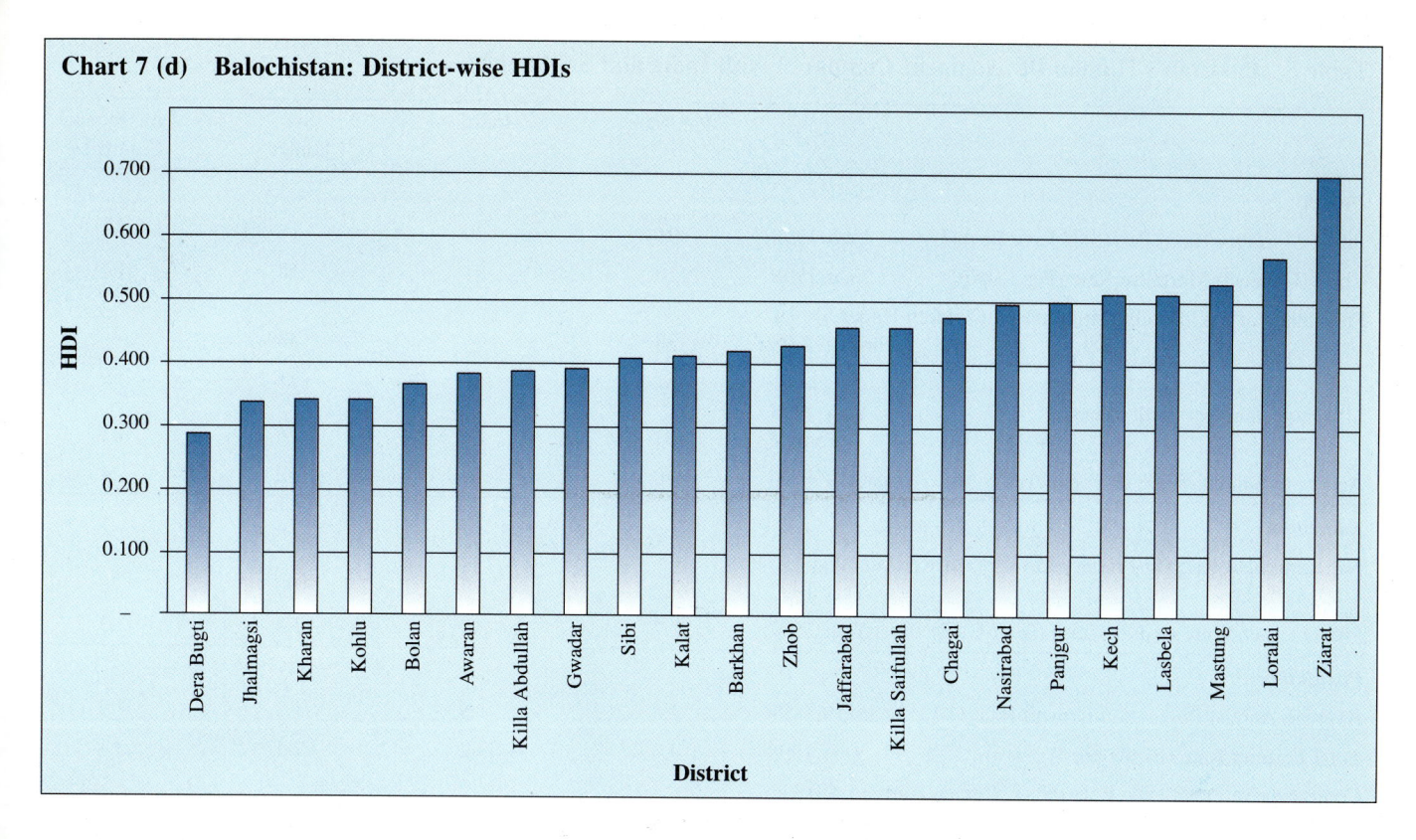

[Bar chart showing HDI values for districts: Dera Bugti, Jhalmagsi, Kharan, Kohlu, Bolan, Awaran, Killa Abdullah, Gwadar, Sibi, Kalat, Barkhan, Zhob, Jaffarabad, Killa Saifullah, Chagai, Nasirabad, Panjgur, Kech, Lasbela, Mastung, Loralai, Ziarat]

relatively high shares, 32 per cent and 29 per cent respectively, while NWFP has 21 per cent and Balochistan 18 per cent.

III.2 Social Indicators in the South Asian Context: The Linkage with Economic Growth and Poverty

Even though the indicators for health, education and population have improved in Pakistan, yet as table 5 shows, they are still far worse than for low income countries, in general, and for some of the other South Asian countries, in particular. For example infant mortality rate in Pakistan was 91 per 1000 live births in 1998, compared to 68 for low income countries, 70 for India and 16 for Sri Lanka. Similarly child mortality rate (under 5 years) is as high as 120 per 1000 for Pakistan compared to 83 for India, 18 for Sri Lanka and 107 for low income countries as a whole. In terms of percentage of population with access over sanitation Pakistan at 30 per cent comes out better than India (16 per cent), worse than Sri Lanka, (52 per cent) but better than low income countries as a whole (24 per cent).

The primary school enrolment rate in Pakistan (62 per cent) again is below India (77 per cent), Sri Lanka (100 per cent) and the average for low income countries (76 per cent). This is to some extent due to the fact that public sector expenditure on education as a percentage of GNP is significantly below its South Asian neighbours (India and Sri Lanka) as well as the average for low income countries.

The average population growth rate at 2.5 per cent (over the period 1990-99), is substantially higher than India (1.8 per cent), Sri Lanka (1.2 per cent) and even the average for low income developing countries (2 per cent).

In terms of the Human Development Index (UNDP Human Development Report 2001) also show that Pakistan lags behind India and Sri Lanka. The HDI for Sri Lanka (0.741) is substantially higher and HDI for India only slightly higher (0.577) than that of Pakistan (0.499).

Pakistan appears to have done badly in terms of human development and reasonably well in terms of GDP growth rates over a protracted period (1950 to 1990). This is indicative of inadequacies in the *content* of growth as much as in the conduct of governance. The capacity of economic growth to benefit the lower income groups was severely constrained by a highly unequal distribution of productive assets reinforced by the government's economic policy.

Regressive tax structures, subsidies, politically motivated bank credit by

Table 5 Pakistan's Human Development Compared with India and Sri Lanka

		Pakistan	India	Sri Lanka	Low Income Countries
Health					
Infant Mortality Rate (Per 1,000 Live Births)	Year 1998	91	70	16	68
Child (Under 5) Mortality Rate (Per 1,000)	Year 1998	120	83	18	107
Prevalence of Child Malnutrition (% of Children Under 5)	Years 1992-98	38		38	
Life Expectancy at Birth (Years)	Male Year 1998	61	62	71	59
	Female	63	64	76	61
Access to Sanitation (% of Population)	Years 1990-96	30	16	52	24
Education					
Net Enrolment Ratio at Primary Level (% of Relevant Age Group)	Year 1997	62*	77	100	76
Public Expenditure on Education (% of GNP)	Year 1997	2.7	3.2	3.4	3.3
Population					
Average Annual Population Growth Rate (%)	Years 1990-99	2.5	1.8	1.2	2.0
Total Fertility Rate (Births per Woman)	Year 1998	4.9	3.2	2.1	3.1
Contraceptive Prevalence Rate (% of Women Ages 15-49)	Years 1990-98	24	41		24
Human Development Index					
Human Development Index,	Year 2002	0.499	0.577	0.741	

Source: (i) World Bank, World Development Report 2000/2001: Attacking Poverty. (New York, Oxford University Press, 2001).
(ii) UNDP Human Development Report 2002.
*For the year 1996.

Improved hygiene, sanitation and preventive health care can lead to reduced frequency of disease, reduced cost of medical treatment and increased productivity and incomes of poor households

nationalized banks and implicit rents served to accentuate income inequality, distort private sector investment decisions and reduce the employment generation capability of GDP growth. In effect, State resources were used to enrich a narrow elite rather than to build the infrastructure of health, education and human development for a broad based and sustainable economic growth. Such policies ended up in lowering GDP growth itself during the 1990s and intensifying poverty and unemployment to a crisis point. The relationship between government policy, the adverse structure of GDP growth and poverty is examined in historical perspective in the next chapter 2 of this Report.

As Pakistan faces a crisis of human development exacerbated by a protracted period of slow GDP growth, it may be time to recognize that initiatives in health and education can play an important role in alleviating poverty and accelerating GDP growth. Paul Streeten et al. have shown in an important study of eighty countries that improvements in literacy for example have made a considerable contribution to economic growth.[26] Similarly improved hygiene, sanitation and preventive health care can lead to reduced frequency of disease, reduced cost of medical treatment and increased productivity and incomes of poor households. Our NHDR/PIDE 2001 survey shows that almost ninety working days per year on average are lost due to illness in poor households. The high cost of medical treatment combine with lowered earnings following illness, to intensify poverty (see chapter 3).

III.3 EDUCATION

III.3.1 *Literacy*: The literacy rate for Pakistan as a whole increased significantly from 33.3 per cent in 1990 to 46.4 per cent in 1999, although it is still below even South Asian standards. According to estimates by the Social Policy and Development Centre

Chart 8   Primary School Enrolment

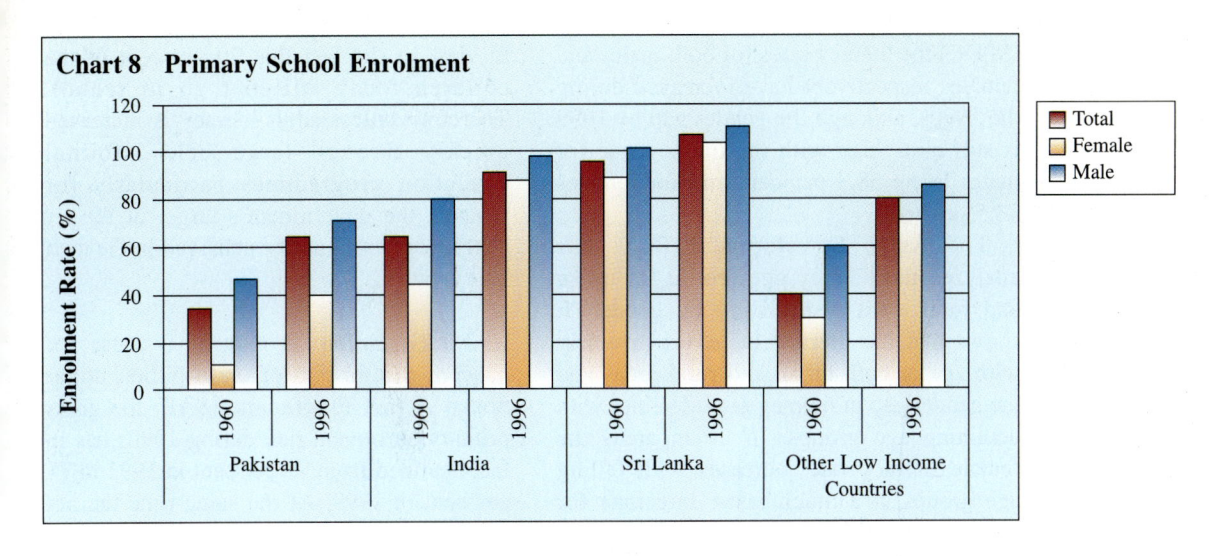

Chart 9   Comparison of Social Development in Health Between Pakistan and other Low Income Countries (%)

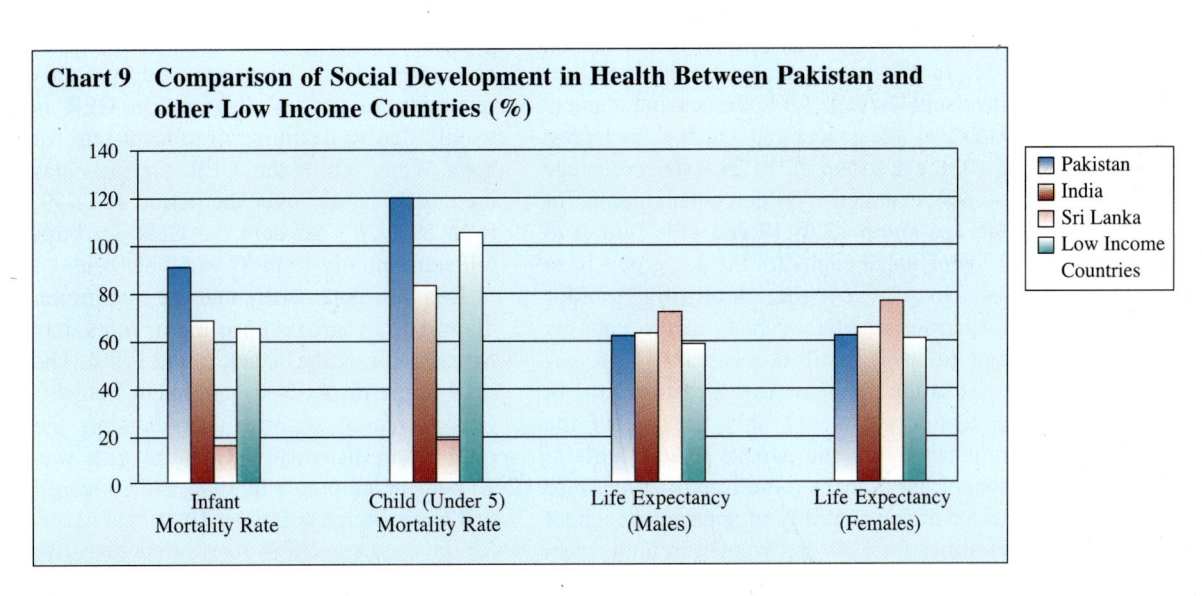

Chart 10   Adult Literacy Rates: Comparison of Pakistan with Other Low Income Countries (1960, 1996)

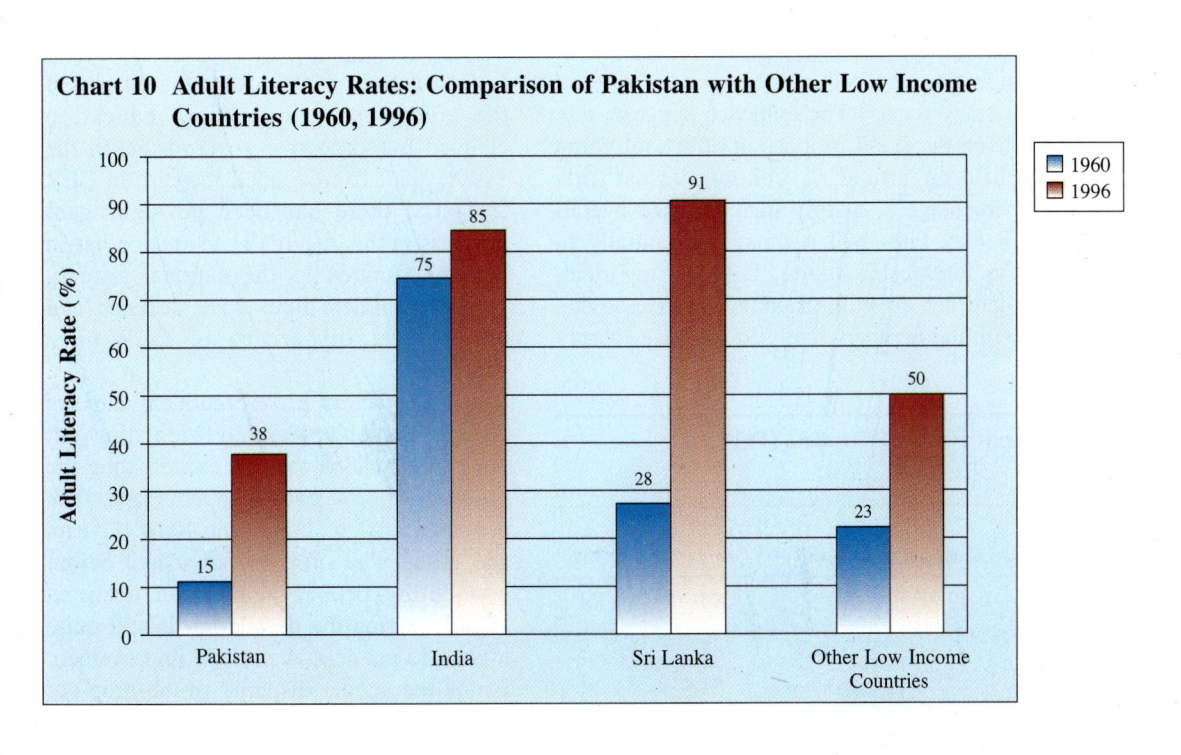

(SPDC) the literacy rates for both males and females respectively have increased during the 1990s, although the gender gap by 1999 is still quite high with the literacy rate for males being 58.3 per cent and for females 33.5 per cent.[27]

The Asian Development Bank has analyzed the literacy age profile for urban and rural areas respectively by gender. It shows that the literacy increases inversely with age in both urban and rural areas and the gender gap in literacy rates declines with declining age groups. In urban areas the female literacy rate increases with falling age groups at a much faster rate than for males so that the gender disparity which is quite high in the 60 plus age group is almost eliminated in the age group 10 to 14 years old. In the rural areas literacy increases inversely with age for both men and women. However, the gender gap which is the largest for the age group 20 to 24, (40 percentage points), declines to 33 percentage points for the age group 15 to 19 and falls further to 22 percentage points for the age group 10 to 14. Inspite of the declining gender disparities of literacy rates in the younger age groups it is still unacceptably high.

It appears that the gender gap in education exists not only because of the reluctance of some parents to send girls to school but perhaps more important because of the non availability of appropriate school facilities for girls and women in both urban and rural areas. Making educational facilities available to girls and women at a relatively faster pace is likely to significantly reduce the gender gap in literacy rates.[28] The evidence suggests that given the small proportion of school going children attending school, unless this percentage is sharply increased the overall literacy rates will not rise substantially in the foreseeable future. Equally important, there are 40 million adult illiterates today with the numbers likely to increase sharply in view of the fact that 29 per cent of the children today will not go to school. Therefore unless adult literacy is increased quickly through large-scale informal education programmes particularly for women, the government's target of 90 per cent literacy will not be achieved in the next half century.

III.3.2 *Education*: It may be a cause for concern that inspite of multi-billion dollar Social Action Programme (SAP) the gross primary enrolment rate during 1990s has in fact declined from 73 per cent in 1991 to 71 per cent in 1999. At the same time the net enrolment rate declined from 46 to 42 per cent for the period.[29] Although the gender gap in the gross enrolment rate (GER) appears to have been reduced, yet this reduction in gender disparity in GER is mainly due to declining enrolment rate for boys. Thus while the GER for girls has increased slightly over the period 1991-99, from 59 to 61 per cent the GER for boys fell substantially from 87 to 80 per cent.

It is also noteworthy that the rural urban disparity in gross enrolment rates has widened during the decade of the 1990s. The rural urban disparity in enrolment rates for girls increased slightly. (For example the rural urban disparity in GER for girls was 40 percentage points in 1991 and increased to 42 percentage points by 1999). However, for boys the growth in rural urban disparity was much greater with the gap being 14 percentage points in 1991 and increasing to 20 percentage points by 1999 (see table 6). It is clear from this evidence that inspite of the commitment to primary education claimed by successive governments in the 1990s, apart from a small increase in GER for girls, there has been no significant progress in this regard: The situation has in fact deteriorated as the national primary school enrolment rates have declined and urban rural disparities in GER have widened.

In Pakistan low gross enrolment rates are accompanied by relatively high drop out rates from school, thereby exacerbating the problem of low education coverage. The percentage of children in the 10 to 18 years age group who drop out of school before completing primary education declined slightly during the decade but is still quite high at 15 per cent. A positive improvement is that the gender disparity in the drop out

Table 6	Gross Primary Enrolment Rate—1991 and 1999					
						%
	1991			1999		
	Overall	Boys	Girls	Overall	Boys	Girls
Pakistan	73	87	59	71	80	61
Urban	92	97	87	94	95	92
Rural	66	83	47	63	75	50

rates narrowed from 5 percentage points in 1991 to 1 percentage point in 1999. However, the urban rural gap in the drop out rates has widened over the decade.

The NHDR 2001 Survey shows that one of the key factors which determines the ability of a poor household to pull out of poverty is whether or not the family has a second earner. It may be important to note that according to our survey data, the magnitude of the second earner's income and therefore his/her ability to pull the family out of poverty, is closely co-related with the educational status of the second earner (see chapter 3). Therefore, given the actual and perceived importance of education in determining the future economic status of a present low income household, parents of even relatively low income families are keen to send their children to school. High drop out rates occur often because the household is facing adversity and gets pushed into such acute poverty that it is forced to send the children to work for a pittance rather than continue with education. Given the high probability of illness in low income families and the high cost of medical treatment such adversity often takes the form of a family member falling sick and the consequent descent of the household into debt and deepening poverty (see chapter 3).

Other factors inducing parents to withdraw children from school include absence of teachers from government schools or such low standards that the parents feel that the opportunity cost of sending the children to school is higher than the perceived benefits of schooling. According to PIHS 1998-99 data, there is a co-relation between household income and school drop out rates. For example 47 per cent of the children from the poorest quintile dropped out before completing primary education as compared to 23 per cent from the richest quintile.

Apart from the poor coverage of education there is a serious problem with the quality of education imparted to students not only with respect to the curricula but also the quality of instruction. A study by the World Bank on the Punjab province illustrates the problem of low educational attainment even within the existing low standards. For example in 1999 only 41 per cent of public school students in the Punjab who took the matriculation examination obtained a passing grade. In view of the fact that only 16 per cent of the age group of 15-19 years reached grade 10 at school, such a low pass percentage should be a cause for concern.

There is an observed tendency of an increasing percentage of students registering in private schools rather than government schools. For example the share of primary school enrolment in government schools fell from 86 per cent in 1991 to 75 per cent in 1999.[30] This increase in the role of private schools in the provision of primary education may be due as much to the higher quality of private schools as the deterioration in the quality of education and the management of government schools.

III.4 HEALTH

III.4.1 *Disease, Health Care and Poverty*: Three factors account for 60 per cent of the burden of disease in Pakistan, when measured in terms of life years lost: (i) Communicable infectious diseases. (ii) Reproductive health problems. (iii) Nutritional deficiencies.[31] Inspite of the fact that all three of the factors are preventable as well as treatable, the incidence of disease and mortality remains high. This is indicative of high levels of poverty (causing poor nutrition, and unhygienic living conditions within the household). Equally important is the continued severe lack of preventive and curative health infrastructure. The seriously inadequate preventive measures include sanitation, safe drinking water, adequate reproductive health care facilities for women and food safety regulations with respect to both raw and cooked food available outside the household.

The curative health care system has expanded substantially during the last decade. For example, the population per doctor has fallen from 2082 in 1990 to 1529 in the year 2000, and the population per nurse has fallen from 6374 to 3732 over the same period. The fact that inspite of this expansion the incidence of disease remains high points to both inadequate coverage and poor quality. According to the National Health Survey of Pakistan there is a high prevalence of ill health particularly amongst women. For example in rural areas prevalence of fair plus poor health for females above 25 years is about 75 per cent,

High drop out rates occur often because the household is facing adversity and gets pushed into such acute poverty that it is forced to send the children to work for a pittance rather than continue with education

There is a serious problem with the quality of education imparted to students not only with respect to the curricula but also the quality of instruction

The data from the survey conducted for this report (NHDR/PIDE 2001), suggests that the high prevalence of disease amongst those who are slightly above the poverty line is a major factor in pushing them into poverty

while for males in the same age group it is about 45 per cent.[32] The high prevalence of disease is also indicated by the fact that visits to a health care provider per person aged 5 years and above, is as high as 6 per year. An increasing proportion of the health care is now being provided by the private sector.[33]

Malnutrition is a major problem in Pakistan and is an important underlying factor in ill health and morbidity. For example for children, protein energy malnutrition is an underlying cause of death in about one-third of all deaths below 5 years of age. For women inadequate intake of energy, protein and micronutrients, compounded by high fertility and unhygienic living conditions associated with poverty, are major factors in the high prevalence of disease. For children, women and men, malnutrition leads to impaired immunity and high susceptibility to infection.

The data from the survey conducted for this report (NHDR/PIDE 2001), suggests that the high prevalence of disease amongst those who are slightly above the poverty line is a major factor in pushing them into poverty. Those who are already poor get pushed into deeper poverty as the result of loss of income and high medical costs resulting from illness. The data show that on average 65 per cent of the extremely poor were ill at the time of the survey and they had on average suffered from their current illness for ninety-five days (see chapter 3). Our survey data show that the poor predominantly go to private allopathic medical practitioners. Many of them are poorly trained and have grossly inadequate diagnostic facilities. Consequently when the poor fall ill they suffer for a protracted period and get locked into a high cost source of medical treatment, which erodes whatever few assets they have, and pushes them into indebtedness and deeper poverty (see chapter 3).

III.4.2 *Infant mortality rates, Immunization and Poverty*: Infant mortality rates have declined over the decade of the 1990s although they are still high compared to other low income countries. The infant mortality rate (IMR) in Pakistan declined from 122 per 1000 live births in 1991 to 89 per 1000 live births in 1999. The IMR for males was 93 per 1000 live births and for females 85 per 1000 live births. Health data suggest that infants born to the least educated mothers have twice the risk of dying within the first year after birth compared to more educated women.[34] However, it is noteworthy that since the percentage of uneducated women is much higher amongst poor households, infant mortality rates may be correlated not simply with the educational status of the mother but also with poverty and hence the inability of the mother to get adequate nutrition, pre natal and post natal care.

The critical determinant of an infant's survival and subsequent health is the nutrition status and health care received by the mother. In Pakistan where 40 per cent of the women are anemic and almost 80 per cent deliver at home without trained assistance, it is not surprising that both infant mortality and maternal morbidity associated with pregnancy are amongst the highest in Asia. (Maternal mortality rates are 300 to 400 per 100,000 live births).

Although the government has not been able to achieve its immunization target rate of 90 per cent, there has been a significant improvement in the immunization rate over the decade 1991 to 1999. The percentage of children between 12 and 23 months who were fully immunized increased from 37 per cent to 49 per cent. The immunization rates in children improved for both genders as well as rural and urban areas. According to PIHS data there is a strong correlation between income levels of household and immunization rates. For example, 75 per cent of the children in the upper income quintile were fully immunized as against only 25 per cent in the lowest income quintile.

III.4.3 *Female Health and Mortality*: Anne G. Tinker[35] in her study on women's health in Pakistan points out that Pakistan together with a number of other Asian countries is one of the few countries in the world where men outnumber women (108 men for every 100 women). She argues that this ratio is mainly due to relatively high mortality rates of young girls and women in the child-bearing age. Also the mortality rate of females in the age group 1 to 4 is 66 per cent higher for girls than boys, suggesting gender discrimination at an early age. Similarly the mortality rate for women in the peak child bearing age group (20 to 29), was more than double the rate during the lowest life time risk period (ages 10 to 19), which indicates poor maternal health services.[36]

Inspite of a substantial increase in immunization rate, maternal pre natal and neonatal rates have remained relatively stagnant. More than half of infant mortality and 45 per cent of under 5 mortality in Pakistan occurs during the first month of life. According to Anne G. Tinker these deaths are 'primarily the result of poor maternal health and nutrition, inadequate coverage of pregnant women with tetanus toxoid immunization and complications at delivery'.

Malnutrition which is widespread amongst the poor, affects adult women more than men. At least 40 per cent of women and 21 per cent of men are anemic. Adult women consume less iron than men in Pakistan even though their requirement is thrice as high as men. Similarly pregnant women receive only 87 per cent of the recommended calories, lactating mothers only 74 per cent and the protein intake for women is about 85 per cent of recommended levels.[37] Such malnutrition has inter generational implications for health, since malnourished mothers face the likelihood of low birth weight babies who often grow up into children with abnormally low height, weight, deficient learning capabilities and susceptibility to disease. (See section III.8 on children). In cases where the babies are girls, on reaching child bearing age they are pre-disposed to giving birth to babies with poor health in the next generation.

III.5 POPULATION

In this section we will briefly examine the problem of Pakistan's high population growth rate and its linkages with health and poverty. The issue of slowing down the population growth rate to achieve demographic stability over the next half century will be highlighted in the context of the government's recently announced Population Sector Perspective Plan.

III.5.1 *Population Growth, Poverty and Health*: Pakistan's population at the last (1998) census was 132.4 million which represents a quadrupling of the population since independence in 1947. With an inter-censal population growth rate of 2.6 per cent, as many as three million people are being added to the population every year. In terms of its contribution to the growth of the world population, Pakistan will have surpassed China and will be second only to India by the year 2035.

Poverty, in so far as it is an underlying factor in high fertility rates, contributes to a high population growth rate. At the same time, a rapidly growing population in turn accentuates poverty. For example, during the process of economic development in Pakistan as the mortality rate decline occurs quicker than the fertility rate decline in poor households, income differentials between poor and non-poor households increase.[38] Poverty, especially the adverse health and socio-economic status of poor women is accentuated as marginal households with given incomes bear the burden of a larger number of children. The consequent constriction of food consumption results in increased malnutrition, greater susceptibility to disease, and hence reduced productivity and intensified poverty.[39] With 40 per cent of children and 45 per cent of women in the child-bearing age (15 to 49 years) suffering from malnutrition, not only is the health and productivity of the existing population adversely affected, but also that of future pregnancy outcomes. As our NHDR/PIDE Survey data shows (see chapter 3), the majority of poor households are suffering from ill health, with a high cost of medical treatment. Illness according to our survey data is a major trigger point that pushes households into deeper poverty. Thus in Pakistan high fertility rates, high population growth rates, ill health and poverty are linked in a vicious cycle. One of the points at which it can be broken is through public action to rapidly reduce fertility rates. Unless this is done urgently there will be an unmanageable increase in the number of young persons deprived of education, health and employment opportunities. This could place overwhelming pressures on the social fabric and the State.

III.5.2 *Achieving Demographic Stability*: Pakistan has a relatively young population, with 41 per cent being below age 15, and as much as 20 per cent of the population in the age group 15 to 24, who would soon contribute to population growth. This is the population momentum, influenced by past

The adverse health and socio-economic status of poor women is accentuated as marginal households with given incomes bear the burden of a larger number of children

In Pakistan high fertility rates, high population growth rates, ill health and poverty are linked in a vicious cycle

**High Population Growth, Poverty and Illness:
A Vicious Circle**

- High Fertility Rates
- High Population Growth Rate
- High Infant Mortality and Lower age of marriage
- For given GDP increase, lower increase in per capita income.
- With given fiscal resources, larger percentage of population without adequate health care, sanitation and primary education
- Deeper Poverty
- **Poverty**
- Lowered Productivity and higher cost of medical treatment per household
- High Frequency of illness

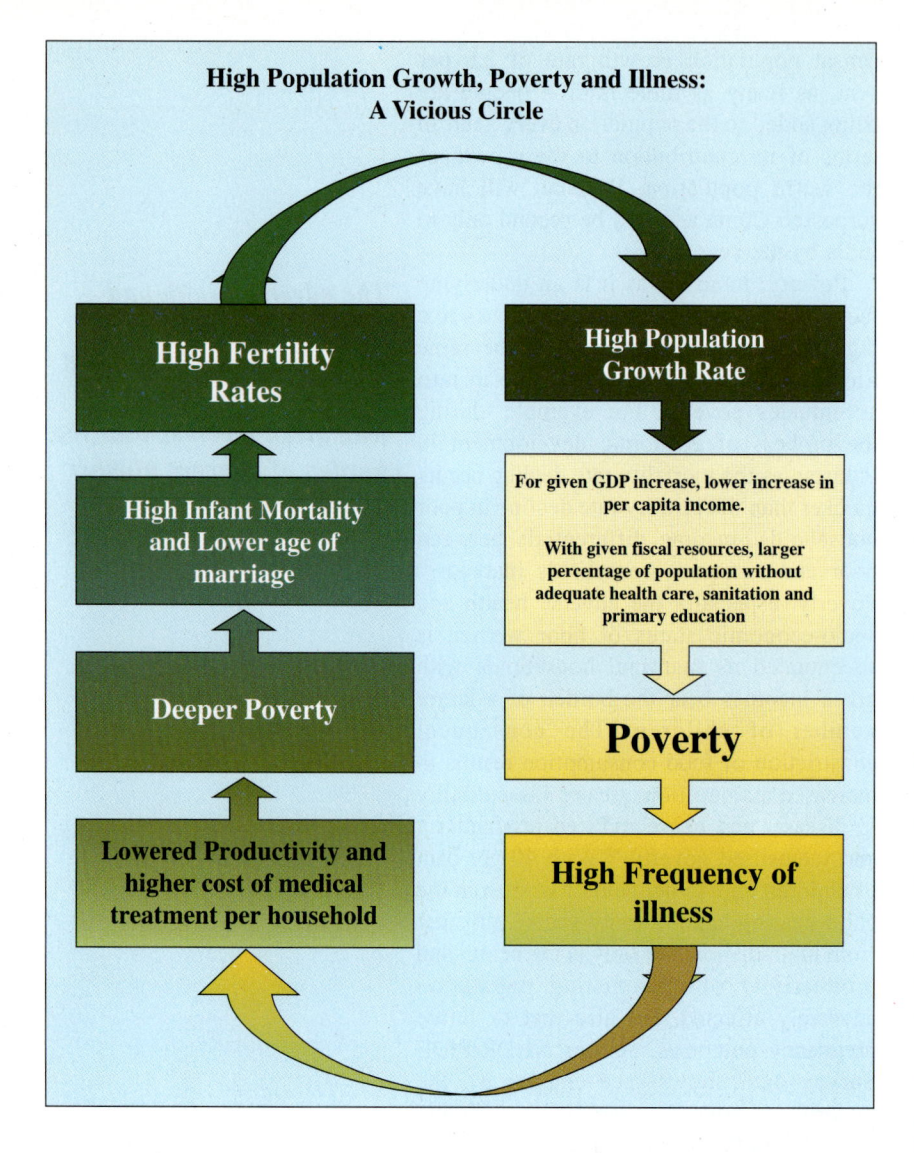

fertility patterns which could generate a relatively high population growth rate for a number of decades. According to a medium level variant of population projection, if the total fertility rate of (TFR) of 5 children per woman were to decline to 2.4 children per woman, Pakistan's population growth rate could decline to 1.4 per cent by 2023, with the total population reaching 212 million.[40] Such an outcome requires continued progress in reducing fertility rates, increases in age of marriage for females, and broad based population planning and development efforts. The government in July 2002 announced a population policy, which aims at an even more ambitious target than that implied in the medium variant projection. It aims to reach a replacement fertility level of 2.1 children per family and a total population of 204 million by the year 2023. This is to be achieved through an energetic and systematic family planning programme integrated with a reproductive health programme using the infrastructure and outreach of both the Ministry of Health and the Ministry of Population Welfare.

The government plans to achieve the long-term objective of population stabilization, by reaching a number of medium term targets. These include an increase in the contraceptive prevalence rate from the present 30 to 57 per cent in 2012, sustaining the increase in age of marriage of girls, fulfilling the existing high unmet need for family planning (33 per cent), and increasing family planning programme coverage from the present 65 to 100 per cent by 2010.

The government's Population Sector Perspective Plan seeks to achieve these quantitative targets through a number of programme interventions which include:
(a) Contribute to improved health, and economic conditions of women by enabling them to avoid 'too many children, too early, too late and too close together'.[41]
(b) Involve males as partners and make family planning service at low cost and of high quality, accessible to couples.
(c) Encourage current users to be continuous users and reach out to younger couples with information and choice of spacing methods.[42]

Even if the ambitious population target of a replacement fertility rate of 2.1 children per family is achieved by 2023, Pakistan's population will continue to grow for another four decades or so, due to the population momentum. This points to the need for systematic and energetic public action combining government with NGOs to be undertaken and maintained so that the aim of population stabilization in the next fifty years can be achieved.

III.6 THE CRISIS OF POVERTY

Poverty has increased sharply during the 1990s. In terms of the calorific norm[43] the percentage of population below the poverty line increased from 26.6 per cent in 1992-93 to 32.2 per cent in 1998-99 (see table 7-a).[44] Similarly, estimates in terms of the poverty gap (which captures the increase in poverty of individual poor households) and in terms of the severity of poverty (which captures the shift of poor households from a relatively better off to a relatively worse off category), both indicate a worsening of the poverty situation during the 1990s (see table 7-a).

Not only has poverty increased but the inequality in the distribution of income in Pakistan has also increased significantly (table 7-b). Income inequality measured in terms of the Gini index for Pakistan as a whole has increased from 26.85 in 1992-93 to 30.19 in 1998-99 (see table 7-b). In urban areas, income inequality which was relatively higher to start with, has increased more sharply compared to rural areas (see table 7-b). For example the Gini index for urban areas of Pakistan has increased from 31.7 in 1992-93 to 35.96 in 1998-99. In rural areas it has increased from 23.89 to 25.21.

As poverty and inequality increased, unemployment and under-employment should also be expected to have increased sharply. This is due to the fact that while GDP growth has declined during the 1990s, there has also been a decline in employment elasticities, labour productivity and real wages in both agriculture and industry (see Table 7 in chapter 2). According to the government,[45] about 0.5 million persons, which is 40 per cent of all new entrants to the labour force, are added to the ranks of the unemployed every year.

While an adverse change in the level and structure of economic growth was a crucial factor in increasing poverty, equally important was the deterioration in the institutions of governance. Due to poor economic management by the government, both the level of development expenditure and the efficiency of its use declined.[46]

Annual development expenditure has historically played a significant role in building infrastructure and generating secondary multiplier effects on GDP and employment. In the period 1980 to 1999, development expenditure fell from 40 per cent of total government expenditure in 1980-81 to 13.5 per cent in 1999-2000. The adverse effects of this trend on the GDP growth was accentuated by the growing inefficiency of the development expenditure induced by politically motivated projects and wide spread corruption.[47] These trends may have been significant factors underlying the phenomenon of deteriorating infrastructure, decelerating growth in the GDP and accelerating poverty.

Deterioration in the institutions of government that were responsible for providing public goods and services, meant

Table 7 (a)   Incidence of Poverty during the 1990s

Poverty Index	1992-93 HIES	1993-94 HIES	1996-97 HIES	1998-99 PIHS
Head-count	26.6	29.3	26.3	32.2
Poverty Gap	4.5	5.5	4.5	6.9
Severity of poverty	1.2	1.5	1.2	2.2

Source: Federal Bureau of Statistics, April 2001.

Table 7 (b)   Income Inequality (Gini Index) during the 1990s

Region and Province	1992-93 HIES	1993-94 HIES	1996-97 HIES	1998-99 PIHS
Pakistan	26.85	27.09	25.85	30.19
Urban areas	31.70	30.70	28.77	35.96
Rural areas	23.89	23.45	22.65	25.21

Source: Federal Bureau of Statistics, April 2001.

Chart 11   Incidence of Poverty During the 1990s

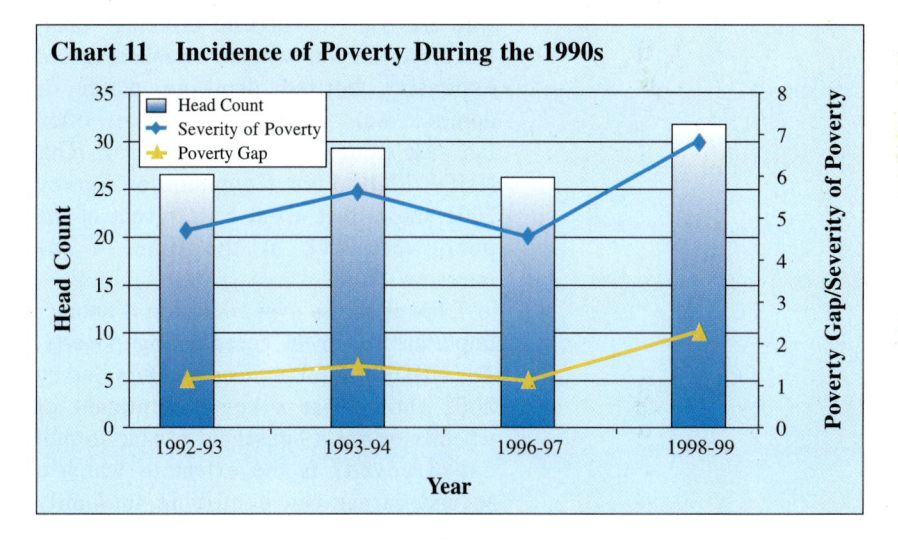

that there was an inadequate coverage and quality with respect to services such as health, sanitation, drinking water, education and transport.

As the quality of basic health units and government hospitals declined, the poor were forced to either shift to expensive private medical services (thereby getting locked into debt dependence) or not having effective access to health services at all (see analysis of NHDR/PIDE Survey results in chapter 3). Similarly even at the end of the decade of the 1990s, 37 per cent of the population did not have access over safe drinking water and 61 per cent of the population did not have sanitation facilities. With the decline in municipal services many

GDP growth has declined during the 1990s, there has also been a decline in employment elasticities, labour productivity and real wages in both agriculture and industry

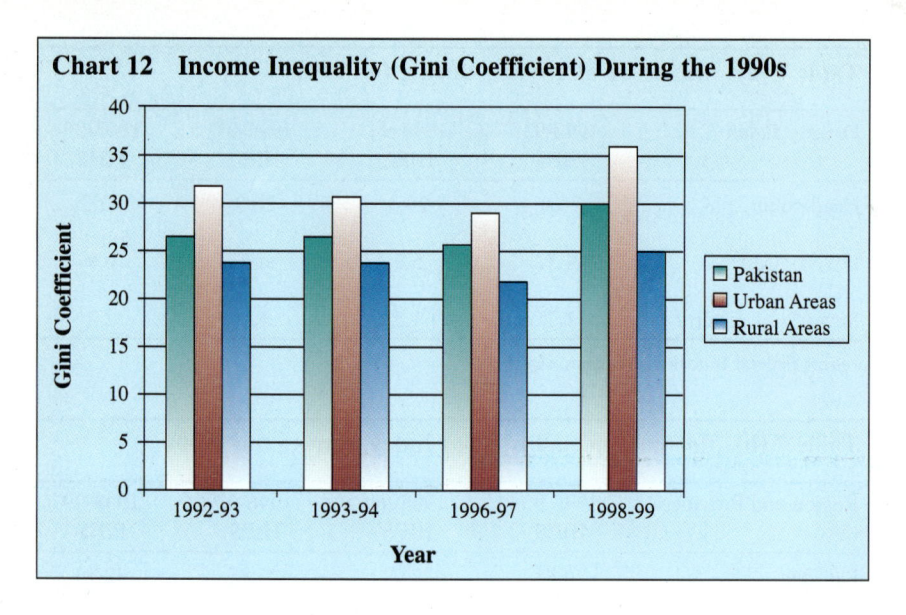

Chart 12   Income Inequality (Gini Coefficient) During the 1990s

[Bar chart showing Gini Coefficient for Pakistan, Urban Areas, and Rural Areas for years 1992-93, 1993-94, 1996-97, and 1998-99]

of those who do get piped drinking water find it unsafe. Those amongst the rural poor who are deprived of safe drinking water, and the urban poor who are unable to afford expensive bottled drinking water or domestic water treatment appliances, often fall sick from water-borne diseases. (Our NHDR/PIDE Poor Communities Survey 2001 shows that about 65 per cent of the poor were sick at the time of the interview).[48]

Lack of access over education is another important factor in accentuating poverty. The NHDR/PIDE Poor Communities Survey 2001 shows that a key determinant of whether or not a household is able to pull out of poverty is the extent to which a second earner can contribute to family income. The evidence shows that the income earning capability of the second earner is closely co-related with her/his education.

We have argued in this section that the slow growth and the adverse structure of the GDP, as well as weaknesses in the institutions responsible for delivering basic services, may have been important factors in the sharply increasing poverty, as indicated by various head count estimates. Yet the poor are not isolated heads to be merely counted. This UNHDR is different from that of most earlier studies on poverty because of the following postulates: The poor exist as living communities who are locked into a structure of power which keeps them dependent on the landlord, the money lender and the local state officials. At the same time the local markets are mediated by the local elites who give the poor unequal access over both the input and output markets. The poor thus face a structure of markets, state and official institutions, which discriminates against their access over resources, public services, and the process of government decision making.[49] The evidence presented in chapter 3, provides support to these propositions.

III.7 WOMEN, POVERTY, ACCESS AND AUTONOMY

A national survey generating gender disaggregated poverty data is required for a systematic gender analysis of the processes of poverty, and the specific determinants of the economic burden on poor women. However, scattered evidence that is available suggests that due to unequal access of women over productive resources and prevailing gender norms within traditional households, women bear a disproportionately higher burden of poverty: Gender discrimination in access over markets, institutions and resources constrain women from overcoming poverty. At the same time lack of autonomy within the household restrains them from increasing and consuming income from even the existing very limited market opportunities. These issues based on the available evidence will be briefly discussed in this sub-section.

III.7.1 *Poverty and the Double Burden on Women*: Poor women in Pakistan have a double burden: the poverty burden and the burden of gender bias against them in social and economic life. This gender bias is reflected in national income statistics which fail to adequately account for the economic contribution of women. It is reflected also in household income and expenditure surveys, which fail to record gender specific distribution of income and consumption *within* the household. This is so inspite of the fact that females constitute 47 per cent of the rural population. Amongst the economically active persons in agricultural households, 42 per cent are women. Evidence of women's economic activities in rural areas comes from district and provincial village level studies. These studies show that the rural Pakistani women are not only completely responsible for time

The poor are not isolated heads to be merely counted

The poor exist as living communities who are locked into a structure of power which keeps them dependent on the landlord, the money lender and the local state officials

and energy consuming household chores, but are also major contributors to the rural economy in three sub sectors: crop production, livestock production and cottage industry.[50] A survey conducted by the Barani Agricultural Research and Development Project in five districts of NWFP shows that 82 per cent of women participate in agricultural work. They spend 45 per cent of their time on agricultural activities and are responsible for 25 per cent of the production of major crops and 30 per cent for food.[51]

In the case of livestock related work, a survey of Barani areas in the Punjab and the NWFP found that out of fourteen livestock production operations covering a complete range of activities, women have primary responsibility for at least eight and are active in the other six.[52] In some activities, such as making *ghee*, and handicraft products manufactured by women often on a piece work basis, including embroidery, tailoring, weaving, leather work, pottery, ceramics and food processing, women have exclusive responsibility. A sample survey of Barani areas found that returns from the sale of animal products by women constitute on average 13 per cent of the total household income. Similarly a household survey of rural working women carried out in forty-two villages of the Punjab showed that 55 per cent of the total respondents were doing cotton embroidery, 20 per cent of women were making straw products and 8 per cent were making mats and baskets. It is clear therefore that women play a vital role in the process of agriculture production, the manufacture of off farm products, performing household tasks, caring for children, and cooking and carrying fuel and water. Yet compared to their male counterparts, they have an inferior social status and a poorer access over services such as health, education, transport, police, and administrative and judicial services. As poverty has increased, persistent inadequacy of basic services and rising violence by religious extremists have combined to intensify the pressure on women. As Khawar Mumtaz points out, women from poor households today are subject to not only the stress from economic deprivation but also: 'loneliness..., violence and fear of violence, depression and resignation...'.[53]

III.7.2 *Gender Discrimination and Market Access*: Due to gender discrimination against women in work roles as well as social restrictions on mobility, women have a relatively poorer access over education, skill training and health facilities as well as over labour markets. Consequently the ability of women to access productive resources, increase their income, improve their health and social status is more limited compared to men. The lack of access over income earning opportunities is reinforced by lack of control over the *utilization* of their earned income within the household. For example a recent research study shows that while women in many poor rural households are making a substantial contribution to family income (16 to 25 per cent), their *control* over intra household consumption decisions is relatively restricted.[54]

III.7.3 *Lack of Access over Education and Skill Training*: This is indicated by the fact that female literacy in Pakistan is over 29 per cent compared to 55 per cent for men. There are only 10 vocational colleges for women, compared to 162 for men and in higher education institutions, women form only 28.9 per cent of the student body in 26 public sector universities.[55]

III.7.4 *Lack of Access over Health Facilities*: This is indicated by the fact that 47 per cent of girl children are fully immunized (compared to 52 per cent of boys) and over 40 per cent of the adult women in the country suffer from anemia. Moreover, households of middle and lower income groups spend considerably less on women than on men in the event of illness and only 20 per cent of women are assisted, by a trained provider during delivery, resulting in not only high infant mortality rates but onset of chronic post natal infections in the case of mothers. Finally information and services to prevent and control reproductive tract infections (including transmission of HIV) and to combat gender based violence are unavailable on any significant scale.[56]

III.7.5 *Gender Discrimination in Labour Markets*: Women's participation in the labour market is adversely affected by the prevalence of traditional gender role norms, restrictions on women's mobility and

Women from poor households today are subject to not only the stress from economic deprivation but also: 'loneliness..., violence and fear of violence, depression and resignation...'

Table 8   Patterns of Female Work Participation by Regions

	Barani	Semi-irrigated	Peri-Urban	Central Punjab	Southern Punjab
All Activities					
Labour force participation rate	75.7	63.4	40.2	66.5	80.9
Unpaid work	61.1	41.6	13.7	29.6	16.6
Paid work	14.6	21.8	26.5	36.9	64.3
Agriculture and Livestock Activities					
Agricultural production	60.4	26.7	5.9	31.5	46.5
Unpaid work on own farm	56.9	17.3	2.0	17.2	12.9
Wage workers	3.5	9.4	3.9	14.3	33.6
Livestock production	66.0	57.4	28.4	57.7	56.0
Non-earning workers	60.4	46.5	17.6	34.5	41.9
Earning income	5.6	10.9	10.8	23.2	14.1
Non-Agricultural Income Earning Activities					
Work outside the home – informal	2.4	3.5	5.9	7.9	3.7
Work outside the home – formal	2.1	–	–	–	–
Home-based income earning activities	4.5	9.4	15.7	7.9	38.2
(N)	(288)	(202)	(102)	(203)	(241)

Source: Zeba Sathar and Shahnaz Kazi, PIDE 1997.

Table 9   Women's Earnings by Principal Activity and Days Worked

	Mean Income (Rs.)	Mean days worked
Agricultural labour	2015	84
Earnings for livestock production	5197	137
Non-agricultural informal sector work	4667	161
Teachers	27411	166
Home-based income earning activities	3148	109
All income earning work	3541	101

Source: Zeba Sathar and Shahnaz Kazi, PIDE 1997.

occupational segregation. Consequently female labour force participation rates in remunerative employment in Pakistan as a whole, are extremely low at 13.7 per cent compared to 70.4 per cent for men. There is also evidence (from a sample survey in rural Punjab) that of the women in farm households who participate in the labour force, as many as 63.5 per cent are engaged in unpaid work, while in landless rural households, of the women participants in the labour force, 34 per cent are engaged in unpaid labour. The data show that due to prevailing seclusion norms, only women from the poorest rural households work in the public space for remuneration and even here their returns are meager since they are relegated to low paid farm labour.

III.7.6 *Women's Work Patterns, Unpaid Work and Women's Autonomy*: Zeba Sathar and Shahnaz Kazi[57] in their study of ten rural regions of the Punjab have shown that while women are predominantly employed in agriculture and livestock, in a large proportion of cases the work is unpaid. The percentage of unpaid farm labour for women varies considerably across regions. In the case of agriculture production, the percentage of unpaid farm work for women is as high as 56.9 per cent in the Barani areas, falls sharply to 17.3 per cent in the semi irrigated areas, and falls further to 12.9 per cent in the irrigated areas of Southern Punjab (see Table 8). Amongst other factors there are two reasons why unpaid farm work for women in the Barani (rain-fed) areas is so high: (i) In these areas the data show that in the sub-group of landowning households nearly 84 per cent of the female respondents were working on their family farm compared to 23 per cent of men.[58] Given the low yield per acre in Barani (rain-fed) areas, the men traditionally seek employment in the military services and trade sector in rural areas. (ii) At a more general level, Barani agriculture with a wheat-pulses cropping pattern, offers fewer opportunities for wage employment compared to the irrigated regions of central and Southern Punjab. In the latter regions, production of cotton and vegetables, which are more labour intensive and where women are traditionally hired for cotton picking and vegetable weeding, there is greater demand for female wage labour.

While agriculture and livestock are the predominant source of women's employment, home based income earning activities are also important. Such activities engage 15.7 per cent of women participants in the labour force, while in Southern Punjab the figure rises to 38.2 per cent.[59]

The Sathar and Kazi study points out that paid employment outside the home is mainly undertaken by women in such low income households that seclusion norms cannot be observed due to economic pressures. In the case of women from landowning families (over 12 acres) seclusion norms are adhered to a greater extent, and here the major source of income for women is sale of livestock products and home based income earning activities.

As table 9 shows the return to women's employment are so low that even though on average they work 101 days a year their average daily income at US$0.15 (Rs.3400 per year), per day is far below the subsistence level. The mean earnings are highest for teachers, and lowest for agricultural wage workers.

An important question investigated for the first time in the Sathar and Kazi study is the control over the income earned by women. As table 11 shows, women engaged in home based income earning activities are able to keep their earnings to a greater extent compared to female agricultural wage labourers. For example, in the former category about 73 per cent keep all their earnings, and 91 per cent have a say in how their income is spent compared to 44.4 per cent and 75.9 per cent respectively in the case of female agricultural wage labourers (see table 11).

In examining the issue of women's autonomy, a range of decision making areas within the household were investigated. These included decisions regarding health, education, marriage of children, food purchase, purchase of household goods, livestock and the issue of women's employment outside the home. The evidence broadly shows that in intra household decisions related with children and food purchase, over 50 per cent of the women reported participation. However on the issue of women's work outside the home, only 38.5 per cent of the women reported participation in the decision, and for other economic issues related with purchases, the figure was less than 21 per cent.

It is significant that paid employment and women's contribution to family income emerge as the most important determinants of women's intra household decision making authority.

III.8 CHILDREN, POVERTY AND HEALTH HAZARDS

The area that is Pakistan today has been the crucible of different civilizations since the last 2,500 years: It has been influenced by the Europeans, West Asia, Central Asia and South Asia. It therefore has not only a rich cultural heritage but also a rich genetic base

Table 10 Contribution of Women's Earnings to Household Income by Total Household Income Quintiles

Total Household income quintiles	Respondent's earnings as % of total household income
I	24.7
II	14.4
III	16.6
IV	14.1
V	10.2

Source: Zeba Sathar and Shahnaz Kazi, PIDE 1997.

Paid employment and women's contribution to family income emerge as the most important determinants of women's intra household decision making authority

Table 11 Women's Control of their Earnings by Selected Employment and Socio-Economic Indicators

	% Who keep all their earnings	% Who have a say how their earnings are spent irrespective of who keeps them
All	52.3	81.9
Type of Income Earning Activity		
Farm Labour	44.4	75.9
Livestock production	42.3	78.5
Non-agricultural work – informal	56.3	87.5
Non-agricultural work – formal	66.7	88.9
Home-based income earnings activities	73.1	91.3

Source: Zeba Sathar and Shahnaz Kazi, PIDE 1997.

which imparts to every generation of children an unusual intellectual and physical potential. Yet poverty and lack of basic services have deprived a large proportion of Pakistan's children of the opportunities of opening their eyes to the world through education, or walking upon it firm of limb and hopeful of heart.

III.8.1 *Children and Health*: Children in Pakistan from lower income families face a high risk of disease and death, suffer stunting and wasting of the body associated with widespread malnutrition and are obliged to work for a living, some times in hazardous occupations. Here they not only work long hours and face a wide range of diseases and injuries, but are also occasionally subjected to physical beating and sexual abuse.

Out of every 1,000 children who survive infancy, 123 die before the age of 5. Of those who survive, a large proportion suffer from malnutrition which leads to impaired immunity and higher vulnerability to infections. The National Health Survey of Pakistan[60] shows that between 30 per cent and 40 per cent of children in Pakistan (6.2 to 8.3 million children) suffer from stunting (i.e. low height for their age). Similarly over 14 per cent (2.9 million) suffer from wasting (i.e. low weight for height). As many as 44 per cent of rural children and 35 per cent of urban children are underweight (low weight for age). All three of these measures of malnutrition (stunting, wasting and underweight) make the children susceptible to repeated infectious diseases. The evidence shows, for example, that about 38 per cent of the children (between 5 to 14 years of age) in the rural areas and about 25 per cent of the children in the urban areas (5 to 14 years of age) have ill health (poor to fair). Thus a large proportion of children are suffering from malnutrition and associated frequent illness. Consequently, they have an impaired ability to learn and play, so crucial to the creative experience of childhood. The ability of children in Pakistan to acquire an education is constrained not only by their malnutrition and the resultant illness but also by the limited opportunities of education: As many as 38 per cent of the children do not get enrolled in primary education because of lack of schools and teachers.

Of those children who come from poor families and are unable to go to school, many are engaged in working for a living. According to the Planning Commission there were in 1991 as many as eight million[61] working children in the 10 to 14 years age group. A large number of these are working in hazardous occupations, even though employment of such children is forbidden under the Employment of Children Act of 1991. We will discuss in this section the hazards faced by such children.

III.8.2 *Hazards at Work Place—Agriculture*: Since the statistics on child workers reflect mainly the numbers in wage employment, child workers in the agricultural sector do not find an adequate place in quantitative estimates. Yet children working alongside their families in agricultural operations such as seed bed preparation, fodder cutting, rice transplanting, weeding and harvesting may constitute the majority of working children in Pakistan. Such children are increasingly exposed without protective devices to toxic substances in pesticides.[62] There is now evidence that indiscriminate use of pesticides many of which are banned in the advanced industrial countries are responsible for growing health hazards in developing countries. For example, although developing countries account for only one sixth of the pesticides users, the rate of poisoning there is thirteen times as great as in some of the developed countries.[63]

Another dimension of the hazards to which rural child workers are exposed, arises out of the production conditions in agriculture: The traditional ties of dependence of poor peasants on landlords in large parts of the Punjab and Sindh have been reinforced by cash indebtedness following the 'Green Revolution'.[64] Children of poor peasant families are often subjected to extra economic coercion. They are in many cases made to work without money wages, as domestic servants in the landlord's manor where they are frequently subjected to humiliation, beating and abuse.

III.8.3 *Hazards at Work Place—Industry*: While the problem of unemployment of adult workers in the informal sector is growing, an increasing number of families under poverty pressure are sending their children to work in the urban informal sector. The reason is that even though child workers are extremely poorly paid, their wages are a significant contribution to

---

Children in Pakistan from lower income families face a high risk of disease and death, suffer stunting and wasting of the body associated with widespread malnutrition

Children in hazardous industries not only work long hours and face a wide range of diseases and injuries, but are also occasionally subjected to physical beating and sexual abuse

Table 12 Percentage of Child Workers Reporting Hazards by Type of Hazard

Hazard	%
Health and Safety Hazards resulting from intrusion of workplace onto the road[1]	8.2
Dangerous Building Structure[2]	11.1
Unsafe Electrical Fittings[3]	3.0
Unsafe Use of Equipment[4]	3.6
Acute Air Pollution[5]	30.1
Handling Toxic Chemicals without protective devices[6]	5.0
Using unsafe Steel Cutting Procedure	0.3
Intense Heat and Glare	7.7
Danger of Falling into furnaces which lack protective devices	1.7
Unhygienic Food at Workplace	8.1
No protection against Welding Sparks	2.6
Excessive Working Hours[7]	9.0
Drain Water spread across Workplace Floor	2.3
Uncovered Manhole on premises, cement, dust and/or Wood Scrap at factory floor where child workers eat food	7.3

Source: Akmal Hussain: Field Survey on Child Workers in Construction and Construction-related Industries, September 1992.

Notes:
1. Includes injuries/deaths caused to child workers by passing vehicles in cases where these workers are employed in open air workshops which intrude onto metalled roads.
2. Includes weak building structure, broken stairs, weak roofs.
3. Includes open switches, electric wires hanging near the workers, naked wires, electric sparks.
4. Includes protruded cutting edges, absence of safety devices on machines.
5. Includes high levels of carbon monoxide, unburnt carbon particles in the air, silica particles in the air (in tiles factories), toxic solvent vapours from paints, dyes and thinners, sulphur compounds in varnish solvents used in furniture manufacture, corrosive acid fumes and cyanide in the air in electroplating units, carcinogenic fumes of vinyl chloride gas (a degraded product of PVC moulding).
6. Toxic dyes, pigments, plasticizers, dryers, acids, mercaptans, acrylic and vinyl resins, used in furniture, paints and plastic moulding units.
7. More than 10 hours of continuous work.

family income. The first survey on child workers in Pakistan was a small sample survey in Lahore conducted in 1985.[65] The survey showed that (on average a child worker was paid Rs.322 per month in 1986) and this constituted 13 per cent of the family income. In the case of children working in hazardous industries like for example construction where the average cash wage of child workers is higher and the total family income lower, the percentage contribution of the child workers wage to family income is 42 per cent.[66]

The poorer the family the greater the marginal significance of money income, and therefore the greater the pressure to send children into even hazardous industries. On the other hand employers in the informal sector find it profitable to hire child workers since they can be paid a wage below the legal minimum of Rs.2,500 per month fixed for adults.

In the urban and semi-urban areas, most of the working children are employed in small scale unregistered establishments in the informal sector where the employers can easily evade the legislative protections granted to working children with respect to protection against hazardous occupations and working hours. While the number of children in the large-scale formal sector may have declined, yet even here child work persists to a significant extent by means of the 'Contract System'. Under this system children remain employees of a contractor in the informal sector while actually

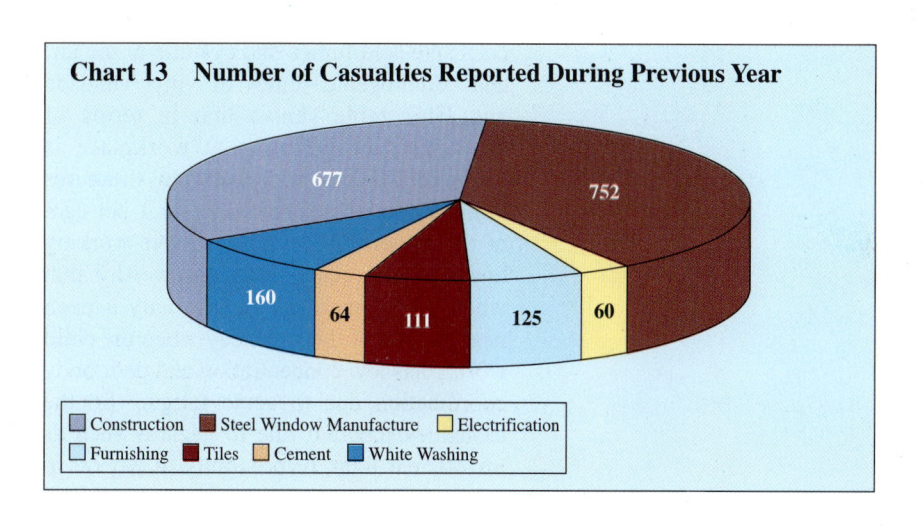

Chart 13 Number of Casualties Reported During Previous Year

- Construction: 677
- Steel Window Manufacture: 752
- Electrification: 60
- Furnishing: 125
- Tiles: 111
- Cement: 64
- White Washing: 160

THE MULTIFACETED CRISIS OF ECONOMY AND SOCIETY   29

working in larger industries, as a device to avoid the law.[67]

A study by Nishtar Medical College, Multan examined twenty-six small establishments in Lahore and showed that all of them were employing one or more children under 15 years of age. In most cases these work places posed several hazards to the health of the child workers including respiratory diseases such as pneumonia, tuberculosis and silicosis, ophthalmic disorders, mental retardation, damage to various body organs and cancer.[68]

The ILO study by Akmal Hussain in 1992 was the first systematic attempt at understanding the nature and the extent of hazards faced by child workers in the construction and related industries. These are perhaps not only growing more rapidly but have far greater hazards than any other set of occupations in which children are employed. The study is based on a field survey of child workers in 200 small-scale establishments in Lahore. Since this study is based on a sample survey in one large city, it cannot be used to draw generalizations at the national level. (A national level survey of children in hazardous industries perhaps needs to be conducted). However, it may be illustrative of the conditions prevailing in some of the other urban centers of Pakistan.[69]

The data show that there were fourteen different kinds of hazards at the workplace with air pollution being by far the hazard most frequently reported by the respondents (30 per cent) (see Table 12). Air pollution includes high levels of carbon monoxide, unburnt carbon particles and silica particles in the air (in tiles manufacture), toxic solvent vapours from paints, dyes and thinners, sulphur compounds in varnish solvents used in furniture manufacture, corrosive acid fumes and cyanide in the air, and carcinogenic fumes of vinyl chloride gas. This table shows that in terms of frequency, air pollution at workplace is followed by dangerous building structures at the workplace (reported by 11.1 per cent of the respondents), and excessive working hours (9 per cent). It is noteworthy that where accidents occur they usually happen near the end of the work day when the child worker has low concentration and poor body coordination due to acute fatigue. So the casualties reported due to hazards such as insufficient light, or proximity of worker to badly insulated electricity wires, may be causally linked with this fatigue factor. Handling toxic chemicals, intensive heat and glare and uncovered manholes in the workplace are also reported by a significant percentage of total respondents interviewed (see table 12).

Annexure II, Table 1 presents the number of casualties reported in each industry due to various hazards. It is important to note that casualties are mainly injuries, and respondents reported that individual child workers underwent repeated injuries during a year.

Annexure II, Table 2 synthesizes the data on hazards and resultant casualties in each industry by constructing a standardized Lethality Index for each category of hazards. Similarly, a standardized Danger Index for industries has been constructed to show how dangerous each category of hazards is in terms of its weight in that industry.

Annexure II, Table 4 presents the percentage of child workers reporting sex abuse in each industry and in each age group. In the case of tiles, cement, furnishing and construction, between 11 per cent to 15 per cent of the respondents (in the respective industries) report sex abuse by their employer. In the case of electrification, steel windows and white washing, the prevalence of sex abuse is at a lower level, ranging from 2 to 4 per cent.

Employer violence, like sex abuse, is prevalent to a significant extent although it varies considerably between industries (see Annexure II, Table 5).

The images of children at work under the scorching sun on building sites or in dark sweat shops lit up by welding sparks, have persisted for two generations. There is a danger of relegating the problem to the deadly realm of 'normalcy'. Yet behind these apparently unchanging images there has been a rapid increase in the number of child workers employed in dangerous occupations in the informal sector. At the same time, as we have shown in this section, a whole range of new hazards have emerged for child workers: toxic chemicals which they handle, and carcinogenic fumes which they breathe, leading to disease and deformity of body and mind. Behind the facade of normalcy, both the scale and intensity of the problem of child labour have reached alarming levels. It is time for policy makers as well as the community to understand and act to arrest this mutilation of a new generation. For specific policies to address the problem, see chapter 5.

III.9 Social Distress

As poverty levels rise, unemployment increases and access to basic services such as health, housing and education continues to remain grossly inadequate, poor households face acute distress. This distress is intensified by a number of additional factors: while malnutrition particularly amongst children from poor families makes them increasingly susceptible to infectious diseases, at the same time unhygienic environmental conditions for the provision of food increase the risk of disease.[70] Yet, due to grossly inadequate public health services, the poor are obliged to turn to expensive private medical services. Distress of extremely poor families associated with sending their children to hazardous work is intensified by injuries and death caused to the children at work places (see preceding Section III.8 of this chapter).

The distress of poor families resulting from injury, disease and death of their children in hazardous work is further intensified by a variety of crimes and human rights violations. Such privations are suffered by citizens, in general, and socially vulnerable poor households, in particular. These range from murder, rape and child abuse to kidnapping of children for sale. Table 14 gives province-wise figures of selected human rights violations in Pakistan for the year 2000, based on data provided by the Human Rights Commission of Pakistan. The data show that in the Punjab province there were 2,144 crimes perpetrated against citizens, 307 in the Sindh province, 88 in the NWFP and 11 in Balochistan. These figures may be biased downward since they are based only on those crimes which are reported in various newspapers in each district. An unknown number of crimes do not get registered at police stations and even a larger number do not get reported in the press. Nevertheless these figures are indicative of the vulnerability of citizens to violent crimes. All these distress factors combine to place family members under acute mental and emotional strain.

It is not surprising, therefore, that for the first time in Pakistan a new phenomenon is being reported in the press: Poverty related suicides. While the data on suicides is inadequate and is not systematically reported either by government agencies or NGOs, nevertheless we have been able to compile from press reports, data on poverty related suicides for the year 1999. While this data cannot be taken to be representative of the country as a whole, it is illustrative of the problem and enables us to apprehend, no matter how inadequately, the intense emotional experience of poverty on the one hand and the poignant sense of responsibility that mothers and fathers feel towards their children and their relatives. Table 13 shows that there were a total of 652 poverty related suicides in poor households. Of these as many as 475 were the result of family tensions related with economic pressure. One hundred and fifty-two suicides were the result of the mental stress of unemployment and twenty-five the result of pressures related with ill health. The gender wise description of suicides suggests that women in poor households take the brunt of mental pressure.

Even this limited evidence indicates the remarkable dignity of the poor, their sense of family responsibility and deep humanity illustrated by taking sick family members to even unaffordable medical facilities, paid for with loans (see chapter 3). Violation of this sense of dignity by brutal economic pressure and humiliating crimes against their family, some times drive the poor to suicide.

Chart 14 Human Rights Violations in Pakistan Number of Persons Affected in 2000

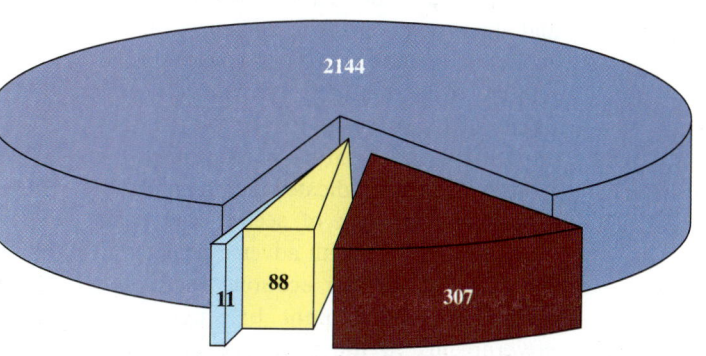

- Punjab: 2144
- Sindh: 307
- NWFP: 88
- Balochistan: 11

Note: Gross under reporting is likely in isolated areas and provinces.

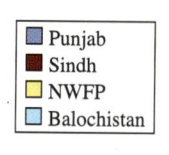

Table 13 Number of Poverty Related Suicides by Cause, by Social Group and Gender in 1999

Reported Cause	Middle Class Male	Middle Class Female	Middle Class Total	Poor Class Male	Poor Class Female	Poor Class Total	All
Family tensions related with economic pressure	64	13	77	220	255	475	552
Mental stress related with unemployment/underemployment	21	0	21	152	0	152	173
Mental stress resulting from economic pressures associated with ill health	5	4	9	17	8	25	34
Total	90	17	107	389	263	652	759

Source: Compiled from news reports in the daily *Jang*, Various issues, 1999.

Table 14 Human Rights Violations in Pakistan for the Year 2000.
Province-wise Breakdown of the Number of Persons Affected*

Province Name	Murder	Kidnapping	Rape	Burn Cases	Sexual Harassment	Child Abuse, Selling & Kidnapping	Total Violations
Punjab Province	605	590	467	223	132	127	2144
Sindh Province	184	53	14	47	2	7	307
NWFP Province	71	10	2	4	0	1	88
Balochistan Province	11	0	0	0	0	0	11
Total Violations (by type of violation)	871	653	483	274	134	135	2550

Source: Human Rights Commission of Pakistan, Lahore.

*Note: The data is collected by the Human Rights Commission of Pakistan's Head Office in Lahore. The source of the data is National and local daily newspapers. The format of the collected data is the number, nature, and place of violation/s per day. This format was converted to represent an annual figure for each District for each nature of violation for this study. The data is for the period 01/01/2000 to 31/12/2000.

CONCLUSIONS

In this chapter we have given a brief snapshot picture of the multi faceted crisis of finance, economy and society. There has been an unprecedented increase in poverty and unemployment. The acuteness of the economic condition of poor households, is reinforced by extremely inadequate access over basic services such as primary education and health, particularly for women. We have indicated that the problem of poverty and lack of access over basic services is related with adverse changes in the structure of the economy and poor economic management by successive governments in the past. We have also indicated some of the structural features in both the financial crisis as well as the crisis in the real economy. Unless these structural and institutional problems are addressed, growth is likely to remain slow and unstable, leading to still greater poverty in the future.

The impact of the crisis of poverty is particularly acute on the most vulnerable sections of society: Women and children. The suffering of women is intensified as they face social discrimination, gender inequality in the access over basic services, employment and income. The data we have presented in this chapter show that a disturbing proportion of poor children face malnutrition, and consequently increased susceptibility to disease. At the same time growing numbers of them instead of going to school are going to work in hazardous occupations where they are subjected to physical injuries and sexual abuse.

Poor households faced with hunger, frequent illness and seeing their children being physically and mentally mutilated, are confronted with the added distress of violence, kidnapping and theft due to the poor law and order situation.

It is clear therefore that in facing this multifaceted crisis of the human condition, the inter-related dimensions of the economy, institutions and governance would have to be simultaneously addressed. In the subsequent chapters we will analyze the dynamics of the crisis in terms of these dimensions to identify the policy actions that can be undertaken to overcome it.

NOTES

1. All figures in this para estimated from various issues of the Economic Survey, GOP, Economic Advisor's Wing, Finance Division.
2. A Debt Reduction and Management Strategy, Summary Report, GOP, March 2001, Table 2, p. 12.
3. Ibid., Table 1, p. 10.
4. Ibid., p. 7.
5. Ibid., Table 2, p. 11.
6. Ibid.
7. See, Hafiz Pasha: 'Fifty years of Public Finance in Pakistan: A Trend Analysis', in Shahrukh Rafi Khan (ed.), *Fifty Years of Pakistan's Economy: Traditional Topics and Contemporary Concerns*, OUP, 1999, p. 207, Table 2.
8. Overcoming Poverty: The Report of the Task Force on Poverty Eradication, May 1997.
9. See, Section II.1 (b).
10. This is elaborated in chapter 2.
11. This is elaborated in chapter 3.
12. See, Akmal Hussain, Employment Generation, Poverty Alleviation and Growth in Pakistan's Rural Sector: Policies for Institutional Change. Report prepared for the International Labour Organization, Country Employment Policy Review, Pakistan, ILO/CEPR, March 1999.
13. Akmal Hussain, ILO/CEPR, op. cit., p. 4.
14. For a more detailed discussion, see: Akmal Hussain, ILO/CEPR, pp. 5-18.
15. Interim Poverty Reduction Strategy Paper, Government of Pakistan, November 2001, p. 23.
16. Mark W. Rosegrant and Robert Evenson: 'Agricultural Productivity Growth in Pakistan and India: A comparative Analysis', presented at Pakistan Institute of Development Economists Ninth Annual General Meeting, Islamabad, 1993.
17. If atmospheric carbon is doubled, the average summer temperatures in Pakistan are expected to increase by 1.5 C to 4.5 C (base average of 2.5 C), over the next seventy years. This could lead to a decline in wheat yields from 10 per cent to 60 per cent, depending on the type of wheat seed, planting time, related atmospheric/weather conditions. See Qureshi, Ata and Iglesias, Implications of Global Climate Change for Pakistan Agriculture: Impacts on Simulated Wheat Production, Climate Institute, Washington, DC USA, 1992.
18. Alim Mian and Yasin Mirza: Pakistan Soil Resources, National Conservation Strategy, Sector Paper IV, Environment and Urban Affairs Division, with IUCN, 1993.
19. Sandra Postel, *Pillar of Sand: Can the Irrigation Miracle Last?*, W.W. Norton & Company (July 1999), New York.
20. Pakistan: A Strategy for Sustainable Agricultural Growth, World Bank Report No. 13092 Pak, November 1994.
21. The discussion on problems of Pakistan's irrigation in this sub-section is drawn from: Pakistan Irrigation and Drainage: Issues and Options, World Bank Report No. 11884-PAK, World Bank, 25 March 1994.
22. See, chapter 2 for a detailed discussion of this issue.
23. See, A.R. Kemal, 'Patterns and Growth of Pakistan's Industrial Sector' p. 162 in Shahrukh Rafi Khan (ed.), *Fifty Years of Pakistan's Economy: Traditional Topics and Contemporary Concerns*, Oxford University Press, Karachi, 1999.
24. Nomaan Majid, op. cit., Table A7, p. 103.
25. For larger districts like Lahore (and Karachi in Sindh) therefore further disaggregation of HDI for sub-districts would be necessary, which existing data does not permit.
26. Paul Streeten et al., *First Things First: Meeting Basic Needs in Developing Countries*, New York, Oxford University Press, 1981. Pages 46-47 cited in S.J. Burki, *Pakistan: Fifty Years of Nationhood*, Vanguard, Lahore, 1999.
27. *Social Development in Pakistan, Annual Review 2002*, Social Policy and Development Centre, Oxford University Press, Karachi 2002, p. 206.
28. Asian Development Bank, *Poverty in Pakistan*, July 2002, pp. 19-20.
29. Ibid., p. 21.
30. Asian Development Bank, op. cit. p. 22.
31. Asian Development Bank, *Poverty in Pakistan*, op. cit., p. 26.
32. National Health Survey of Pakistan, Pakistan Medical Research Council, Federal Bureau of Statistics, Pakistan and the Department of Health and Human Services, USA, 1998, p. 127.
33. Ibid., p. 2.
34. Naqvi and Zareen, Poverty in Pakistan: Review of Recent Literature. South Asia Poverty Reduction and Economic Management Unit, The World Bank, Islamabad.
35. Anne G. Tinker, *Improving Women's Health in Pakistan*, Human Development Network, The World Bank, 1998.
36. Anne G. Tinker, op. cit. p. 6.
37. Anne G. Tinker, op. cit. p. 8.
38. Population Sector Perspective Plan 2012, p. V.
39. Data from the NHDR/A.I. Hamid Spot Survey 2001 shows that large family size is one of the factors which accentuate poverty in low income families. It can be argued that the relatively larger family size in poor households makes them more vulnerable to economic shocks resulting from medical expenses following illness in the family, or bad harvests. (For a discussion on the relationship between the impact of sickness and the process of poverty creation see chapter 3).

40. Interim Population Sector Perspective Plan 2012, Government of Pakistan, February 2002, p. 6.
41. Ibid., p. vii.
42. Ibid.
43. The calorific norm is translated into monthly per equivalent adult expenditure of Rs.682 in 1998-99 crisis.
44. Inter-temporal comparison of household income and expenditure survey data (HIES) is somewhat compromised by the fact that the sample size in 1990-91 was much smaller than in subsequent years and also the average household sizes particularly in the lowest expenditure categories are higher in the 1998-99 PIHS compared to the HIES during 1992-93 to 1996-97. However, these qualifications not withstanding the general conclusion that poverty has increased substantially during the decade of the 1990s is robust and is supported by other poverty studies using different poverty lines and methodologies (See, Poverty in Pakistan: Vulnerabilities, Social Gaps, and Rural Dynamics, World Bank Report, 31 May 2002).
45. Pakistan Interim Poverty Reduction Strategy Paper (I-PRSP), Government of Pakistan, November 2001, p. 7.
46. A Debt Burden Reduction and Management Strategy, op. cit., p. 1.
47. For a detailed discussion of this issue, see chapter 2.
48. See, Table 25, in chapter 3 of this Report.
49. For a more detailed discussion of this approach see, Akmal Hussain, 'Pro-Poor Growth, Participatory Development and Decentralization, Paradigms and Praxis', in P. Wignaraja and S. Sirivardana, *Pro-Poor Growth and Governance in South Asia*, Zed Press, London (forthcoming), Part-III.
50. World Bank, *Women in Pakistan: An Economic and Social Strategy*, 1990.
51. Cited in Akmal Hussain, *Poverty Alleviation in Pakistan*, Vanguard Books, 1994, p. 17.
52. World Bank, *Women in Pakistan*, op. cit.
53. Khawar Mumtaz, 'Poverty: The Gender Perspective', Research Input for the UNHDR 2002.
54. Zeba A. Sathar and Shahnaz Kazi, *Women's Autonomy, Livelihood and Fertility*, PIDE, 1997.
55. See, *Poverty in Pakistan*, Asian Development Bank, July 2002.
56. See, Anne G. Tinker, *Improving Women's Health in Pakistan*, Human Development Network, The World Bank, Washington, DC, May 1998.
57. Zeba Sathar and Shahnaz Kazi in a recent study based on a sample survey of rural communities in ten Punjab districts, have for the first time, systematically investigated the patterns of women's employment and issues of women's employment. This sub-section draws on their work.
Zeba Sathar and Shahnaz Kazi, *Women's Autonomy, Livelihood and Fertility*, PIDE, 1997.
58. Ibid.
59. Ibid.
60. See, *National Health Survey of Pakistan – 1990-94*, Pakistan Medical Research Council, Health Profile of the People of Pakistan, Published: 1998.
61. This figure even for 1990 is an under estimate since it does not take account of working children in the age group 14 to less than 15. A revised estimate to take account of this bias is 8.65 million children in the year 1990. Assuming a 2.8 per cent population growth rate with the percentage of working children remaining constant (the percentage should be expected to because of sharply increasing poverty during the 1990s), the number of working children in the year 2001 may be approximately 12 million.
62. See, Akmal Hussain, 'Women, Environment and Development'. Paper presented to the Centre for Research and Management, Islamabad, 12 February 1991.
63. Catherine Canfield, 'Pesticides Exporting Death', *New Scientist*, 16 August 1984.
64. For a detailed analysis of this issue see, Akmal Hussain, 'Technical Change and Social Polarization in Rural Punjab', in *Strategic Issues in Pakistan's Economic Policy*, Progressive Publishers, Lahore, 1988.
65. Akmal Hussain, 'Economic Growth, Poverty and the Child', Paper presented at the Harvard Conference on *Who speaks for the Child*, Harvard University, Cambridge, Mass, 11-12 August 1986.
66. See, Akmal Hussain, 'Child Workers in construction and related industries in Pakistan', ILO/ARTEP, Geneva, 1 October 1992 (Mimeo). A summarized version was published in the *Journal of Lahore School of Economics*, Volume 2 No.2, July-December 1997.
67. *Situation Analysis of Children and Women in Pakistan*, UNICEF, 1992, p. 84.
68 Study by Nishtar Medical College, Multan, cited in *Discover the Working Child*, 1990, UNICEF, Islamabad.
69. The study may also be useful in that it developed a methodology for estimating the lethality index of each kind of hazard faced by working children and also for a standard danger index of industry with varying composition of hazard types.
70. The NHDR/PIDE 2001 Poor Communities Survey shows that as many as 65 per cent of poor respondents were sick at the time of the interview. These findings are corroborated by the *National Health Survey of Pakistan – 1990-94*, Pakistan Medical Research Council, Health Profile of the People of Pakistan, 1998.

CHAPTER 2

ECONOMIC POLICY, ECONOMIC STRUCTURE AND POVERTY

Photograph by Keith Stanley

**There is always another death to die
beyond the death you know**

**Always another door of scars
opening into another room**

– RUMI
13th Century Sufi Poet
(Translation, Lawrence Harvey)

CHAPTER 2

Economic Policy, Economic Structure and Poverty

INTRODUCTION

In chapter 1, we identified the elements of the crisis of the human condition in Pakistan. In this chapter we attempt to explain this crisis through a historical analysis of the impact of economic policy on the structure of the economy, as it developed a tendency for increasing poverty and loan dependence. These processes accelerated during the 1990s and began to be manifested in terms of acute poverty, sharp slow down in the GDP growth, unsustainable fiscal deficits and intense pressures on governance. The analysis in this chapter therefore focuses on the pattern of growth, fiscal deficits and poverty creation in the context of the economic policy of various regimes in the period 1958 to 1999.

I. THE AYUB REGIME 1958-69: ECONOMIC GROWTH, INEQUALITY AND THE ROOTS OF FINANCIAL DEPENDENCE

The economic strategy undertaken by the Ayub regime, while it accelerated GDP growth, sharply accentuated inter-personal and inter-regional economic inequalities. In this section, we will briefly examine the economic policies of the Ayub regime to indicate how an economic structure emerged in this period that was to lock Pakistan's economy into a narrow and inefficient industrial base, slow export growth and increasing loan dependence in the next four decades.

Following the Korean boom in 1953, the government introduced a policy framework for inducing the large profits of traders in jute and raw cotton to flow into the manufacturing sector. This was done through a highly regulated policy framework for import substitution industrialization in the consumer goods sector. The policy combined tariff protection for manufacturers of consumer goods together with direct import controls on competing imports. It has been estimated that the average rate of effective protection was as high as 271 per cent in 1963-64, and fell to 125 per cent in 1968-69.[1] This enabled the emerging industrial elite to make large profits from the domestic market without the competitive pressure to achieve higher levels of efficiency and an export capability.

During the 1960s import substitution industrial growth in the consumer goods sector, was more systematically encouraged by the government. This was done by means of high protection rates to domestic

The economic strategy undertaken by the Ayub regime, while it accelerated GDP growth, sharply accentuated inter-personal and inter-regional economic inequalities

Chart 1 Period Averages of Exports of Various Commodity Groups as a % of Total Exports of Pakistan

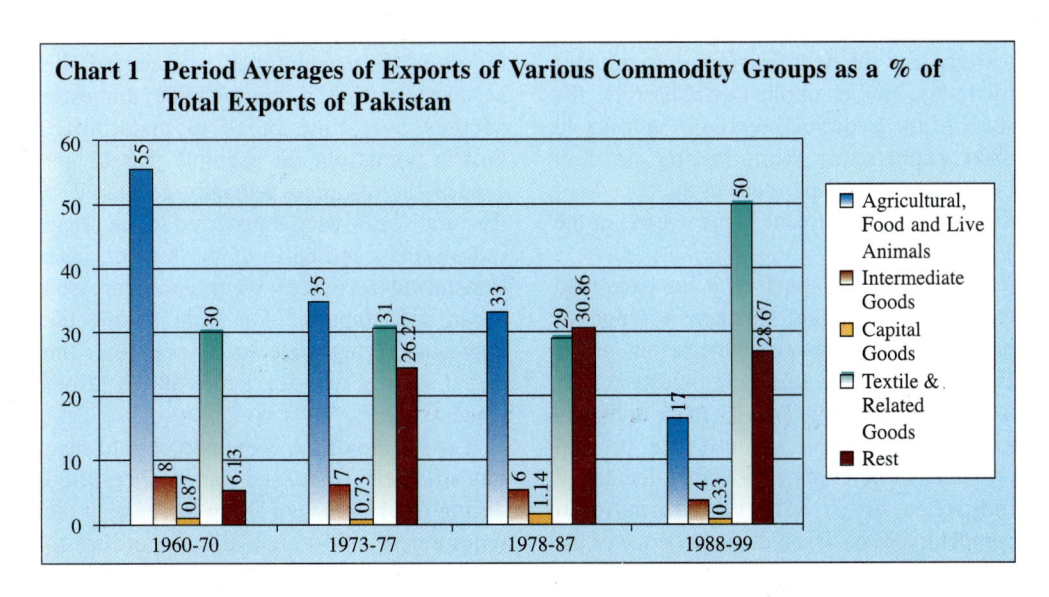

Period	Agricultural, Food and Live Animals	Intermediate Goods	Capital Goods	Textile & Related Goods	Rest
1960-70	55	8	0.87	30	6.13
1973-77	35	7	0.73	31	26.27
1978-87	33	6	1.14	29	30.86
1988-99	17	4	0.33	50	28.67

> *The government through a range of protection measures and concessions in the 1960s, enabled the emerging industrial elite to make large rupee profits from domestic and export sales, without the market pressures to diversify into high value added industries or to achieve international competitiveness*

manufacturers of consumer goods, cheap credit, and direct import controls on competing imports. At the same time, there was removal of import controls (established earlier in the 1955) on industrial raw materials and machinery. In addition to various forms of protection, new incentives were offered for exports. These included the Bonus Voucher Scheme, tax rebates, tax exemptions and accelerated depreciation allowances to increase post tax profits.

The Bonus Voucher Scheme enabled exports of certain manufactured goods to receive in addition to the rupee revenue of their exports, bonus vouchers equivalent to a specified percentage of the foreign exchange earned. The vouchers could be sold in the market (to potential importers) for a price usually 150 to 180 per cent above the face value. Thus, the exporter not only earned the rupee revenues from exports but also an additional premium through sale of the bonus vouchers.

The Bonus Voucher Scheme essentially constituted a mechanism for enabling domestic manufacturers to earn large rupee profits on exports which brought no gain to the economy in terms of foreign exchange. Soligo and Stern[2] estimated that during the 1960s, Pakistan's main industries (when input costs and output values are both measured in dollar terms) were producing negative value added.

It has been argued that the phenomenon of negative value added in industry was an important reason why during the 1960s, despite import substitution and large export volumes, foreign exchange shortages persisted.[3] He suggests that this set the 'mould' for Pakistan's narrow export base (concentration on low value added end of textiles) and the debt problem, that remains till today. For example (see Chart 1), the share of the traditional textile in industry in total exports far from falling, in fact increased from 30 per cent in the decade of the 1960s to 50 per cent in the decade of the 1990s.

In a broader perspective, it can be argued that the government through a range of protection measures and concessions in the 1960s, enabled the emerging industrial elite to make large rupee profits from domestic and export sales, without the market pressures to diversify into high value added industries or to achieve international competitiveness. Thus, the experience of the 1960s is illustrative of the nature of both government and the economic elite. In the pursuit of securing its power base, the government by means of subsidies, manipulation of tariffs and the exchange rate mechanism, transferred rents to the industrial elite. This reinforced the tradition bound propensity of the economic elite for risk aversion, lack of innovative dynamism and dependence on governmental patronage.

The economic policies and processes during the 1960s, illustrate the sociological propensity of the ruling elite to seek rents from government which in turn reinforced its power through such patronage. These sociological propensities are rooted in the region's history stretching back to the eighteenth century (see box titled: Government Patronage and Rent Seeking Elites: A Longer Historical View). These tendencies persisted in varying degrees for the next four decades. Yet they were at an economic cost that became a growing burden on an increasingly fragile economy: It has been estimated for example that even in 1990-91 by which time the rates of effective protection had been considerably reduced, the increase in the share of manufacturing attributable to protection amounted to 5 per cent of GNP.

As we have seen, the government during the 1960s adopted a deliberate policy of concentrating national income in the hands of the upper income groups.[4] The economic basis of this policy was the assumption that the rich save a larger proportion of their income and hence a higher national savings rate could be achieved with an unequal distribution of income (the target savings rate being 25 per cent of GDP). In practice while the policy of distributing incomes in favour of the economic elite succeeded, the assumption that it would raise domestic savings over time failed to materialize. Griffin points out for example that 15 per cent of the resources annually generated in the rural sector were transferred to the urban industrialists and 63 to 85 per cent of these transferred resources went into increased urban consumption.[5] Far from raising the domestic savings rate to 25 per cent, the actual savings rate never rose above 12 per cent.[6]

The failure of the economic elite to save out of their increased income resulted during the 1960s, in a sharp increase in the requirement of foreign aid. According to

> *The phenomenon of negative value added in industry was an important reason why during the 1960s, despite import substitution and large export volumes, foreign exchange shortages persisted*

official figures, gross foreign aid inflows increased from US$373 million in 1950-55 to US$2,701 million in 1965-70. The rapid increase in foreign aid was accompanied by a change in its composition from grants to higher interest loans.[7] Consequently, the debt-servicing burden rose dramatically. Debt servicing as a percentage of foreign exchange earnings was 4.2 per cent in 1960-61 and increased to 34.5 per cent by 1971-72. The magnitude of this figure did not fall for the next three decades and by the year 2000, it was even higher at 40 per cent.

Given the policy of re-distributing incomes in favour of the rich, it is not surprising that by the end of the 1960s a small group of families with inter-locking directorates dominated industry, banking and insurance in Pakistan. In terms of value added 46 per cent of the value added in the large scale-manufacturing sector originated in firms controlled by only forty-three families.

In banking, the degree of concentration was even greater than industry. For example, seven family banks constituted 91.6 per cent of private domestic deposits and 84.4 per cent of earning assets. Furthermore, State Bank compilation of balance sheets of listed companies indicates that the family banks tended to provide loans to industrial companies controlled by the same families.[8] The insurance industry, although smaller in size than banking, also had a high degree of concentration of ownership. The forty-three industrial families controlling 75.6 per cent of the assets of Pakistani insurance companies tended to favour industrial companies owned by the same group.[9]

The major industrial families and entrepreneurs were a fairly closely-knit group. Not only did many of them have caste and kinship relations, but also members of the families tended to sit on each other's boards of directors. For example about one-third of the seats on the boards of directors of companies controlled by the forty-three families were occupied by members of other families within the forty-three.

Not only were the forty-three families dominating industry, insurance and banking, but also had considerable power over government agencies sanctioning industrial projects. PICIC (Pakistan Industrial Credit and Investment Corporation) was the agency responsible for sanctioning large-scale industrial projects. Out of the twenty one directors of PICIC, seven were from the forty three leading industrial families and were actively involved in the public sector financial institutions that directly affected their private economic interests.

During the process of rapid economic growth of the 1960s, while an exclusive and highly monopolistic class was amassing wealth, the majority of Pakistan's population was suffering an absolute decline in its living standards. For example, the per capita consumption of foodgrain of the poorest 60 per cent of Pakistan's urban population declined from an index of 100 in 1963-64 to 96.1 in 1969-70. The decline was even greater over the same period in the case of the poorest 60 per cent of rural population. In their case, per capita consumption of foodgrain declined from an index of 100 in 1963-64 to only 91 in 1969-70.[10] There was an even larger decline in the real wages in the industry: Griffin suggests that in the decade and a half ending in 1967, real wages in the industry declined by 25 per cent.[11] An ILO/SAAT study has estimated that in 1971-72, poverty in the rural sector was so acute that 82 per cent of rural households could not afford to provide even 2,100 calories per day per family member.[12]

In an economy where there were significant differences in the infrastructure facilities available in the different provinces, there was a tendency for investment based on private profitability to be concentrated in the relatively developed regions. Consequently, regional disparities would tend to widen over time. This is in fact what happened in the case of Pakistan. The Punjab and the Sindh provinces, which had relatively more developed infrastructure, attracted a larger proportion of industrial investment than the other provinces. In Sindh, however, the growth in income was mainly in Karachi and Hyderabad. Thus, economic disparities widened not only between East and West Pakistan, but also between the provinces within West Pakistan.

During the 1960s, the factor which accelerated the growth of regional income disparities within what is Pakistan today was the differential impact of agricultural growth associated with the so-called 'Green Revolution'. Since the yield increase associated with the adoption of high yield varieties of foodgrain required irrigation,

During the process of rapid economic growth of the 1960s, while an exclusive and highly monopolistic class was amassing wealth, the majority of Pakistan's population was suffering an absolute decline in its living standards

and since the Punjab and the Sindh had a relatively larger proportion of their area under irrigation, they experienced much faster growth in their incomes, compared to the Balochistan and the North West Frontier Province.[13]

In a situation where each of the provinces of Pakistan had a distinct culture and language, the systematic growth of regional disparities created acute political tensions. Addressing these tensions required a genuinely federal democratic structure with decentralization of political power at the provincial level.[14] Only such a polity and large federal expenditures for the development of the under-developed regions could ensure the unity of the country. In the absence of such a polity, the growing economic disparities between provinces created explosive political tensions.

The failure to conduct an effective land reform in Pakistan has resulted in a continued concentration of landownership in the hands of a few big landlords. Thus, in 1972, 30 per cent of total farm area was owned by large landowners (owning 150 acres and above). The overall picture of Pakistan's agrarian structure has been that these large landowners have rented out most of their land to small and medium-sized tenants (i.e., tenants operating below twenty-five acres).

In an earlier doctoral study it was shown that given this agrarian structure, when the 'Green Revolution' technology became available in the late 1960s the larger landowners found it profitable to resume some of their rented out land for self-cultivation on large farms using hired labour and capital investment. Consequently there was a growing economic polarization of rural society.[15] While the landlords' incomes increased, those of the poor peasantry declined relatively, as they faced a reduction in their operated farm area and in many cases growing landlessness.[16] For example in the case of farms in the size class 150 acres and above, the increase in the farm area during the period 1960 to 1978, constituted half their total farm area in 1978. In terms of the source of increase, 65 per cent of the increase in area of large farms came through resumption of formerly rented out land. That this resumption was accompanied by growing landlessness of the poor peasantry is indicated by the fact that in the period 1960 to 1973 about 0.8 million tenants became landless wage labourers. Of the total rural wage labourers in Pakistan in 1973, as many as 43 per cent had entered this category as the result of proletarianization of the poor peasantry.[17]

The polarization of rural society and increased landlessness of the poor peasantry was associated with increased peasant dependence in the face of rural markets for agricultural inputs and outputs that were mediated by large landlords. In the pre 'Green Revolution' period, the poor tenant relied on the landlord simply for the *use* of the land but used the government's canal water, his own seeds and animal manure. In the post 'Green Revolution' period however, since the political and social power of the landlord remained intact, the peasant began to rely on the landlord for the *purchase of inputs*. (For example, HYV seeds, chemical fertilizers, pesticides, the landlord's tube-well water, for a seasonally flexible supply of irrigation, and credit). Thus in many (though not all) cases, the dependence of the poor peasant intensified with the commercialization of agriculture in the sense that now his very *re-constitution of the production cycle* annually depended on the intercession of the landlord. At the same time due to the reduction in his operated area following land resumption, the tenant was obliged to complement his income by working as a wage labourer part of the time at a wage rate below the market rate in deference to the landlord's power. (Conversely, the landlord's management of the owner cultivated section of his land was facilitated through this tied source of labour supply). These phenomena persist till today. (They were first analyzed by Akmal Hussain in a doctoral study 1980,[18] and current empirical evidence is provided in chapter 3, Section-IV). Finally, the peasant's income was further constricted as he was obliged to sell a large part of his output at harvest time when prices were low (in order to pay back loans for input purchase). Near the end of the year, when he ran out of grain, he had to purchase his remaining consumption requirements at high prices from the market.[19]

Thus the 'commercialization of agriculture' in a situation where landlords and the local power structure controlled markets for inputs and outputs, brought new mechanisms for the reproduction of rural poverty, although overall agricultural growth accelerated. As we will see, the high

While the landlords' incomes increased, those of the poor peasantry declined relatively, as they faced a reduction in their operated farm area and in many cases growing landlessness

rate of agricultural growth of the Ayub period could not be sustained in subsequent years. Yet, the mechanisms of reproducing rural poverty that had emerged in this period, persisted over the next four decades. They are analyzed with supportive field survey data in chapter 3.

II. THE BHUTTO REGIME 1973-77: INVESTMENT, GROWTH AND THE BUDGET DEFICIT

One of the most important initiatives of the Bhutto regime was the nationalization in 1972 of forty-three large industrial units in the capital and intermediate goods sectors such as cement, fertilizers, oil refining, engineering and chemicals. Just three years later the government nationalized the cooking oil industry and then flour milling, cotton ginning and rice husking mills.

While the first set of nationalizations impacted the 'monopoly capitalists', the second set of nationalizations in 1976 by contrast hit the medium and small sized entrepreneurs. Therefore, nationalization in the Bhutto regime cannot be seen in terms of state intervention for greater equity. Rather the rapid increase in the size of the public sector served to widen the resource base of the regime for the practice of the traditional form of power through state patronage.[20]

Let us now briefly indicate the implications of the economic measures in this period on investment, growth and the budget deficit. Private investment as a percentage of GDP in the Bhutto period (1973/74 to 1977/78) declined sharply to 4.8 per cent compared to 8.2 per cent in the preceding period 1960/61 to 1972/73 (see Table 1). The nationalization of heavy industries shook the confidence of the private sector and was a factor in the declining investment. The trend may have been reinforced by a second set of measures during the Bhutto regime. These included a devaluation of the exchange rate which placed large and small scale industry at par with respect to the rupee cost of imported inputs (i.e., the indirect subsidy provided to large scale manufacturing industry through an overvalued exchange rate, was withdrawn). At the same time, direct subsidies to manufacturing were significantly cut down, import duties on finished goods were reduced and anti-monopoly measures along with price controls were instituted. It is not surprising that domestic manufacturers who had been bred on government support, responded by further reducing investment.

It may be pertinent to point out here that the decline in private sector manufacturing as a percentage of the GDP, had already begun eight years before the Bhutto period, after the 1965 war.[21] Therefore, while the nationalization and subsequent economic measures cannot be said to have *caused* the decline in private investment, they certainly intensified it.

The decline in private sector investment in the post 1965 period as a whole, (as opposed to its sharp deceleration during the nationalization phase), can be attributed[22] to three underlying factors: (i) foreign capital inflows fell sharply after the 1965 war, (ii) the manufacturing sector in a situation of declining domestic demand was unable to meet the challenge of exports due to high production costs in traditional industries, and (iii) entrepreneurs did not diversify into non traditional industries where there was considerable growth potential. Thus, the declining trend in private sector manufacturing investment in the post-1965 period, a trend that persisted right into the 1990s, can be said to be rooted in certain sociological features that characterized most of Pakistan's entrepreneurial elite: (a) its reliance on foreign savings rather than its own thrift, (b) its dependence on state patronage and subsidies of various kinds, and (c) its tradition bound nature, risk avoidance and in many cases lack of innovativeness for breaking new ground.

The rapid increase in the size of the public sector served to widen the resource base of the regime for the practice of the traditional form of power through state patronage

Table 1 Period Averages of Gross Investment* as a % of GDP

Average During	GFCF (Total) as % of GDP (Current Prices)	GFCF (Private) as % of GDP (Current Prices)	GFCF (Public) as % of GDP (Current Prices)
1960-1973	15.28	8.21	7.26
1973-1978	15.50	4.79	10.71
1978-1988	16.77	7.10	9.66
1988-1993	17.95	9.22	8.73
1993-1998	16.31	9.32	7.36
1998-2000	13.26	8.10	5.31

Source: Economic Survey, Government of Pakistan (GOP), Economic Advisor's Wing, Finance Division, Various Issues.
Note: *GFCF is Gross Fixed Capital Formation.

Apart from the increased expenditures on defence and administration, the budget was additionally burdened by the losses of the public sector industries

We find that unlike manufacturing investment, the decline in the *total* private sector investment as a percentage of the GDP was more than compensated by an increase in the total public sector investment. Thus the overall investment/GDP ratio during the Bhutto period reached 15.5 per cent, which was slightly higher than in the preceding period (see Table 1). Yet, despite an increase in the total investment/GDP ratio, the growth rate of GDP declined compared to the preceding period (as Table 2 shows, GDP growth during the Bhutto period was about 5 per cent compared to 6.3 per cent in the earlier 1960-73 period). This is indicative of a decline in the productivity of investment (i.e., an increase in the incremental capital output ratio). The question is what caused the decline in the capacity of investment to generate growth? The answer lies in the fact that not only was most of the investment in the period emanating from the public sector, but that a large proportion of this investment was going into unproductive spheres: Defence and public administration were the fastest growing sectors of the economy (11.4 per cent) while the commodity producing sector was growing at only 2.21 per cent during the period. Even in the productive sector, the lion's share of the public investment went into the Steel Mill project beginning in 1973. The project using an obsolete Soviet design, involved a technology that was both capital intensive and inefficient. Consequently, the tendency of declining productivity of investment was exacerbated.

Even in the existing manufacturing industries in the public sector while some industries showed good profits to start with, there was a sharp decline in the rates of return on investment, due to a combination of poor management of existing units and improper location of new units on political grounds.[23] Thus, the lowering of GDP growth despite an increase in investment in the Bhutto period occurred because of two sets of factors: (a) concentration of public sector investment in the unproductive sectors of defence and administration, and (b) economically inefficient investment decisions in the public sector industries based on political considerations, with respect to technology choice, geographic location, and production management.

Let us now briefly discuss the implications of economic measures of the Z.A. Bhutto regime for the budget.

The problem of the government's dependence on financial borrowing as we have indicated, started in the Ayub period, when the obligation of maintaining a large military and bureaucratic apparatus combined with the imperatives of providing huge subsidies to both agriculture and industry: For agriculture in the form of subsidized inputs (water, fertilizer, pesticides) as part of the elite farmer strategy; for industry in terms of explicit and implicit subsidies such as an over-valued exchange rate, subsidized credit and tax incentives to an industrial sector that was inefficient and lacked export competitiveness.

In the Z.A. Bhutto period, budget deficits widened further as expenditures on defence and administration increased sharply. Higher defence expenditures were part of Bhutto's policy of refurbishing the defence establishment in the hope of winning it over after his hand picked appointment of General Ziaul Haq as the Army Chief. Large expenditures on government administration arose mainly out of Bhutto's decision to build new para military institutions such as the Federal Security Force which he expected to be personally loyal to him.[24] He also enlarged and re-structured the bureaucracy through the policy of 'lateral entry' which enabled loyalists outside the civil services cadre to be appointed at the upper and middle echelons. Bhutto's attempt to build a demesne of patronage within the state apparatus had huge financial consequences. For example, defence expenditure as a percentage of GDP increased from 2.7 per cent in 1965 to 6.7 per cent in 1974-75. Similarly general administration as a percentage of GDP increased from 1.1 per cent in 1964-65 to as much as 1.8 per cent in 1974-75.[25]

Apart from the increased expenditures on defence and administration, the budget was additionally burdened by the losses of the public sector industries. The deficits in these industries were generated by their poor performance on the one hand and the pricing policy on the other. Nationalized units under official pressure to suppress price increases despite rising costs, were recovering not much more than their operating costs.

Consequently, internally generated funds could finance only 7 per cent[26] of the investment undertaken, thereby necessitating heavy borrowing from the government.

As government expenditures increased, the ability to finance them from tax revenue was constrained by two factors: (a) The slow down in the GDP growth, and (b) the government's inability to improve the coverage of direct taxation. Consequently, the deficit increased rapidly. The government attempted to control the rising budget deficit by reducing subsidies on consumption goods and increasing indirect taxation. However, even these measures failed to reduce the budget deficit in the face of rising current expenditures. So monetary expansion was resorted to, resulting in accelerated inflation.

The financial constraint following the large non development expenditures, severely restricted the funds available for development, and hence enfeebled the two initiatives that were designed to benefit the poor: the National Development Volunteer Programme (NDVP) and the Peoples Work Programme. The former aimed at providing employment to the educated unemployed and the latter to generate employment for the rural poor through labour intensive projects. Both programmes were marginalized due to budgetary constraints.[27]

III. THE ZIA REGIME 1977-89: ECONOMIC GROWTH AND THE PRELUDE TO RECESSION

The rapidly growing debt servicing burden together with a slow down of GDP growth and government revenues that had occurred at the end of the Bhutto period would have placed crippling fiscal and political pressures on the Zia regime but for two factors: (a) the generous financial support received from the West, and (b) the acceleration in the inflow of remittances from the Middle East which increased from US$0.5 billion in 1978 to US$3.2 billion in 1984. These remittances not only eased balance of payments pressures, but also potential political pressures, directly benefiting about 10 million people, predominantly in the lower middle class and working class strata.[28]

As it was, the easing of budgetary pressures together with good harvests and the construction and consumption booms associated with Middle East remittances, helped stimulate economic growth. As table 2 shows, GDP growth increased from about 5 per cent during the Z.A. Bhutto period, i.e. (1973-77) to 6.6 per cent during the Zia period (1978-88). The data show that this acceleration in the GDP growth was induced to some extent by increased investment: The gross fixed capital formation as a percentage of the GDP increased from 15.5 per cent in the Bhutto period to 16.8 per cent in the Zia period (Table 1).

There was a strategic shift from the 'socialist' policies of nationalization, and the large public sector in the Bhutto period, to denationalization and a greater role assigned to the private sector in the growth process. In this context the Zia regime offered a number of incentives to the private sector such as low interest credit, duty free imports of selected capital goods, tax holidays and accelerated depreciation allowances. These inducements combined with high aggregate demand associated with consumption expenditures from Middle East remittances, and increased investment in housing, created a favourable climate for new investment. Private sector

Table 2 Period Averages of the Percentage Share of Selected Macro-Economic Indicators in the GDP of Pakistan

Average During	Real GDP Growth % (Market Prices)	Domestic Savings as % of GDP	Average Export Growth %	Exports as % of GDP	Trade Balance as % of GDP	Workers Remittances as % of GDP	Debt Servicing as % of GDP
1960-1973	6.26	12.99	16.19	4.57	−5.11	—	1.28
1973-1978	4.99	7.29	10.31	8.79	−7.27	—	2.04
1978-1988	6.6	8.15	14.33	9.59	−8.66	7.71	2.44
1988-1993	4.92	12.99	9.19	13.01	−5.00	4.54	3.02
1993-1998	3.14	14.98	5.15	13.50	−3.99	2.55	3.48
1998-2000	4.17	—	0.16	13.69	−2.33	1.71	2.55

Source: Economic Survey, Government of Pakistan (GOP), Economic Advisor's Wing, Finance Division, Various Issues.

When the cushion of foreign loans and debt relief was withdrawn at the end of the Afghan War, the underlying structural constraints to GDP growth began to manifest themselves

gross fixed investment increased from 7.1 per cent of the GDP in the Bhutto period to 9.2 per cent in the Zia regime (see Table 1). The public sector gross fixed capital formation as a percentage of the GDP however declined slightly from 10.7 per cent in the preceding period to 9.7 per cent in the Zia period. The data on the manufacturing sector is also consistent with these findings and show a substantial acceleration in the growth of overall manufacturing from 5.5 per cent in the 1970s to 8.21 per cent in the 1980s (see Annexure Table 1). In terms of the composition of investment in the large scale manufacturing sector as table 3 shows, there appears to be a significant acceleration in the investment in the intermediate and capital growth sectors, whose percentage share in the total manufacturing increased from about 43 per cent at the end of the Bhutto period to about 50 per cent in the mid-1980s. (The share fell again in the late 1980s and 1990s). This is consistent with the boom in the construction sector and the secondary multiplier effects in the intermediate and capital goods sectors.

Although the GDP growth rate during the Zia period did increase, yet this higher growth rate could not be expected to be maintained because of continued poor performance of three strategic factors that sustain growth over time: (i) The domestic savings rate continued to remain below 10 per cent compared to a required rate of over 20 per cent. (ii) Exports as a percentage of GDP continued to remain below 10 per cent and did not register any substantial increase (see Table 2). (iii) Inadequate investment in social and economic infrastructure. As defence and debt-servicing expenditure increased, the Annual Development Programme (ADP) through which much of the infrastructure projects were funded, began to get constricted. As table 4 shows, ADP expenditure as a percentage of GDP fell from an average of 7.4 per cent in the Z.A. Bhutto period, to 6.2 per cent in the Zia period.

It is not surprising that when the cushion of foreign loans and debt relief was withdrawn at the end of the Afghan War, the underlying structural constraints to GDP growth began to manifest themselves: Debt-servicing pressures resulting from the low

Table 3 Total Investments in Various Industries as a Percentage of Total Investment in All Industries in the Large Scale Manufacturing Sector of Pakistan*

Years	Investment in All Consumer Goods	Investment in Intermediate & Capital Goods	Investment in Textile & Related Goods	Investment in all other Industries
1964-65	22.7	25.2	41.1	11.1
1966-67	28.7	30.8	37.3	3.1
1970-71	31.8	27.3	38.0	2.9
1976-77	31.2	22.1	17.9	28.8
1977-78	23.6	43.2	23.7	9.6
1982-83	18.0	49.7	21.5	10.7
1983-84	24.5	57.2	17.9	0.3
1987-88	29.4	21.8	37.4	11.4
1990-91	28.7	24.6	44.4	2.2

Source: Census of Manufacturing Industries, FBS, Statistics Division, GOP. Various Issues.

Notes:
1. The CMI data represents only the large scale manufacturing sector in the economy.
2. The compilation of CMI data is conducted through mail enquiry supplemented by field visits. The questionnaires are issued to the factories as per list of manufacturing establishments maintained on the basis of monthly statements of registrations and cancellations received from the provincial Chief Inspectors of Factories, Directorates of Labour Welfare of the Provinces.
3. Large scale manufacturing industries are those which employ twenty workers or more on any one given day of the year for manufacturing activity.
4. Investments here refer to all fixed assets consisting of land and building, plant and machinery and other fixed assets which are expected to have a productive life of more than one year and are in use by the establishment for the manufacturing activity.
5. Investments for a year include additions made during the year minus any sales of fixed assets during that year. These consist of, both Pakistan made and imports, and assets made for own use.

* Data refers to the figures obtained from the industries/establishments included in the census and does not represent the figures as a whole for the economy of Pakistan.

savings rates, high borrowings and balance of payments deficits related with low export growth and poor infrastructure, combined to pull down the GDP growth into a protracted economic recession in the 1990s.

IV. THE DEEPENING CRISIS 1989-99: ECONOMIC GROWTH, EMPLOYMENT AND POVERTY IN THE DECADE OF THE 1990s

During the decade of the 1990s, political instability, the use of public office for private gain and the worsening *law and order* situation perhaps had a significant adverse effect on private investment and GDP growth. Yet these factors merely accentuated the tendency for declining growth that was rooted in structural factors, which were manifest even in the 1980s. The failure of successive governments in this period to address the deteriorating infrastructure and the emerging financial crisis further exacerbated the unfavourable environment for investment. As table 1 shows, total investment (as a percentage of GDP) declined from 17.9 per cent in the period 1988-93 to 16.3 per cent in the period 1993-1998. The decline in the overall investment was due to the fact that while the private sector investment did not increase (it remained around 9 per cent),

Table 4   ADP as a Percentage of GDP (Period Averages)

Average During	ADP as a % of GDP
1972/73 to 1976/77	7.4
1977/78 to 1986/87	6.24
1987/88 to 1996/97	4.26
1997/98 to 1999/2000	3.5

Source: Economic Survey, GOP, Economic Advisor's Wing, Finance Division, Various Issues.

the public sector investment declined sharply from 8.7 per cent at the end of the 1980s to 5.3 per cent at the end of the 1990s. The decline in the public sector investment was to an extent due to 'budgetary constraints': successive governments being unable to reduce their unproductive expenditures chose instead to reduce development expenditure which fell from an average of 7.4 per cent of GDP in the Z.A. Bhutto period (1973-77) to only 3.5 per cent of GDP in the last Nawaz Sharif regime, 1997-98 to 1999-2000 (see Table 4). By contrast, chart 3 shows that unproductive expenditure on government remained at a high level.

The sharp decline in the investment and the GDP growth for such a protracted period in the 1990s though unprecedented in Pakistan's history, had nevertheless been predicted. A study in 1987 argued that the high growth experience of the preceding three decades may not be sustainable in the

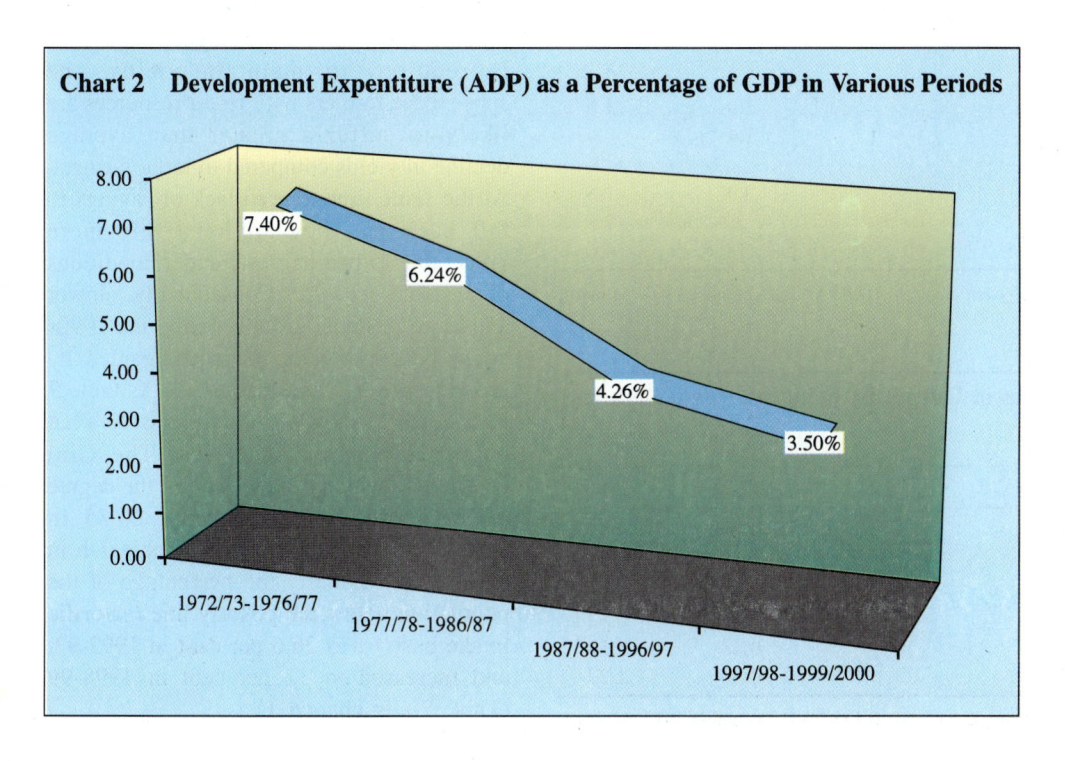

Chart 2   Development Expentiture (ADP) as a Percentage of GDP in Various Periods

Period	%
1972/73-1976/77	7.40%
1977/78-1986/87	6.24%
1987/88-1996/97	4.26%
1997/98-1999/2000	3.50%

next decade due to structural constraints rooted in the deteriorating infrastructure, low savings rates and slow export growth: '...if present trends continue, we may be faced with the stark possibility that high GDP growth may not be sustainable over the next *five years*...' (Emphasis added).[29]

While GDP growth declined during the 1990s (from 6.3 per cent in the 1980s to 4.2 per cent in the 1990s), employment growth has continued to remain at a low level of 2.4 per cent since the 1980s. This indicates that the employment problem persisted during the 1990s. At the same time the growth of labour productivity declined (see Table 5), which would be expected to push real wages downwards. The available evidence shows that this is indeed what happened in the 1990s: An ILO study suggests that real wages of casual hired labour (which is the predominant form of hired labour in Pakistan) declined in both agriculture and industry, during the 1990s.[30]

An examination of the evidence on employment elasticities in various sectors shows that the employment elasticity in the manufacturing sector declined sharply from 0.17 in the 1980s to minus 0.10 in the 1990s, while in agriculture it declined only slightly. However, employment elasticities in construction and trade increased substantially over the two decades (see Table 6). This evidence of declining employment elasticities in agriculture and manufacturing when combined with the evidence of declining output growth in these two sectors, suggests a crisis of employment and poverty emerging during the 1990s.[31] Our NHDR/PIDE 2001 survey shows that supplementary income contributed through wage employment of a second member of low income agricultural households was critical in pulling the household just above the poverty line (see chapter 3). The fact that there were slower economic growth rates, declining employment elasticities and falling real wages in both agriculture and industry during the 1990s, had an important implication for the mechanism of poverty creation: It meant that increasingly, the second family members of households on the margin of poverty could not get adequate wage employment. This could have been a significant factor in pushing increasing numbers of households into poverty.

A second important dimension of the dynamics of poverty creation in this period was located in the increased fluctuations in agricultural output which was pointed out in the study by Akmal Hussain.[32] The study indicates that under conditions of declining input productivity, when higher input/acre is required to maintain yields, the subsistence farmers with fewer resources are likely to suffer a greater than average decline in yields compared to large farmers. At the same time, due to lack of savings to fall back on, they are relatively more vulnerable to bad harvests under conditions of unstable growth.[33] Consequently, slower and more unstable growth during the 1990s could be expected to be accompanied by growing poverty and inequality. As table 7 in chapter 1, shows, this is precisely what happened during the 1990s: The Gini coefficient, which is a measure of the degree of inequality, increased from 26.85 in 1992-93 to 30.19 in 1998-99 (Table 7-b in chapter 1). Similarly the percentage of the population below the poverty line (calorific intake basis) was 26.6 per cent in 1992-93, and increased to 32 per cent in 1998-99 (Table 7-a in chapter 1).

Table 5   Growth of GDP, Employment and Productivity in Two Decades

%

Growth	1980s	1990s
1. GDP Growth	6.3	4.2
2. Employment Growth (Total)	2.4	2.4
(i) Agriculture	1.9	1.6
(ii) Manufacturing	1.4	−0.4
3. Productivity Growth (Total)	3.9	1.8
(i) Agriculture	2	1.7
(ii) Manufacturing	7	4.6

Source: Nomaan Majid, *Pakistan: An Employment Strategy*, ILO/SAAT, December 1997 (Mimeo), Table A5, p. 58.

Table 6   Employment Elasticities of Output by Sectors in Two Decades

%

Employment Elasticity	1980s	1990s
Agriculture	0.49	0.48
Manufacturing	0.17	−0.10
Construction	1.05	1.81
Electricity & Gas	−0.39	0.32
Transport	0.48	0.14
Trade	0.37	1.22

Source: Nomaan Majid, *Pakistan: An Employment Strategy*, ILO/SAAT, December 1997 (Mimeo), Table A5, p. 48.

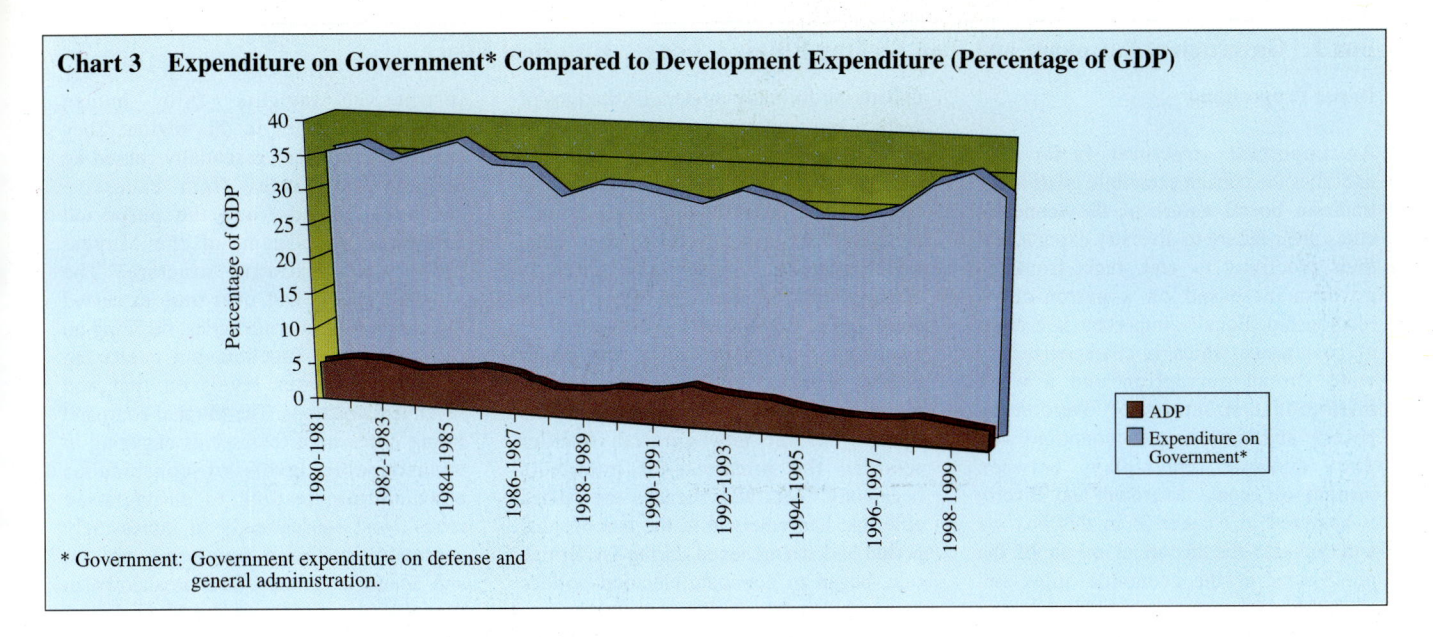

Chart 3   Expenditure on Government* Compared to Development Expenditure (Percentage of GDP)

* Government: Government expenditure on defense and general administration.

CONCLUSIONS

In this chapter we have analyzed investment, growth and poverty in historical perspective. The purpose was to understand the emergence of the process of increasing poverty, the tendency for loan dependence and slow GDP growth.

The Ayub regime was characterized by economic policies that induced acute social and regional economic disparities. We saw how the mechanisms of rural poverty observable today,[34] were rooted in the increased peasant dependence on the landlord, and asymmetric markets for inputs and outputs that resulted from a particular form of agricultural growth during the Ayub period. The analysis also showed how the tendency for the economy's loan dependence so manifest today, may have originated in the policies of the Ayub regime. The government by providing state subsidies locked the economy into an industrial structure which was dominated by low value added industries, incapable of generating adequate foreign exchange for the country.

The structural constraints to fiscal space were exacerbated as successive governments engaged in financial profligacy, and allocation of state resources based on considerations of political patronage rather than economic efficiency. Nationalization of industries during the Z.A. Bhutto period enlarged the domain of power and patronage for the regime. However, the consequent growing losses of nationalized units laid the basis of subsequent fiscal hemorrhaging of the government. The sharply rising budget deficits during the Z.A. Bhutto period were accentuated by a huge increase in expenditures on the State apparatus.

During the Zia regime State funds were directed for unproductive political purposes instead of urgently needed investment in the maintenance of the irrigation system and technical training of the human resource base. Consequently, when the cushion of foreign financial assistance was withdrawn after the Afghan war, investment and growth declined, budget deficits increased sharply, and poverty intensified.

During this period, the structure of GDP growth also underwent further adverse changes as both capital and labour productivity fell sharply, together with declining employment elasticities. A reduction in capital productivity lead to slower growth, while reduction in labour productivity lead to falling real wages. As both GDP growth and real wages fell, poverty tended to increase. This tendency was reinforced by declining employment elasticities. Thus bad governance and associated adverse changes in the structure of the economy, in this period, laid the basis for a rapid increase in poverty and unemployment.

Box 1 Government Patronage and Rent Seeking Elites: A Longer Historical View

Initial Propositions

An important structural factor that underlies the current economic crisis is the tradition bound nature of the economic elites, their failure to diversify exports, and their proclivity to seek rents from the government based on a patron-client relationship. Equally important is a crisis of governance which is characterized by wide spread corruption and a weak institutional structure for overcoming poverty and sustaining economic growth. The dynamic inter-play between institutions, economic growth and poverty is analyzed in chapter 2. In this box we will indicate the historical origin of the proclivities of the economic elites and weaknesses of governance within a longer term perspective.[1]

Why, and from which segment of its historicity, should it be assumed that culture, society, psyche and deeper-rooted values in Pakistan have changed significantly enough to rearrange the pre-existing 'ordering of things'? Could it be that the arrangements are coded through modernized terminology, whereas the content and substance have remained traditional?

A number of propositions, arising from the above questions, can be put forward. Hence, at a more empirical level, the lack of change can translate into an accommodation of the upper social levels with arrangements that are traditional and even atavistic. The ruling elite of the country could not only have adjusted itself to the old order, but in its core values and actions could continue to represent and uphold the old order.

Emphatic manifestations of this resistance to change may have come from another theme having a major bearing on human development in this region. This has been the cycles of political response to the emerging forces of the market economy, which in recent history has been a most powerful force in the dissolution of the old order. These responses can be traced to the eighteenth century (agrarian revolts), the late nineteenth century (the Land Alienation Act), the entire colonial period (emergence of a hydraulic society), the mid-twentieth century (communal conflict and national independence) and the 1970s (nationalization). In the process, the Pakistani world has not been transformed as it was in Europe. Indeed, over time, these permutations have led to a tendency towards retention of traditional structures, underlying formally modern institutions of politics and market economy.

The initial colonial goal was the incorporation into a supportive mode of a largely militarized and autonomous peasantry, and a newly arisen rural elite, which were the legacy of eighteenth century Punjab. The process of agricultural colonization then created an even stronger alignment with rural elites and upper peasant groups.

At an even more significant level, the opening of the new agrarian frontier retarded the prospects of bourgeois hegemony. This was because the landed elite that had emerged in the late Mughal period and strengthened during the British rule, began to dominate electoral politics in post independence Pakistan.

An industrial class emerged in Pakistan through the 1950s and 1960s. Yet, the behavioural culture of the industrial elite, might well have remained non-market and mercantilist. Deeply rooted was the rent-seeking behaviour, the reliance on anti-competitive policy interventions, and the retention of patron-client relationships.

The study of not only colonial, but even pre-colonial, processes and structures can help to identify continuities into the modern period. These can in turn help us to better understand the political, economic and social configurations in the contemporary period.

The Rural Elite and the Transition from Mughal to British Rule

Only in the Punjab (and perhaps in the areas of western India overrun by the Marathas), were the upper echelons of the social hierarchy extensively displaced[2] during the extended transition from the Mughal to the British empire. The growing momentum of peasant uprisings in the eighteenth century culminated, after the collapse of the Mughal control, in the virtual physical effacement of the old rural elite. The upper village groups, or landholding segments of the peasantry, were in the forefront of this armed rebellion. These peasant war bands, ultimately asserted autonomous control over land and political authority. The rebel leadership emerged as a new class of superior landholders, later to be acknowledged as such, and even as native princely states, by the British.

The causes of the agrarian uprisings of the eighteenth century also throw instructive insights into human development issues in this region. They appear to have been essentially caused by economic pressures from excessive revenue demands, and the purported economic parasitism, of the Mughal military-administrative structure.[3] The Mughal 'peace' had over time expanded the numbers of intermediaries, fulfilling no real productive function, but exercising liens at numerous levels on rent and revenue extractions. The Mughal court and ruling elites were themselves engaging in unsustainable levels of conspicuous consumption, leading to an 'agrarian crisis', and subsequently to increasingly successful retaliation from upper peasant and *zamindar* groups. The breakdown in the relationship between the Mughal state and the local agrarian order led to a collapse of the state itself. This was a lesson, not lost on the British, and perhaps not properly grasped by the fledgling Pakistani state.

Having thrown off the old ruling order, the upper peasantry consolidated its autonomous position, while its leaders emerged as a new agrarian elite. Evidence of the displacement of the older Mughal period elite comes from British documentation such as the District Gazetteers and Griffin and Massy's tome, *Chiefs and Families of Note in the Punjab*.[4] Hardly any families identified at the district level as of elite status, and worthy of description in these documents, had such antecedents prior to the late eighteenth century.[5]

The Landed Elite, Military and Bureaucracy during the Raj

The strategic directions of colonial policy are best understood when compared with other parts of South Asia. In the British period there occurred a further consolidation of the agrarian hierarchy in the area that later came to constitute Pakistan. ('The Pakistan area'). In Sindh, the British pursued the policy of retaining the agrarian elite, and accommodated large landholder families, the so-called *waderas*, into the new arrangements. In the Punjab, the effacement of the old elite in the previous century had already 'rationalized' the problem of intermediaries. The incorporation of the peasant landholding lineages and newly arisen *zamindars* took place through revenue settlements, which also formalized their proprietorship over land.

Further bonding in the latter decades of the nineteenth century occurred with the upper Indus basin being converted into a logistical base for the 'great game' strategy against the Russian empire in central Asia. This region became a major recruiting area for the British Indian army, and for forces operating in many other parts of the British empire.

Such processes led to the further consolidation of the agrarian hierarchy in the 'Pakistan area'. The military recruitment took place almost exclusively from landholding lineages, which were also the revenue payers and were accorded property rights.

By 1900 the British adopted a quite remarkable piece of legislation in the Punjab, which further protected the position of agricultural owners. This was the Alienation of Lands Act, under which lists of 'agricultural castes' were drawn up for each Punjab district; and non-agriculturists were prohibited from purchasing land from these castes.

The Act of 1900 was followed by other pro-agriculturist legislation, ameliorating the threats to mortgaged land. Indeed, during the depression of the 1930s several large estates were brought under direct administrative protection, through the Court of Wards, as they moved towards heavy indebtedness and insolvency, owing to the downturn in agricultural prices and rents. Had the British not overtly safeguarded these large landholdings, the political economy of Pakistan might well have been quite different.

The most far-reaching and historically important form of cooperation between dominant agrarian groups and the colonial state occurred through the development of canal irrigation, and the process of agricultural colonization that accompanied it in the late nineteenth century. This opening of a new agrarian frontier brought about radical changes in the economy and ecology of the Indus basin, and created the foundations of the existing Pakistan economy.

In the agricultural colonization schemes, the British once again chose as grantees of land those who were exclusively from the 'agricultural castes'.

The military and bureaucracy were the other institutions strengthened through the new canal economy. Large areas of canal land were devoted for military usage. Extensive land grants were made to army pensioners and world war veterans, in a form of tangible resource gratification that no other part of British India was able to match.

The more pervasive hold of the military over economic resources under colonialism, and the more binding nexus between military service, social authority and state power, served as a precursor to the direct exercise of political control by the military in Pakistan after 1947.

The civil bureaucracy also emerged with greater authority. Canal irrigation created a truly hydraulic society in the Indus basin, in which water, the scarce and vital resource, was under administrative control. Not only was the cultivator more dependent on the government than under rain-fed agriculture, but the centralized nature of gravitational flow irrigation furthered the dependence of the citizen on the State. However, all did not need to be equally obedient. The more powerful landholders were able to manipulate and bribe the local officials to divert water to their lands, either out of turn or in unfair proportions. The power of public office was tempered, and indeed delegitimized, by private vice.

The state of Pakistan as it emerged in 1947, inherited various institutions of the State, structures of power, economy and behavioural proclivities in the economic elites. These historical attributes profoundly impacted on issues of equity and exclusion, just as much as they influenced economic policies.[6]

After independence the triad of military, bureaucracy and landlords, greatly strengthened in the hydraulic society of the Indus basin, continued to exercise inordinate influence over public and economic affairs. The issue that arises here is whether the strong rent-seeking model established in colonial political economy was to replicate itself in the new state. The concentration of power created a not dissimilar environment for decision-making. The British had consolidated a recent elite, through a sharing of military and agrarian resources with intermediaries. The Pakistani state endeavoured to maintain existing stakeholders, essentially through the patron-client nexus and the diversion of state resources. It also began to constitute a new elite, in the commercial and industrial spheres, but again through resource transfer mechanisms (For an analysis of this phenomenon see chapter 2). In both the colonial and post-colonial cases, rent seeking behaviour, rather than income and wealth generating capabilities, appears to have been the critical impulse. The result could be an inability to achieve competitive efficiency, which became an endemic constraint to export diversification, economic growth, and financial stability during the five decades after independence.

NOTES

1. This box is based on the research paper presented by Professor Imran Ali, for the UNHDR.
2. The Punjab experienced a greater degree of social change than other areas, where the transition from Mughal rule appeared to be more 'orderly'. When some decades later the British were expanding into the former provinces of the Mughal empire, they encountered successor kingdoms ruled by none other than the descendents of former Mughal viceroys and governors. These regional entities had assumed independence as the empire receded, providing a large degree of continuity in the social structure. Under the ruling lineages, the agrarian hierarchy remained largely undisturbed, with no major effacement or turnover in the position of rural magnate elements. Lower levels of the social structure, both urban and rural, also failed to achieve any significant breaks in the traditional patterns of caste and class hierarchy. Thus changes in social relationships, the power structure and economic organization, were minimal, and major continuities remained in the extended transitions from the Mughal to the British rule.
3. See, T. Raychaudhuri, 'The Mughal Empire', in Cambridge Economic History of India (Cambridge, Cambridge University Press, 1982), Vol. I, pp. 172-92.
4. For a discussion of the eminent families of the Punjab, by districts and princely states, see, L.H. Griffin and C.F. Massy, *Chiefs and Families of Note in the Punjab*, 2 vols. (Lahore, 1940).
5. One of the most spectacular examples, albeit from a part of Punjab now in India, came from the Phulkian war band. This was named after a Sidhu Jat peasant called Phul, whose descendents in British times ruled the princely states of Patiala, Nabha and Jind, and the fiefs of Bhadour, Maloudh and Badrukhan. Other Sidhu Jat families established the state of Faridkot, the *jagirs* of Kaithal and Arnauli, and a large number of smaller fiefs. The ruling family of Kapurthala State were descended from the Sikh war band leader, Jassa Singh, who belonged to the lowly caste of Kalal, or liquor producers. The ruling family of Bahawalpur State emerged from the upper peasant Daudpotra caste. In Griffin and Massy's book case after case is described of an elite that had recently risen from upper peasant ranks.
6. See, D.A. Low (ed.), *The Congress and the Raj* (New York, 1977).

NOTES

1. Dr A.R. Kemal, 'Patterns of Growth in Pakistan's Industrial Sector', in Shahrukh Rafi Khan (ed.), *Fifty Years of Pakistan's Economy*, OUP, Karachi, p. 165.
2. Soligo, and J.J. Stern, 'Tariff Protection, imports substitution and investment efficiency', *The Pakistan Development*, 1965, p. 249-70.
3. Sikander Rahim, 'Myths of Economic Development', Lahore School of Economics, Occasional Paper No.10, February 2001.
4. 'It is clear that the distribution of national production should be such as to favour the savings sectors', Government of Pakistan, Planning Commission, The Third Five Year Plan, 1965-70, Karachi, p. 33.
5. K. Griffin, 'Financing Development Plans in Pakistan', in K. Griffin and A.R. Khan, *Growth and Inequality in Pakistan*, Macmillan, London, pp. 41-42.
6. Ibid., p. 133.
7. For example, during 1950-55 grant and grant type assistance constituted 73 per cent of total foreign aid. By 1965-70, this type of assistance had declined to only 9 per cent of total foreign aid. See: Economic Survey, Government of Pakistan, Finance Division, Islamabad, 1974, p. 133.
8. L.J. White, *Industrial Concentration and Economic Power in Pakistan*, Princeton University Press, p. 63.
9. Ibid., pp. 74-75.
10. N. Hamid, 'The Burden of Capitalist Growth, A study of Real Wages in Pakistan', *Pakistan Economic and Social Review*, Spring 1974.
11. K. Griffin and A.R. Khan, op. cit., pp. 204-205.
12. S.M. Naseem, Rural Poverty and Landlessness in Asia, ILO Report, Geneva, 1977.
13. Naved Hamid and Akmal Hussain, 'Regional Inequalities and Capitalist Development', *Pakistan Economic and Social Review*, Autumn 1974.
14. Akmal Hussain, 'Civil Society Undermined', in *Strategic Issues in Pakistan's Economic Policy*, op. cit., p. 374.
15. This was first established on the basis of field survey data and census data by Akmal Hussain, 'Impact of Agricultural Growth on changes in the Agrarian Structure of Pakistan, with special reference to the Punjab Province', D.Phil. Thesis, University of Sussex 1980. Also see, Akmal Hussain, *Strategic Issues in Pakistan's Economic Policy: Technical Change and Social Polarization in Rural Punjab*, Chapter 4, Progressive Publishers, June 1988.
16. See, Akmal Hussain, D. Phil Thesis, op. cit.
17. See, Akmal Hussain, *Strategic Issues in Pakistan's Economic Policy*, op. cit., p. 187.
18. See, Akmal Hussain, D. Phil Thesis, op. cit.
19. For a more detailed analysis of the new squeeze on poor peasant incomes, see, Akmal Hussain, 'Technical change and Rural Polarization' in *Strategic Issues in Pakistan's Economic Policy*, op. cit., pp. 150-156.
20. Omar Noman, *The Political Economy of Pakistan*, op. cit., p. 79.
21. See, A.R. Kemal, 'Patterns of Growth in Pakistan's Industrial Sector', in Shahrukh Rafi Khan (ed.), *Fifty Years of Pakistan's Economy*, OUP, Karachi 1999, p. 158.
22. Ibid., p. 158.
23. Omar Noman, *The Political Economy of Pakistan*, op. cit., p. 80.
24. For a more detailed discussion on the nature of changes within the state structure see, A. Hussain, *Strategic Issues in Pakistan's Economic Policy*, op. cit., pp. 378 and 379.
25. Hafiz Pasha, p. 209, Table-3.
26. Omar Noman, op. cit., p. 82.
27. Omar Noman, op. cit., p. 122.
28. As many as 78.9 per cent of emigrants to the Middle East were production workers, see, Jillani et. al., Labour Migration, PIDE, Research Report No. 126.
29. Akmal Hussain, *Strategic Issues in Pakistan's Economic Policy*, Progressive Publishers, Lahore 1988. Introductory Essay: Is Pakistan's Growth Path Sustainable?, p. xviii.

    Declining growth in the next decade could be predicted because: '...the strategic variables and sectors through which growth is sustained over time seem to show a declining trend: For example the growth rate of fixed investment, the domestic savings rate, the growth rate in the value of exports, and finally the weight of the commodity producing sectors in the economy...', Akmal Hussain, op. cit., p. 4.
30. Nomaan Majid, ILO/SAAT, op. cit., pp. 34, 35.
31. Agriculture and manufacturing have historically absorbed the bulk of the employed labour force in Pakistan. For example in 1969-70, 72.6 per cent of the total employed labour force was employed in these two sectors. By the mid-nineties this percentage fell, but was still over 60 per cent.
32. Akmal Hussain, 'Employment Generation, Poverty Alleviation and Growth in Pakistan's Rural Sector: Policies for Institutional Change'. The study analyses the structural factors that slowed down agricultural growth and increased its variability from year to year.
33. Ibid., p. 4.
34. The mechanisms of poverty are analyzed in chapter 3 on the basis of the NHDR/PIDE 2001 Survey.

CHAPTER 3

THE STRUCTURE OF POVERTY AND THE PROCESS OF POVERTY GENERATION

Photograph by Sami-ur-Rehman

**Now my being is caught in a vice,
Like sugar cane in the cane crusher,
The challege is to still remain true**

– MIAN MUHAMMAD BAKHSH
19th Century Sufi Poet
(Translation)

CHAPTER 3

The Structure of Poverty and the Process of Poverty Generation

I. INTRODUCTION: A CONCEPTUAL AND EMPIRICAL PERSPECTIVE ON POVERTY

The poor in Pakistan like all human beings have a creative potential. Yet, by being denied the minimum of food and basic necessities, such as health, education and employment opportunities, they are rendered incapable of actualizing their human potential.[1]

In understanding this constraint to human development, the poor in Pakistan cannot simply be seen as individuals with certain adverse 'resource endowments', making choices in free markets. Poverty occurs when the individual in a fragmented community is locked into a nexus of power, which deprives the poor of their actual and potential income. The poor face markets, state institutions and local power structures, which discriminate against access of the poor over resources, public services and governance decisions which affect their immediate existence.[2]

Most studies on poverty in Pakistan have examined the problem simply in terms of measuring the number of people below certain poverty lines. However, if poverty is to be overcome, what may now be important is to understand the processes of poverty creation and to identify points of intervention in the process through which the poor can be enabled to overcome poverty on a sustainable basis. In the pursuit of this objective, the NHDR study for the first time undertook to establish a new data set to be able to conduct an analysis of the mechanisms through which poverty is perpetuated and the possible routes out of it. Any data set contains information within certain specific classifications. The particular classifications emerge from the questions posed. The NHDR data set is new, simply because the underlying questions have not been asked before. Some of the questions raised are: How do distorted markets for inputs and outputs of goods and services result in the loss of the actual or potential income of the poor? If this is indeed the case then what is the magnitude of the income loss? How do local structures of power with respect to landlords, local administrative officials, and institutions for the provision of health, credit and dispute resolution, deprive the poor of their income, assets and the fruits of their labour? who are the poor, what kind of occupations and institutions are they engaged in, and what are the constraints to increasing their incomes?; to what extent are urban poor engaged in micro enterprises, and what are the problems that prevent an increase in their profitability?; where do the poor borrow from and how do they use their loans?; finally, how do the poor finance their budget deficit? Almost every study on poverty in Pakistan shows that the consumption level of a large proportion of households fall below certain calorific norms. However they fail to ask, when incomes of the poor fall below their minimum consumption levels, how is consumption financed? The mode of financing consumption in excess of their income levels has a strong bearing on the future income levels and the probability of either moving out of poverty or falling deeper into it. In the pursuit of these questions it is hoped to develop for the first time an understanding of the dynamics and concrete nature of poverty, rather than merely its magnitude. These broad questions specified by Akmal Hussain were the basis of the survey.

The survey was conducted by A.R. Kemal and his team at PIDE. Since the poor exist not as isolated individuals but as family households living in communities, no matter how fragmented, therefore the survey focused on eliciting

Poverty occurs when the individual in a fragmented community is locked into a nexus of power, which deprives the poor of their actual and potential income.

The poor face markets, state institutions and local power structures, which discriminate against access of the poor over resources, public services and governance decisions which affect their immediate existence

information from eight poor communities in seven carefully selected districts. The study is called the NHDR/PIDE Poor Communities Survey of Pakistan 2001. Since this is a sample survey of seven districts of Pakistan it cannot be claimed that it is representative of the entire country. However, systematic and careful selection of poor communities from all provinces of the country provides a rich source of data to examine the factors responsible for poverty generation.

The survey design for data collection on the eight communities is discussed in Annexure-I of this chapter. However, it may be pertinent to point out here that the survey was focused on poor communities. Consequently, the non-poor category in the income classes shown in the ensuing tables, refers not to affluent people but those who are 'not so poor'. The average annual household income of the non-poor being only four times that of the poor is on average still only Rs.123,273 (US$2,055 per year). In section-II, poverty levels and modes of financing consumption expenditure in the eight poor communities are examined. In section-III, the implications of the employment status and education level of the earning members of the household for its ability to pull out of poverty are discussed. In section-IV, an analysis is presented, of how local power structures and distorted markets for inputs impact the process of poverty creation. Apart from this, the process of income loss to the poor resulting from distorted markets for farm output is analyzed and its magnitude estimated. In section-V, the nature of disputes which the poor are undergoing and the erosion of incomes associated with existing forms of dispute resolution are briefly discussed. In section-VI, the data on the health of the poor is analyzed to show how vulnerability of low income groups to disease and associated medical expenses could be a major factor in pushing non poor households into poverty and poor households into extreme poverty. In section-VII, the employment status of the non-farm households with respect to micro enterprises is examined and the problems related with their functioning with associated implications for poverty are specified. In section-VIII, the role of corruption, credit and indebtedness in the poverty process are examined.

II. POVERTY AND MODES OF FINANCING CONSUMPTION

The basic difference between the extremely poor and the poor categories is that in the former, the total annual household income (Rs.15,350) is substantially less than the food consumption requirement (Rs.18,497), while in the latter the annual total household income (Rs.40,566) is sufficient to fulfill the food consumption requirement, although not enough to fulfill the total consumption requirements (excluding durables) (Rs. 41,092). Therefore the distinguishing feature between these two classes of the poor is that the extremely poor are obliged to use loans for food consumption requirements, while those in the poor category do not have to do so. Similarly in the extremely poor category the total consumption requirements (excluding durables) (Rs.23,722) is greater than the annual total household receipts including transfers and remittances received. In the poor category, by contrast, the total receipts (Rs.45,818) are greater than the total consumption requirements. In the non-poor category, annual total household income is not only enough to fulfill food consumption, but also more than enough to finance total consumption (excluding durables).

The extremely poor, whose incomes and receipts fall below the poverty line, tend to use loans and sale of assets to increase their consumption level. Since availability of loans to the extremely poor is constrained and they often do not have substantial assets, they suffer from extreme nutritional deficiencies. Total available resources of the extremely poor are 84.0 per cent of the poverty line.

In urban areas, the total household incomes of the extremely poor and the poor of Rs.30,266 and Rs.53,830, were only 39.5 and 70.9 per cent of the poverty line, respectively. In the rural areas, household income levels of the extremely poor and the poor are 21.6 and 61.9 per cent of the poverty line, respectively.

Transfers, especially the remittances, supplement considerably the total income of both the extremely poor and the poor categories. For the extremely poor, remittances account for 16 per cent and total transfers 20.9 per cent, and for the poor, remittances account for 4.2 per cent and total transfers 5.3 per cent of the total

Table 1 Average Household Income, Receipts and Total Available Resources

	Extremely Poor	Poor	Non-Poor	Total
Pakistan				
Total Household Income	17,397	41,093	115,690	42,972
Total Receipts of the Households	20,170	43,925	123,273	46,506
Total Resources available to the Households	25,184	52,624	147,382	56,079
Total Consumption by the Households	24,152	41,764	85,217	41,330
Food Consumption by the Households	19,041	32,381	62,325	31,599
Urban				
Total Household Income	30,266	53,830	110,804	51,007
Total Receipts of the Households	30,691	54,207	110,894	51,370
Total Resources available to the Households	33,030	57,000	114,061	54,024
Total Consumption by the Households	28,740	44,562	63,002	40,354
Food Consumption by the Households	23,465	36,229	49,200	32,612
Rural				
Total Household Income	12,495	35,704	116,992	39,918
Total Receipts of the Households	16,162	39,575	126,574	44,657
Total Resources available to the Households	22,195	50,773	156,267	56,860
Total Consumption by the Households	22,405	40,580	91,141	41,701
Food Consumption by the Households	17,356	30,753	65,824	31,214

Source: NHDR/PIDE Survey 2001.

Table 1 (a) Average Household Income, Receipts, and Total Available Resources by Economic Status

Economic Status	Total Household Income (including) Imputed Rent and Profit)	Other Transfers (excluding (Remittances)	Total Receipts H.H. income + Transfers Received + Remittances	Net Credit during Last Year	Total Available Resources	Food Consumption	Total Consumption Excluding Durables
Extremely Poor	15,350	684	21,738	3,998	24,547	18,497	23,722
Poor	40,566	456	45,818	4,800	51,165	32,203	41,092
Non-Poor	106,100	1,078	118,492	10,886	132,798	57,794	78,790
Average	42,972	666	—	5,639	56,079	31,599	41,330

Source: NHDR/PIDE Survey 2001.

receipts. Despite the large transfers the current receipts of the extremely poor fall short of their consumption levels by 35 per cent and they have to resort to credit and sale of assets to finance their meager consumption levels. As much as 17 per cent of total consumption of the poor is financed through credit and 5 per cent through the sale of land. Even though the poor on average spend less than the total receipts, yet a large number of households amongst them do use credit and proceeds from the sale of assets to finance their consumption; 10 per cent of the consumption of the poor is financed through net credit and 2 per cent through the sale of assets. The deficit between food consumption requirements and total household receipts of the extremely poor is much higher in the rural areas than in urban areas.[3]

The pattern is observed in all the communities covered in the survey. The highest level of poverty is observed in Lahore urban and Khuzdar where 93.5 and 91.3 per cent of the households were poor and the minimum in Lahore rural where 66.9 per cent of the households were poor (see Table 3). While the poverty levels have been high across all the areas, the abject poverty levels do differ. For example both in Karachi and Lahore urban, the average level of income of the poorest has been 5 to 6 times that of the rural areas. Even more important, it is the inequality of incomes within the community that underlies poverty; average incomes of the richest

Table 2 Transfers and Financing of Consumption (Proportion)

	Extremely Poor	Poor	Non-Poor	Total
All Pakistan				
Remittances/Total Receipts	0.12	0.05	0.07	0.08
Other transfers/Total Receipts	0.04	0.01	0.01	0.02
Consumption/Total Receipts	1.24	0.96	0.74	1.02
Net Credit/Consumption	0.14	0.13	0.15	0.14
Land Sale/Consumption	0.05	0.03	0.04	0.04
Urban				
Remittances/Total Receipts	0.00	0.00	0.00	0.00
Other transfers/Total Receipts	0.02	0.00	0.00	0.00
Consumption/Total Receipts	0.95	0.83	0.59	0.83
Net Credit/Consumption	0.07	0.06	0.04	0.06
Land Sale/Consumption	0.00	0.00	0.00	0.00
Rural				
Remittances/Total Receipts	0.20	0.08	0.08	0.13
Other transfers/Total Receipts	0.05	0.01	0.01	0.03
Consumption/Total Receipts	1.44	1.04	0.76	1.13
Net Credit/Consumption	0.18	0.17	0.16	0.17
Land Sale/Consumption	0.07	0.05	0.05	0.06

Source: NHDR/PIDE Survey 2001.

10 per cent of the households in the eight communities is 16.1 times that of the poorest 10 per cent of the households.[4]

Transfers take various forms such as boarders and lodgers, *zakat* from government, *zakat* and *ushr* from private sector and remittances from within and outside Pakistan. Boarders and lodgers, (i.e., households who earn rental income from those who stay on a 'paying guest' basis), is most common amongst the extremely poor who accounted for 63.1 per cent of all households providing the boarding and lodging facility; 31.8 per cent were poor and 4.5 per cent were non-poor. However, the boarding and lodging supplemented the incomes of the extremely poor to the extent of only Rs.7,904. Such supplementary income in the case of the poor and the non-poor is Rs.18,364 and Rs.65,000 respectively. Another aspect of significance in the case of boarders and lodgers is that it is more common in rural areas than in urban areas.

Zakat, ushr, fitrana and *nazrana*, (different forms of charity), have been quite significant for both the extremely poor and the poor. The two most important aspects that emerge from the analysis are that the assistance from charity in the private sector is three times that in the public sector, and that the non-poor are also recipients of government *zakat* indicating the widespread corruption generally alleged in this sphere. The extremely poor accounted for 66.7 per cent of government *zakat* recipients, which rises to more than 80 per cent in the case of private sector zakat recipients.

The remittances constitute a major supplement to their incomes but mainly in rural areas. The proportion of the households that received remittances is almost evenly distributed amongst all the three categories of households. Remittances are received from both within and outside Pakistan. Pension and gift receiving households have been relatively few especially among the poor because they rarely have government jobs or pensions [see Annexure-3 (b)].

Since remittances constitute a major supplement to household incomes, any policy that helps in increasing the remittances could be quite potent in poverty

Table 3 Poverty Levels, Incomes and Receipts in Various Communities

	Poverty Levels (%)	Mean Income Poorest	Mean Income Richest	Ratio of Richest to Poorest	Mean Total Receipts Poorest	Mean Total Receipts Richest	Ratio of Richest to Poorest
Karachi	83.1	17,900	129,007	7.2	19,225	129,123	6.7
Badin	85.0	3,902	130,957	33.6	6,430	130,957	20.4
Mirpur Khas	96.7	4,187	183,162	46.1	4,969	193,162	38.9
Muzaffar Garh	86.1	8,259	161,211	19.5	14,081	169,196	12.0
Lahore Urban	93.5	21,233	110,895	5.2	22,142	110,895	5.0
Lahore Rural	66.9	10,023	178,298	17.8	77,200	190,042	11.0
Dir	80.1	2,197	182,103	82.9	28,909	194,392	6.5
Khuzdar	91.3	4,061	92,945	22.9	5,345	92,945	17.4
Total	83.7	8,764	140,972	16.1	14,448	147,679	10.2

Source: NHDR/PIDE Survey 2001.

reduction. The characteristics of migrants, therefore, can be rather helpful in devising emigration policy. The young, males and married persons, form the bulk of migrants. Since as much as 73.9 per cent of the migrants were illiterate or had just primary education, their earnings have been rather low; the non-poor migrants earn more because of their better human resources [see Annexure-3 (c)].

III. POVERTY ALLEVIATION AND NUMBER OF EARNERS IN THE HOUSEHOLD

The number of earners in a household is one of the major determinants of the income level and the probability of falling below the poverty line. The key factor that determines whether a poor household shifts out of poverty or moves deeper into poverty is the share of household income contributed by the second earner. As table 4 shows the percentage share of the second earner in household income is 13.4 for the poor category. When this share increases the household enters the category of non-poor (17.8 per cent) and when it falls substantially (4.0 per cent) the household becomes extremely poor.

The low levels of income of the extremely poor and the poor, and the low probability of getting employed are reflective of their low human resource development. This is also manifested in the fact that as many as 83.4 per cent of the extremely poor and 73.5 per cent of the poor are illiterate and another 7.6 and 13.9 per cent in the two categories of poor, respectively, have merely primary education. Only 2.3 per cent of the extremely poor and 3.5 per cent of the poor have higher level of education and they are poor because of their inability to get a job.

Table 4 The Incomes of the Principal and Second Earners

	Extremely Poor	Poor	Non-poor	Total
Total earned income	15,339	35,550	96,109	36,685
Major earner income	14,608	29,566	69,447	29,652
Second earner income	617	4,759	17,119	4,983
share of major earner (%)	95.2	83.2	72.3	80.8
share of second earner (%)	4.0	13.4	17.8	13.6

Source: NHDR/PIDE Survey 2001.

The women in the sample contribute only 4 per cent to the incomes of the households. (see Table 6). This is mainly because of the fact that only earned money income is considered and also because the women from poor households due to asymmetries in market access, get very low wages. They are also unable to work much of the time due to frequent illness. The share of women in household income of the poor and the extremely poor is higher than their contribution in the non-poor segment of the population. Whereas the share in the household income of women in the non-poor households in the urban areas is higher, in the rural areas it is even smaller.

Besides education, productivity depends on learning by doing, on the job training and experience. Whereas there is not much variation in the period of experience, (each category has 14 to 16 years of experience), it has been their low level of education and lack of improvement in skills that is responsible for the low levels of productivity and incomes. The proportion of persons who got on the job training is rather small in the case of the extremely poor. Moreover, the poor do not have sufficient work; number of hours worked is relatively much lower for the poor and the extremely poor (see Table 7).

As we have mentioned above, the share of household income contributed by the

The key factor that determines whether a poor household shifts out of poverty or moves deeper into poverty is the share of household income contributed by the second earner

Table 4 (a) Percentage of Second Earners within Each Economic Category by Education Level

Economic Status	No Education (%)	Upto Primary (%)	Middle (%)	Matric (%)	Higher (%)	Total
Extremely Poor	81.4	13.4	1	1	3.1	100
Poor	77.5	10.9	4.7	4.4	2.5	100
Non Poor	58.9	14.4	8.7	8.7	9.1	100

Source: NHDR/PIDE Survey 2001.

Table 5 The Education Levels of the Various Sections of Population

Average of Sample	Extremely Poor	Poor	Non-Poor	Total
All Pakistan				
Education Level of Major Earner	(%)	(%)	(%)	(%)
No education	83.4	73.5	50.3	73.6
Primary	7.6	13.9	14.6	11.6
Middle	3.6	4.2	10.7	5.0
Matric	3.1	5.0	11.0	5.2
Higher education	2.3	3.5	13.4	4.6
Education Level of Second Earner				
No education	84.0	78.5	51.4	70.9
Primary	10.6	11.4	15.7	12.6
Middle	2.1	4.5	9.5	5.7
Matric	1.1	3.5	11.4	5.6
Higher education	2.1	2.1	11.9	5.1
Pakistan (Urban)				
Education Level of Major Earner				
No education	83.2	82.8	68.1	81.2
Primary	7.0	8.1	16.7	8.6
Middle	3.7	5.4	5.6	4.7
Matric	2.0	1.7	2.8	2.0
Higher education	4.1	2.0	6.9	3.4
Education Level of Second Earner				
No education	94.7	88.9	71.2	86.0
Primary	2.6	6.5	9.6	6.6
Middle	2.6	3.3	5.8	3.7
Matric	—	1.3	5.8	2.1
Higher education	—	—	7.7	1.6
Pakistan (Rural)				
Education Level of Major Earner				
No education	83.4	69.4	45.5	70.5
Primary	7.9	16.4	14.0	12.8
Middle	3.5	3.7	12.1	5.1
Matric	3.5	6.4	13.3	6.5
Higher education	1.6	4.1	15.2	5.1
Education Level of Second Earner				
No education	76.8	71.3	44.9	62.5
Primary	16.1	14.8	17.7	16.0
Middle	1.8	5.4	10.8	6.9
Matric	1.8	4.9	13.3	7.6
Higher education	3.6	3.6	13.3	7.1

Source: NHDR/PIDE Survey 2001.

> **Box 1 Moving out of Poverty**
>
> Rehman-ud-Din, Village Shah Alam Baba, District Dir: Rehman-ud-Din's family has moved out of poverty. His father, who died twenty years ago, was an Imam in the local mosque. He depended upon the grain received as charity from the community. Rehman has been a hard worker since his childhood. In the morning, he used to go to school and in the afternoon he worked in the fields. When his father died he was quite young. He continued his education and work in the field. He was able to complete his MA although his mother had to sell their land to finance his education.
>
> Rehman was lucky in getting employment in the forest department as a forest officer. Rehman worked hard and got rapid promotion. At present the government has given him a house and a car. His salary is sufficient for his household needs. Although he does not live in the village he is an active member of the joint family and he visits his mother and brothers once a week.
>
> Rehman's mother says that her family came out of poverty due to her son's education and hard work. She never lost courage after the death of her husband. Now she is contended with life and she has no more wishes except going for Haj. All her sons are employed. Rehman's family is not in any dispute. In short this family came out of poverty due to hard work, education and employment. Rehman played the key role in pulling his family out of poverty.

second earner is an important factor in the household's shifting out of poverty or being pushed into deeper poverty. Therefore, it may be pertinent to point out that an important determinant of the income share contributed by the second earner is the education level of the second earner. As table 4 (a) shows only 1 per cent of the second earners in the extremely poor category are matriculates while 4.4 per cent of second earners are matriculates in the poor category. The percentage doubles to 8.7 per cent in the case of non-poor households.

Both because of the low level of education as well as little improvement in their skills, they are absorbed only in the occupations where the productivity levels, and hence wages and incomes, are rather low. As much as 66.7 per cent of the major earners in the urban areas belonging to the extremely poor are unskilled workers. In the rural areas, 53.4 per cent are unskilled and 30.4 per cent are agricultural workers (see Table 8). These ratios are significantly higher than that in the case of the poor, and even higher when compared to the non-poor. The mobility of workers across various occupations seems to be low. Vocational training and apprenticeship programmes to impart training to the workers after the primary education may therefore be helpful in reducing poverty levels.

Whereas education level amongst the poor and extremely poor is rather low, there are some highly educated persons in the categories of the poor and the extremely

Table 6 Contribution of Women in Total Earned Income

Average of Sample	Extremely Poor	Poor	Non-Poor	Total
All Pakistan	0.04	0.05	0.04	0.05
Urban	0.01	0.03	0.07	0.02
Rural	0.06	0.06	0.04	0.06

Source: NHDR/PIDE Survey 2001.

Table 7 Hours Worked, Experience, On-Job Training and Second Occupation

	Extremely Poor	Poor	Non-Poor	Total
Pakistan				
No. of hours worked last week	46.7	49.0	50.3	48.3
Experience	13.1	14.6	15.1	14.1
On-Job Training	9.5	46.3	44.2	100.0
Urban				
No. of hours worked last week	49.6	53.2	59.6	52.5
Experience	11.1	13.1	15.1	12.5
On-Job Training	7.7	38.5	53.8	100.0
Rural				
No. of hours worked last week	45.4	47.2	47.8	46.6
Experience	14.0	15.3	15.1	14.8
On-Job Training	9.8	47.6	42.7	100.0

Source: NHDR/PIDE Survey 2001.

poor households. Amongst the educated youth, 78.5 per cent of the extremely poor and 60.0 per cent of the poor were unemployed. They have been so

Table 8 The Occupation of the Major Earners

Average of Sample	Extremely Poor	Poor	Non-Poor	Total
Pakistan				
Professional workers	2.4	2.4	4.8	2.8
Clerical & Service workers	6.4	12.6	13.9	10.4
Agriculture/Livestock workers	21.8	24.9	28.5	24.2
Business/salesmen/milkmen	3.4	6.5	13.6	6.4
Skilled workers	8.0	12.3	14.5	11.0
Unskilled workers	57.5	40.2	23.9	44.3
Miscellaneous	0.6	1.2	0.6	0.9
Urban				
Professional workers	1.7	0.7	1.4	1.2
Clerical & Service workers	14.2	20.8	15.7	17.6
Agriculture/Livestock workers	1.7	0.7	1.4	1.2
Business/salesmen/milkmen	5.0	6.1	11.4	6.3
Skilled workers	9.6	16.4	31.4	15.4
Unskilled workers	66.7	55.3	38.6	57.9
Miscellaneous	1.3	—	—	0.5
Rural				
Professional workers	2.7	3.1	5.8	3.4
Clerical & Service workers	3.0	9.0	13.5	7.6
Agriculture/Livestock workers	30.4	35.4	35.8	33.6
Business/salesmen/milkmen	2.7	6.7	14.2	6.5
Skilled workers	7.3	10.5	10.0	9.2
Unskilled workers	53.6	33.7	20.0	38.0
Miscellaneous	0.4	1.6	0.8	1.0

Source: NHDR/PIDE Survey 2001.

Table 9 Educated Persons by Employment Status

Average of Sample	Extremely Poor	Poor	Non-Poor	Total
Pakistan				
Govt. Employee	8.9	19.4	17.0	16.8
Private Employee	10.7	7.5	14.5	11.6
Self-Employment	1.8	10.0	16.6	12.5
Retired	—	3.1	1.7	2.0
Tried to get Employment	32.1	35.6	24.5	29.3
Did not try to get Employment	46.4	24.4	25.7	27.8
Urban				
Govt. Employee	8.3	13.3	—	6.4
Private Employee	33.3	20.0	25.0	25.5
Self-Employment	—	6.7	—	2.1
Retired	—	—	—	—
Tried to get Employment	33.3	33.3	60.0	44.7
Did not try to get Employment	25.0	26.7	15.0	21.3
Rural				
Govt. Employee	9.1	20.0	18.6	18.0
Private Employee	4.5	6.2	13.6	10.0
Self-Employment	2.3	10.3	18.1	13.7
Retired	—	3.4	1.8	2.2
Tried to get Employment	31.8	35.9	21.3	27.6
Did not try to get Employment	52.3	24.1	26.7	28.5

Source: NHDR/PIDE Survey 2001.

disheartened that 46.4 per cent of the extremely poor and 24.4 per cent of the poor did not even try to get a job, probably because of the experience of those who tried to get a job but did not succeed. In the urban areas, 33.3 per cent of the extremely poor educated tried to get employment but could not, while 25 per cent never applied for a job; the comparable proportions for the poor were 33.3 and 26.7 per cent. In the rural areas the situation is even worse, where 31.8 per cent of the extremely poor did not get a job and 52.3 per cent did not even apply for the job. Of those who succeeded in getting a job they got it in the private sector rather than in government (see Table 9).

It is noteworthy that the poor are mostly illiterate, but those who do get education do not find jobs and some are so frustrated that they do not even apply for a job. The presumption that jobs cannot be obtained without bribe or strong 'connections' has been the main reason for not applying for a job; as many as 83.3 and 91.1 per cent of the educated from the extremely poor and the poor households, respectively, cited this to be the reason for not getting a job, and 50.0 and 47.4 per cent respectively cited it as a reason for not applying (see Table 10).

IV. LOCAL POWER STRUCTURES, MARKETS AND POVERTY

Various forms of dependency of the peasant on the local power structures and the distortions in the input and the output markets, functioning against the poor, constitute the elements of the process of poverty generation amongst the peasantry. A substantial proportion of the potential as well as actual income of the poor peasantry is lost to the increasingly adverse tenancy arrangements and the obligation to sell labour at less than market wage rates or without any wages at all, to the landlords. This is because of the social and economic leverage that the landlords exercise over the poor peasants. At the same time, there is unequal access over both the input and the output markets, as well as over services such as credit, dispute resolution and health facilities. In this section, we will present evidence from the NHDR/PIDE Survey to analyze the nature of the process of poverty generation and the magnitude of peasant income lost due to various forms of dependence and market distortions. In the small farm households, the most significant constraint to increasing income is the non-availability of land and the income losses associated with land use within the structure of dependence. Amongst the non rural farm households, the principal constraint to poverty alleviation is the limited possibility of remunerative jobs and the low ability to initiate self-employment projects. In the urban areas, the employment status, informalization of the work force and the low level of productivity of micro enterprises constrain income levels and give rise to poverty.

IV.1 SMALL LANDHOLDERS AND LANDLESSNESS

Farmers' income not only depends on the production of various crops, tenancy arrangements, and marketing arrangements but also on other agricultural activities, such as livestock, and non-agricultural activities. The poor and the extremely poor households have a very small amount of owned land. Poverty and land ownership are positively correlated: Compared to the non-poor's land ownership that exceeds six acres; for the extremely poor and the poor it was only one acre and two acres, respectively.[5] Such land holdings are uneconomical and, as such, a sizable proportion of the extremely poor and the poor rent out the land and undertake non-agricultural activity.[6] The others rent-in the land both on share-cropping and cash rent basis and increase the operated holdings to around three acres (see Table 11). While this does help in increasing the production levels, their incomes would not necessarily rise proportionately, through increasing operated holdings. The increase in income would largely depend on the share-cropping arrangements.

Instead of buying land, the poor were forced to sell their land. As many as 76.5 per cent of the extremely poor and 38.9 per cent of the poor sold their land over the last ten years. Even more important, the poor had to sell land for urgent consumption needs, marriage expenditure and health expenditures (see Table 12). In the process, the productive assets of the poor get depleted, adversely impacting their future streams of incomes and reducing the probability of getting out of poverty.

Table 10 Reasons for not Applying and Reasons for not Getting the Job

	Extremely Poor	Poor	Non-Poor	Total
Reasons for not getting a job				
High merit/competition	11.1	3.6	6.8	6.0
No Safarish/Money	83.3	91.1	86.4	88.0
Others	5.6	5.4	6.8	6.0
Total	100	100	100	100
Reasons for not applying				
Low Marks/High merit	15.4	2.6	6.6	7.2
No Safarish/Money	50.0	47.4	16.4	32.8
Had to work in family enterprise	—	7.9	16.4	11.2
Lack of information	7.7	10.5	4.9	7.2
Others	23.1	31.6	55.7	41.6
Who helped in getting Employment				
No one	44.4	54.8	59.7	56.8
MPA/MNA/Chairman	11.1	11.9	9.0	10.2
Relative/Friend	11.1	9.5	4.5	6.8
Person already in the Department	22.2	2.4	6.0	5.9

Source: NHDR/PIDE Survey 2001.

Table 11 Land Owned and Operated by Economic Status (Rural Farm Households)

(in acres)

	Extremely Poor	Poor	Non-Poor	Total
Land owned	1.07	2.06	6.09	2.72
Land rented out	0.11	0.37	1.19	0.49
Land rented-in on share-crop basis	1.85	0.99	0.92	1.22
Land rented-in on cash rent basis	0.04	0.14	0.71	0.25
Any other land	0.08	0.26	0.11	0.17
Total land	2.93	3.09	6.65	3.88

Note: There are non-farm households who own land and because of that total land exceeds the land owned.
Source: NHDR/PIDE Survey 2001.

Table 12 Land Obtained and Sold by Economic Status

	Extremely Poor	Poor	Non-Poor	Total
Made any plan to buy land (Proportion)	1.7	4.6	7.5	3.9
If yes, reasons for not buying				
Too expensive	90.9	93.1	83.3	89.7
Land not available	9.1	6.9	—	5.2
Did you sell any land (Proportion)	2.5	5.0	10.4	4.9
Acres of land sold	2.0	4.3	13.6	7.03
Reasons for selling land				
Urgent consumption need	46.2	23.5	29.2	29.6
Marriage expenditure	30.8	26.5	12.5	22.5
Health expenditure	23.1	17.6	4.2	14.1
To purchase other property	—	11.8	20.8	12.7
To return debt	—	17.6	25.0	16.9
To establish business	—	2.9	8.3	4.2
Sold any land during last few years as well (Proportion)	76.5	38.9	42.3	48.1
Money received from land sale last year	1522	1458	6126	2261

Source: NHDR/PIDE Survey 2001.

Under asymmetric tenurial arrangements, the extremely poor farmers are obliged to pay a larger proportion of their farm produce compared to the poor and the non-poor categories

IV.2 Poverty and Unequal Access over the Land Rental and Credit Markets

As table 13 shows, the average farm size of owner-cum-tenant households is higher compared to any other category of tenurial status. This is true for all the income classes, the extremely poor, the poor and the non-poor. This suggests that, ceteris paribus, the ability of farm households to increase their farm size and income depends upon the ability to rent-in additional land. It is interesting that the average farm size of owner-cum-tenant operators amongst the non-poor is more than twice that of poor households. This indicates that the non-poor are able to rent-in more land than the poor to enlarge their operated holdings and incomes. It also suggests a certain asymmetry in the rural land rental market as between the poor and the non-poor households, as also the relative shortage of working capital amongst the former arising from unequal access over the credit market. Yet it is precisely the poorest farm households with an average farm size of only 2.3 acres (compared to 7.03 acres for the non-poor households) who have a greater need for renting-in land than the non-poor.

IV.3 Power, Economic Dependence and Poverty

Table 15 shows the impact of the landlord's power on the disposal of produce by the poor farm households, and its direct consequence for their consumption. Under asymmetric tenurial arrangements, the extremely poor farmers are obliged to pay a larger proportion of their farm produce compared to the poor and the non-poor categories. For example, the extremely poor have to pay 28.21 per cent of their production value to the landlord, compared to 13.39 per cent by the poor households and only 8.41 per cent by the non-poor households. Consequently, the extremely poor households are forced to keep only 39.59 per cent of their crop output for household consumption, compared to 48 per cent by poor households and 54 per cent by non-poor households. This suggests that the extremely poor and the poor households are likely to run out of their household stock of food grain and would be obliged to purchase grain in the market near the end of the year when market prices are relatively higher.[7] Such households are then faced with the necessity of borrowing for food consumption. Where this is not possible the peasant household faces starvation. This is also suggested by the evidence in table 1, which shows that the extremely poor households borrow for food consumption. Poor farm households are placed under a double squeeze: First by the power of the landlord, who obliges them to hand over a relatively larger proportion of their crop output as a crop share to the landlord. A second squeeze is placed by the seasonal variation in the market price of grain, which obliges the extremely poor households to purchase a relatively larger proportion of their food consumption requirements from the market when prices are high (see chapter 2 for an analysis of how this phenomenon emerged in the agrarian structure).

Given their food budget deficit, many tenant households in the poor and the extremely poor categories are obliged to supplement their incomes by working part

The resultant leverage and additional social control acquired by the landlord obliges many poor households to work for the landlord without any wage at all

---

Box 2 Wage Labourer on Landlord's Farm

Muhammad Ibrahim: This case study was carried out in a village, Bajori Kallan, some 40 km away from district Khuzdar. Muhammad Ibrahim is 35 years old. He is married and has four children. He is the only earning member of the household.

He works as a labourer on the farm of the local landowner and also cultivates his own small piece of barani land.

Relations with the landlord are tense, because he makes unfair demands on Ibrahim in terms of giving him a wage much below the market rate when he works on the landlord's farm. His annual income is about Rs.12,000 which is not enough to cover his consumption needs. There are also other expenditures on buying seeds, fertilizer and other inputs. He manages his expenditures by taking loans from the landowner and some relatives.

Ibrahim also took a loan of Rs.75,000 from his relative to establish his own tea shop on the RCD (Regional Cooperation for Development) highway. However, his business failed. He is now paying his debts in installments.

time on the landlord's owner-cultivated piece of the land holding. Such poor tenants thereby constitute a convenient source of tied labour supply to the landlord. It is convenient not only in the sense that their labour is easily accessible during peak seasons when many farmers experience a temporary labour shortage. Perhaps equally important, landlords are able to pay a lower than market wage rate to their dependent tenants.[8] Table 14 for example, shows that a substantial proportion of the poor households work as wage labourers for the landlord and that the wage rates of the poor and the extremely poor households are almost half the wage rates at which the non-poor households are able to sell their labour in the market.

Apart from the income loss of the poor households emanating from adverse crop sharing contracts, an additional squeeze on their income results from *loan* dependency on the landlord. Table 14 shows that as many as 50.8 per cent of the extremely poor farm households borrow a loan from the landlord.

The resultant leverage and additional social control acquired by the landlord obliges many poor households to work for the landlord without any wage at all. For example, table 14 shows that 57.4 per cent of extremely poor households worked for the landlord without wages. Similarly amongst poor households, as many as 29.4 per cent have borrowed a loan from the landlord and 38 per cent are obliged to work for the landlord without wages.

IV.4 Impact of Adverse Changes in Tenancy Arrangements on Input Costs of the Poor

The incomes of households depend on the proportion of the land owned, tenurial status and productive use of assets. Majority of the extremely poor (52.5 per cent) and the poor (30.6 per cent) are tenants. Any deterioration in the tenancy arrangements for the tenant would therefore tend to increase poverty. As shall be seen later, the tenants over time have to bear a higher proportion of the cost of inputs thereby reducing the incomes of the poor. No doubt, 36.2 and 56.4 per cent of the extremely poor and the poor are owner-operators but because of very small land holdings they

Table 13 Farm Size by Tenurial Status

	Extremely Poor	Poor	Non-Poor	Total
Farm Size (Acres)				
Owner Operator	2.32	3.43	7.03	3.92
Tenant	3.28	3.38	3.66	3.34
Owner Operator-cum-Tenant	3.68	4.11	8.94	5.92
Others	1.07	6.59	19.08	7.30
Total	2.85	3.62	7.67	4.16
Percentage of Households				
Owner Operator	41.1	58.6	58.3	51.7
Tenant	45.8	25.5	10.3	30.3
Owner Operator-cum-Tenant	9.8	11.9	27.6	14.3
Others	3.4	4.0	3.8	3.7

Source: NHDR/PIDE Survey 2001.

Table 14 Loan Dependence on the Landlord and Labour Exploitation of the Poor Peasantry

	Extremely Poor	Poor	Non-Poor	Total
Loan from landlord (%)	50.8	29.4	11.7	34.4
Work for landlord against wages (%)	14.0	24.3	5.1	16.9
Daily wages (Rupees)	28.0	436.0	60.0	40.0
Work for landlord without wages (%)	57.4	38.5	25.4	43.5

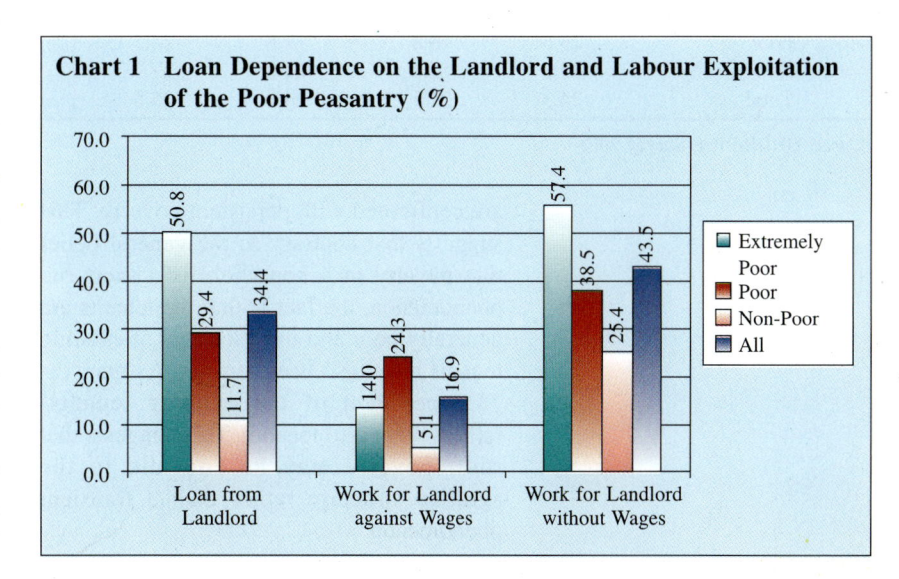

Source: NHDR/PIDE Survey 2001.

Chart 1 Loan Dependence on the Landlord and Labour Exploitation of the Poor Peasantry (%)

Table 15 Disposal of Crop Harvest by Income Class

	Total Production Value	Paid in kind to labour (Value)/Total Production Value* 100	Paid as rent (Value)/Total Production Value* 100	Paid to landlord under share cropping agreement (Value)/Total Production Value* 100	Given to Relatives (Value)/Total Production Value* 100	Crop Sold (Value)/Total Production Value* 100	Crop Kept for Own Use/Total Production Value* 100
Extremely Poor	13864	1.45	1.10	28.21	0.09	29.57	39.59
Poor	22538	2.76	1.40	13.39	1.06	33.27	48.12
Non-Poor	37626	4.70	0.83	8.41	1.61	30.02	54.43

Source: NHDR/PIDE Survey 2001.

Table 16 Contribution of Tenants in Inputs

(%)

	1990-91 Tractor	Labour	Seeds	Fertilizer	2000-2001 Tractor	Labour	Seeds	Fertilizer
Wheat								
Extremely Poor	58	43	45	43	70	51	56	50
Poor	55	45	52	48	75	65	72	60
Non-Poor	93	59	62	57	84	69	75	64
Total	63	47	51	47	74	60	67	57
Cotton								
Extremely Poor	41	20	24	24	52	28	34	34
Poor	21	8	15	15	46	31	41	38
Non-Poor	21	15	21	19	42	32	42	36
Total	30	15	20	20	48	30	38	36
Rice								
Extremely Poor	24	17	16	20	29	20	19	25
Poor	22	14	13	18	25	15	14	19
Non-Poor	28	18	22	21	32	18	25	25
Total	24	16	16	19	28	18	18	23
Sugarcane								
Extremely Poor	22	15	14	17	23	15	15	18
Poor	20	8	11	17	19	11	11	19
Non-Poor	17	11	10	12	20	12	13	13
Total	20	12	12	16	21	13	13	17
Total								
Extremely Poor	36.3	13.8	24.8	26.0	43.5	28.5	31.0	31.8
Poor	29.5	18.8	22.8	24.5	41.3	30.5	34.5	34.0
Non-Poor	39.8	25.8	28.8	27.3	44.5	32.8	38.8	34.5
Total	34.3	22.5	24.8	25.5	42.8	30.3	34.0	33.3

Source: NHDR/PIDE Survey 2001.

are confronted with persistent poverty. This suggests that contrary to the general belief that poverty of a household is a short run phenomenon, the fact is that the tenants are generally poor and the ancestors of existing tenants have also been tenants. As many as 78.7 per cent of the existing tenants' fathers were also tenants. This suggests that rural poverty may be endemic to the agrarian structure rather than a transient phenomenon.

Changes in tenancy arrangements with respect to the financial contribution of the tenants to input use on the tenant operated farm have become a significant factor in generating poverty. The contribution of tenants to input costs in the case of tractor rental, labour, seeds and fertilizer has increased during the period 1990-91 to 2000-2001. For example as table 16 shows, in the case of wheat, the contribution of the tenants in the provision of tractors increased

Table 17 Percentage Loss in Prices of Inputs Used for Selected Inputs by Economic Status

	DAP	Urea	Potash	Nitrogen	Pesticide #1	Pesticide #2	Total
Extremely Poor	7.11	14.65	—	4.23	18.57	28.57	11.78
Poor	7.98	9.74	2.86	6.67	20.29	—	9.03
Non-Poor	8.27	10.56	—	6.67	4.76	—	9.41
Total	7.81	11.32	2.86	5.45	16.84	28.57	9.89

Source: NHDR/PIDE Survey 2001.

from 63 to 74 per cent, labour from 47 to 60 per cent, seeds from 51 to 67 per cent and fertilizer from 47 to 57 per cent. The increase in the proportion of tenant's contribution to inputs for cotton has been 30 to 48 per cent in the case of tractors, from 15 to 30 per cent in the case of labour, from 20 to 38 per cent in the case of seeds, and from 20 to 36 per cent in the case of fertilizer. For rice the tenant's share in input costs has increased in the case of tractors hiring from 24 to 28 per cent, labour from 16 to 18 per cent and fertilizer from 19 to 23 per cent.

The burden of financing input costs in percentage terms even in 1990-91 was higher for the extremely poor and poor categories compared to the non-poor (see Table 16). With the increase in this burden over the decade of the 1990s, the squeeze on tenant income has been intensified.

While the financial burden and input costs on the poor tenants has increased, their lack of control over timing of water application, combined with adulterated inputs, keeps the yield per acre of poor peasants at a low level, thereby reducing their net income.

IV.5 Income Loss Resulting from Unequal Access over Input Markets

The source of input procurement also impacts adversely the cost of production and hence on incomes of the poor. As many as 28.2 per cent of the extremely poor have to buy the inputs from the landlords and the proportion falls to only 8.7 and 2.7 per cent in the case of the poor and the non-poor. On average, the poor have to pay 11.8 per cent more than the actual amount which they would have to pay in case these inputs were procured from the least cost sources. Compared to the extremely poor, this proportion for the non-poor is only 9.41 per cent (see Table 17).

Irrigation is basic to the productivity in the agriculture sector. As many as 54 per cent of the extremely poor households do not have any source of irrigation and the proportion falls to 45.8 per cent in case of the poor and 30.3 per cent in case of the non-poor. Whereas the proportion of households using canal as the only source of irrigation is not much different, it is significantly different in the case of other irrigation facilities. Moreover, most of the extremely poor households are at the tail end of the irrigation channel.

IV.6. Income Loss Resulting from Unequal Access over Output Markets

As we have seen in the preceding Section IV.5, unequal access over input markets squeezes the income of the poor since the inputs they purchase have a higher price and poorer quality compared to those which the more influential large farmers are able to acquire. Similarly the income of the poor farmers is further squeezed due to unequal access over markets for farm output. The government fixes the support prices for some of the major crops but the small farmers seldom receive these prices because government agencies procure output from commission agents rather than directly from small farmers. The following table 18 shows the distribution of four major crops sold in the market by type of buyer.

It shows that an overwhelming proportion of output sold in the case of rice, cotton and wheat, is sold to traders and landlords who constitute an important element in the local power structure in many areas, rather than directly to the government or semi-autonomous government organizations. It is

While the financial burden and input costs on the poor tenants has increased, their lack of control over timing of water application, combined with adulterated inputs, keeps the yield per acre of poor peasants at a low level, thereby reducing their net income

Table 18 Distribution of Four Major Crops Sold in the Market by Type of Buyer (Rural Pakistan)

To whom Sold	Rice	Cotton	Wheat	Sugarcane	Total
Trader	37.5	78.2	49.7	1.9	56.9
Relative/Friend	14.1	1.6	15.6	—	7.1
Neighbour	4.7	—	4.1	—	1.8
Mill Owner	28.1	0.4	—	88.5	12.8
Government	1.6	—	—	1.9	0.4
PASCO	—	—	1.4	—	0.4
Food Department	—	—	2.7	—	0.8
Landlord	7.8	18.1	13.6	5.8	14.2
Others	6.3	1.6	12.9	1.9	5.5
Total	100.0	100.0	100.0	100.0	100.0

Source: NHDR/PIDE Survey 2001.

Table 19 Income Loss due to Distortions in Output Markets by Economic Status

	Loss/Value Sold* 100
Extremely Poor	7.44
Poor	6.42
Non-Poor	5.65
Total	6.55

Source: NHDR/PIDE Survey 2001.

pertinent to point out that the traders and the landlords give a lower price than the official purchase price of the government, since, in most cases, either the poor peasants do not have direct access over government agencies, or are tied into various forms of dependence (on the landlord through tenancy and loans dependence, and on traders through loan dependence and protection rackets). For example of the total output sold, the percentage sold to traders and landlords is 45.3 per cent in the case of rice, is 96.3 per cent in the case of cotton and 67.3 per cent in the case of wheat. Only in the case of sugarcane, as much as 88.5 per cent of the total output was sold directly to the mill owners. However even in this case, mill owners enjoy a virtually monopsonistic position vis-à-vis the farmers in the local area. They are able to push down prices of sugarcane simply by delaying purchase in a situation where delay in the opportunity to sell the sugarcane places the small farmer under intense pressure. This is partly because of his urgent requirements at harvest time and partly because the sucrose content of the sugarcane falls over time thereby reducing its value.

As seen in table 19, the income of the poor is reduced by 7.44 per cent of the total value of sales for the major crops because they were unable to get the minimum ruling market price. These four crops account for 85 per cent of the total output in the crop sector. If the loss of income in the other sub sectors resulting from such market distortions, is also taken into account, then the loss would be almost doubled. If the increase in the cost of input procurement is also taken into account, then the small

Table 20 Place Where Livestock Produce Sold by Economic Status

Where Sold	Extremely Poor	Poor	Non-Poor	Total
Milk				
Village	33.3	33.0	16.3	26.9
Town	21.2	19.1	16.3	18.4
Middleman	36.4	44.3	61.6	49.6
Others	9.1	3.5	5.8	5.1
Total	100.0	100.0	100.0	100.0
Butter/Ghee				
Village	100.0	100.0	—	80.00
Town	—	—	100.0	20.0
Total	100.0	100.0	100.0	100.0

Source: NHDR/PIDE Survey 2001.

Table 21 Livestock by Economic Status

	Currently Owned	Owned in the Start of Last Year	Value of Animals (Rs.) Sold during Last Year	Slaughtered/ Consumed during Last Year	Purchased during Last Year	Received as Gift during Last Year
Extremely Poor	17048	12641	1106	51	1706	19
Poor	23990	19438	2114	163	2103	220
Non-Poor	47414	39631	3624	303	3118	206
Total	27268	22050	2165	163	2218	159

Source: NHDR/PIDE Survey 2001.

farmers are deprived of about 20 per cent of their potential income from crop production. If the income loss resulting from the pressure to bribe local administration officials through provision of milk and ghee is included, then as much as one-third of the potential income of small farmers is lost (see following sub-section, table 22).

IV.7 MILK AND MILK PRODUCTS AND INCOME LOSS TO THE LOCAL POWER STRUCTURE

Besides land, livestock is another major asset of the farming community especially of the poor. It plays a major role in providing nutrition to the farming community. Whether the farmers are poor or extremely poor, they do own some animals; ownership of animals is less skewed than the ownership of land. Value of animals owned by the extremely poor and the poor ranges between Rs.17,000 to Rs.24,000, compared to Rs.47,400 for the non-poor. It is noteworthy that the value of animals owned has increased over the years for all the three categories.

Milk is the major product, and the quantity produced per year varies from 702 litres of milk annually in case of the extremely poor to 2,463 litres in case of the non-poor (see Table 22). The extremely poor households consumed 84 per cent of the total milk they produced. The ratio declines to 76 and 66 per cent for the poor and the non-poor, respectively. Since the extremely poor have a small amount to sell, they are able to earn from the sale of milk only Rs.1,898 compared to Rs.5,980 by the poor and Rs.19,202 by the non-poor. Whereas production of the extremely poor and the non-poor has a ratio of 1 to 3.5, the sales ratio is 1 to 10. Another interesting feature is that whereas the extremely poor and the poor are pressurized to provide a relatively large proportion of their milk

Table 22 Production and Income from Livestock by Economic Status

	Extremely Poor	Poor	Non-Poor	Total
Milk				
Quantity produced (Litres)	701.85	1079.96	2463.72	1380.56
Quantity consumed from own production (%)	83.83	75.60	66.35	74.92
Quantity sold (%)	12.39	23.63	33.78	23.85
Sale value (Rs.)	1898	5980	19202	8672
Value of produce given to Patwari (Rs.)	0	0	8	2
Value of the produce given to other officials (Rs.)	72	197	7	116
Value of produce given to Imam Masjid (Rs.)	35	10	51	27
Butter/Ghee				
Quantity produced (Kg.)	24.89	47.42	73.00	51.21
Quantity consumed from own production (%)	94.12	89.24	95.80	92.49
Quantity sold (%)	5.88	11.07	3.33	7.47
Sale value (Rs.)	26	203	43	114
Value of produce given to Patwari (Rs.)	0	0	0	0
Value of the produce given to other officials (Rs.)	0	0	0	0
Value of produce given to Imam Masjid (Rs.)	0	4	0	2

Source: NHDR/PIDE Survey 2001.

In the relatively few cases where the extremely poor do engage in disputes, the cost of mediation (Rs.18,333) places a crippling burden on them since it is more than their annual household income

output to the officials in the area, it does not form a significant proportion in the case of the non-poor (see Table 22).

All the three income classes also produce butter and ghee. The annual quantity is 25 kg in case of the extremely poor and 73 kg in case of the non-poor. Most of this is consumed and it is only the poor who sell 11 per cent of the total quantity (see Table 22).

V. DISPUTES AND THE ECONOMIC COST OF SEEKING RESOLUTION

Given the powerlessness of the poor and their vulnerability to social and economic injustice within the local power structure, the poor are engaged in a variety of disputes. The NHDR/PIDE Survey 2001 has investigated the frequency and type of disputes for various income classes of the poor and the cost of mediation as well as the rate of successful resolution.

As table 23(a) shows, the highest frequency of reported disputes occurs in the case of the poor, while the extremely poor, perhaps due to their acutely constrained economic circumstances, are often not prepared to take on the burden of a dispute. Their disputes as a percentage of the total disputes is 17.1 per cent, with the figure for the non-poor being 34.2 per cent. In the relatively few cases where the extremely poor do engage in disputes, the cost of mediation (Rs.18,333) places a crippling burden on them since it is more than their annual household income. Yet inspite of having spent such a large amount of money, usually by taking out loans or selling whatever few assets they have, the percentage of successful resolution of disputes in the case of the extremely poor is the lowest amongst the three income classes (38.5 per cent). In the case of the non-poor, the percentage of reported disputes resolved is much higher at (80.8 per cent) indicating the role of their relatively greater social influence in dispute resolution.

As table 23(b) shows, the greatest proportion of disputes related with money/credit occurs in the case of the poor (61.2 per cent) and to a much lesser extent in the other two income classes, being 22.2 per cent for the extremely poor and 16.7 per cent for the non-poor. In the case of land disputes, again the highest proportion occurs in the case of the poor (42.9 per cent) with the extremely poor also facing a substantial proportion of land disputes (21.4 per cent). In disputes related with honour or 'loss of face', again the greatest percentage occurs amongst the poor (47.1 per cent) with the figure in the case of the extremely poor being 17.6 per cent, and in the case of the non-poor being 35.3 per cent.

The data show that in all the three income classes, the poor by and large tend

Table 23 (a) Frequency of Disputes, Resolution and Cost of Resolution by Economic Status (Cases Reporting Disputes only)

Economic Status	Distribution of Reported Disputes	Amount Spent on Mediation (Mean)	Reported Disputes Resolved (%)
Extremely Poor	17.1	Rs. 18,333	38.5
Poor	48.7	Rs. 12,074	59.5
Non-Poor	34.2	Rs. 18,264	80.8
Total/Average	100	Rs. 15,123	63.2

Source: NHDR/PIDE Poor Communities Survey 2001.

Table 23 (b) Type of Dispute by Economic Status (Dispute Reporting Cases only)

Economic Status	Land Dispute	Water Dispute	Money/Credit Dispute	Honour Dispute	Other
Extremely Poor	21.4	—	22.2	17.6	13
Poor	42.9	—	61.2	47.1	47.8
Non-Poor	35.7	100	16.7	35.3	39.1
Total	100	100	100	100	100

Source: NHDR/PIDE Survey 2001.

to avoid involving the police. This is indicative not only of the perceived inefficiency of the police in handling disputes, but also the danger of harassment by them. This is quite apart from the bribe money that has to be paid to register and pursue a case with the police, whether it is theft, violence or kidnapping. As table 24 shows, the extremely poor involve police in only 1 per cent of the disputes, the poor to the extent of 2.8 per cent and the non-poor to the extent of 4.9 per cent. The relatively low involvement of police in the disputes of the poor is explained to some extent by the fact that a relatively large amount of bribe money has to be paid to the police just to register a case. In the case of extremely poor the bribe money paid to police, in cases where it was involved was Rs.16,171, in the case of the poor, it was Rs.14,517 and in the case of the non-poor, it was Rs. 35,558.

VI. POVERTY AND ILLNESS

The NHDR/PIDE Survey 2001 shows that the poor are not only afflicted by a high frequency of illness but also, the high cost of medical treatment constitutes a major factor in pushing people into poverty.

The poor due to inadequate nutrition and hence lowered immunity are relatively more susceptible to disease. Moreover the lack of access over safe drinking water as well as unhygienic conditions of production, storage and consumption of food would be expected to result in a relatively high frequency of disease amongst the poor. It is not surprising that our data show that 55 per cent of the poor and 65 per cent of the extremely poor in the NHDR/PIDE 2001 poor communities survey, were ill at the time of the survey (see Table 25). The high prevalence of poor health amongst the poor is also borne out by the National Health Survey of Pakistan. It shows that in rural areas, amongst low income women of 45 years age and above as many as about 45 per cent suffer from poor health and over 80 per cent suffer from poor to fair health.[9] Amongst men in rural areas, almost 60 per cent suffer from poor to fair health. Similarly children under 5 years of age in rural Pakistan have on average six episodes of cough and fever during the year.[10]

Table 24 Police Involvement in Disputes and Amount of Bribe Money Paid by Economic Status

Economic Status	Police Involvement in any Dispute (%)	Bribe Money Paid to Police
Extremely Poor	1	Rs.16,171
Poor	2.8	Rs.14,517
Non-Poor	4.9	Rs.35,558
Average	2.5	Rs.22,648

Source: NHDR/PIDE Survey 2001.

Box 3 Moving into Deep Poverty

Shehnaz Bibi: She lives in Mohalla Shamspura which is an impoverished urban neighbourhood (Lahore). Her husband, Niamat felt pain in his kidneys a few years ago. He took medicine from a local private practitioner irregularly. With the passage of time, his kidney problem became serious and he was admitted to a hospital for two months last year. When he recovered from the kidney problem he returned home. After some days, he was struck by an unknown disease and had to be carried to the Mayo Hospital. In the evening of the second day, a little blood came out of his mouth and he passed away.

Shehnaz spent sixty thousand rupees on her husband's treatment. Twenty thousand rupees were household savings while forty thousand rupees were borrowed from relatives. Besides the loss of her husband, Shahnaz had also to bear the loss in goods which Niamat had sent to other cities for sale. Now, she is in debt of nearly forty thousand rupees and is worried about paying it back.

She is living in this household with her six children, three sons and three daughters. At present, Shehnaz Bibi, is earning a livelihood for her family. She takes a few goods from the mandi (market) and then carries them on her head in a wicker basket for sale. She earns sixty to seventy rupees daily.

Table 25 Percentage of Poor Who are Sick, Number of Days of Sickness, Treatment Expenses and Distance Travelled for Medical Consultation (Head of Household only)

Economic Status	Sick at the Time of Survey (%)	Number of Days in Current Sickness (Mean)	Treatment Expenses (Rs.)	Patients Travelling over 6 kms. (%)
Extremely Poor	65.1	94.9	1885	49.4
Poor	55.6	27.4	497	29.5

Source: NHDR/PIDE Survey 2001.

Chart 2 Type of Health Facility Used by Sick Persons within Each Economic Category

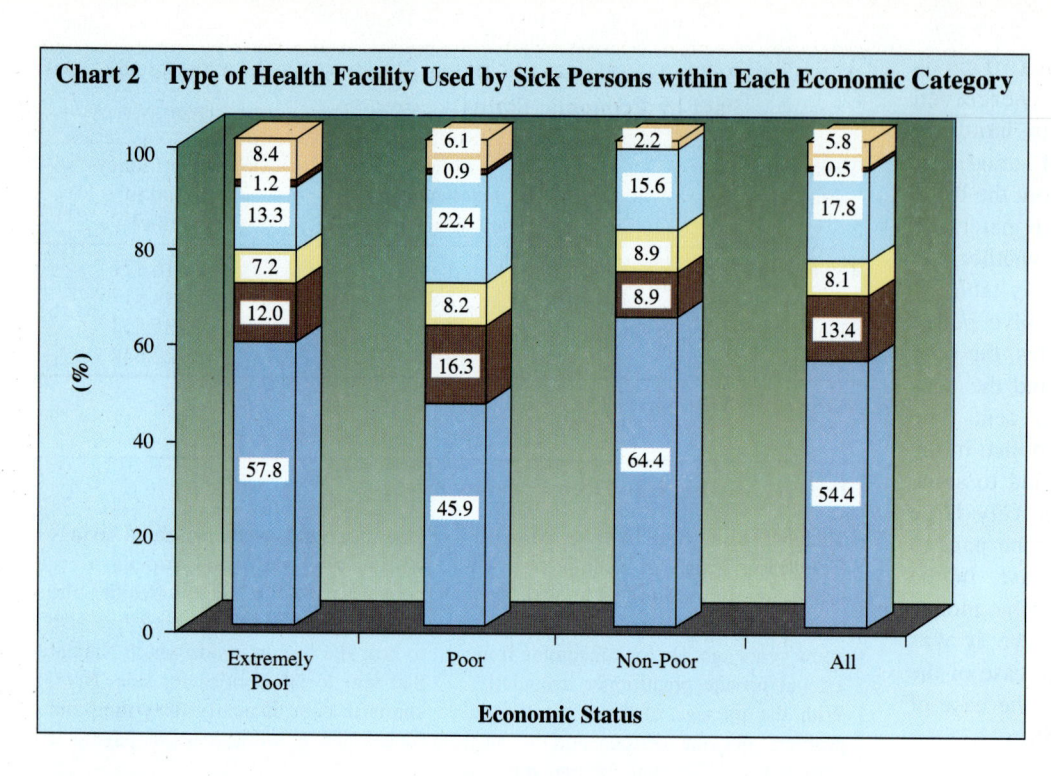

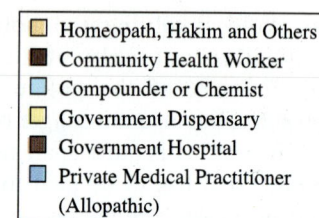

	Extremely Poor	Poor	Non-Poor	All
Homeopath, Hakim and Others	8.4	6.1	2.2	5.8
Community Health Worker	1.2	0.9	—	0.5
Compounder or Chemist	13.3	22.4	15.6	17.8
Government Dispensary	7.2	8.2	8.9	8.1
Government Hospital	12.0	16.3	8.9	13.4
Private Medical Practitioner (Allopathic)	57.8	45.9	64.4	54.4

Economic Status

The NHDR/PIDE Survey 2001 shows that not only 65.1 per cent of the extremely poor respondents were sick at the time of the survey but that they had on average suffered from their current sickness for the last ninety-five days

The NHDR/PIDE Survey 2001 shows that not only 65.1 per cent of the extremely poor respondents were sick at the time of the survey but that they had on average suffered from their current sickness for the last ninety-five days (see Table 25). The NHDR/PIDE Survey shows that rather than going to homeopaths, *hakims* or even government hospitals and dispensaries, the poor predominantly go to private allopathic medical practitioners. This is reflective of the desire of the poor to get the best possible medical treatment for their loved ones. It is also reflective of the poor quality of most government medical facilities and of the lack of access of the poor over the better ones. As table 26 and chart 2 show, of the poor in the various income classes, on average, 54 per cent go to private medical practitioners, 13.3 per cent to government hospitals, 8.0 per cent to government dispensaries and only 5.6 per cent to homeopaths, *hakims* and others.

Ironically, a large number of private allopathic medical practitioners who are conducting private practices in the rural areas, are poorly trained and have grossly inadequate diagnostic facilities. The result is that when the poor fall ill they suffer for a protracted period and get locked into a high cost source of medical treatment. As table 25 shows, the extremely poor spend Rs.1,885/ on their current illness and 49.4 per cent of the patients have to travel over six kilometers for their medical consultation. Given the high cost of medical treatment and protracted illness due to inadequate diagnostic facilities, in many cases the poor are forced to sell whatever few assets they have and to finally borrow money to finance

---

Table 26 Type of Health Facility used by Sick Persons within each Economic Category

Economic Status	Private Medical Practitioner (Allopathic)	Govt. Hospital	Govt. Dispensary	Compounder or Chemist	Community Health Worker	Homeopath, Hakim and others	ROW TOTAL
Extremely Poor	57.8	12.0	7.2	13.3	1.2	8.4	100
Poor	45.9	16.3	8.2	22.4	0.9	6.1	100
Non-Poor	64.4	8.9	8.9	15.6	—	2.2	100
Average	54.0	13.3	8.0	17.7	0.4	5.6	100

Source: NHDR/PIDE Survey 2001.

the treatment of their loved ones. The poignancy of the human condition of the poor in this context is that as they undertake the noble act of providing succour to their family members, they get pushed deeper into poverty.

VII. MICRO-ENTERPRISES AND POVERTY ALLEVIATION

Whereas land ownership has been a major factor in determining the probability of being poor in the farm sector, productivity of micro-enterprises would be important for the large proportion (42.7 per cent) of the work force that is engaged in the non-agricultural sector [see annexure 3(e)]. In general, productivity of micro-enterprises in which most of the poor work, is low, and therefore, the employees have low incomes and tend to fall below the poverty line.

VII.1 Occupational Status of the Poor in the Non-Agricultural Sector and the Types and Profitability of Micro-Enterprises

Whereas non-agriculture enterprises account for almost 40 per cent of the total enterprises in the rural areas, almost all the labour force (in our sample) in the urban areas, is engaged in non-farm enterprises. In the rural areas, as many as 57.2 per cent of the extremely poor are farmers and another 32.4 per cent are absorbed in the household establishments employing less than ten persons, or carry out other manual work [see annexure 3(f)]. Most of the poor in small establishments are employees rather than employers, and as such, the probability of falling below the poverty line is quite high.[11] Similarly, in the urban areas, most of the extremely poor and the poor are in micro-enterprises; the proportion being 57.0 and 52.1 per cent respectively. Location of these enterprises also plays an important role in determination of income levels. Most of the enterprises of the extremely poor and the non-poor are located in the house itself or in a small shop. A large proportion of them are also street vendors. None of the extremely poor run a micro-enterprise unit of their own in the industrial sector. Enabling the poor to set up their own micro enterprise units

Table 27 Duration of Operation, Sale and Net Profit of Non-Agricultural Enterprises by Economic Status

	Extremely Poor	Poor	Non-Poor	Total
All Pakistan				
Duration of Operation (Months)	11	11	11	11
Sales (Rs.)	76438	121698	173261	12922
Net Profit (Rs.)	43670	29689	63160	42673
Urban				
Duration of Operation (Months)	11	11	11	11
Sales (Rs.)	93930	169470	198355	154161
Net Profit (Rs.)	55395	36686	53373	44147
Rural				
Duration of Operation (Months)	12	11	10	11
Sales (Rs.)	32125	46999	164897	102574
Net Profit (Rs.)	13185	19131	66422	41102

Source: NHDR/PIDE Survey 2001.

would be an important factor in poverty reduction.

Non-farm enterprises are about two-fifth of the total enterprises. [See annexure 3(f)]. The poor and the extremely poor are associated with those organizations which employ less than ten employees. The productivity levels and employment generating capacity of these enterprises are significant determinants of the poverty levels. Whereas the households involved in operation of these enterprises reported operations of eleven months, effective work seems to be much less when their sales and net profits are taken into consideration. The enterprises run by the extremely poor (all Pakistan) have annual sales of Rs.76,438 and net profit of Rs.43,670 (see Table 27). The sales volume in the rural areas of micro enterprises run by the extremely poor is only Rs.32,000 and profits merely about Rs.13,000 annually (Table 27). The volume of business is rather small. Enhancing sales and net profits of enterprises run by the poor could contribute significantly to poverty reduction.

VII.2 Problems in Running Micro-Enterprises

Most of the enterprises have not reported any specific problem out of a sense of utter frustration. However, little less than half of the extremely poor have been able to voice their problems which relate to lack of funds,

Enhancing sales and net profits of enterprises run by the poor could contribute significantly to poverty reduction

Table 28 Type of Help Needed to Expand Business/Enterprise by Economic Status

Location of Enterprise	Extremely Poor	Poor	Non-Poor	Total
Pakistan				
Credit	62.5	65.3	65.5	64.7
Better Location	25.0	18.4	20.7	20.6
Recovery Loan	—	2.0	—	1.0
Transport	12.5	6.1	10.3	8.8
Others	—	8.2	3.4	4.9
Urban				
Credit	63.2	72.4	71.4	69.1
Better Location	26.3	17.2	14.3	20.0
Transport	10.5	6.9	—	7.3
Others	—	3.4	14.3	3.6
Rural				
Credit	60.0	55.0	63.6	59.6
Better Location	20.0	20.0	22.7	21.3
Recovery of Loan	—	5.0	—	2.1
Transport	20.0	5.0	13.6	10.6
Others	—	15.0	—	6.4
Total	100.0	100.0	100.0	100.0

Source: NHDR/PIDE Survey 2001.

high costs, police harassment, Municipal Corporation/Committee harassment, uncertainty in supply of inputs, uncertainty of earnings, sale on credit, government disturbance, transportation problems, locality problems and others [see Annexure 3 (a)].

Lack of funds has been reported as a major problem by both the rural as well as the urban enterprises. The problems were similar in all the three categories, as were reasons given for the decline in business. An overwhelming proportion felt that enhanced availability of credit would be helpful in the business. Better location has been the second most important factor and lack of transport facilities as the third. The last two in fact are related to marketing problems (see Table 28).

VII.3 MICRO-ENTERPRISES, LOCAL POWER STRUCTURE AND CORRUPTION

Running a small business without social influence over the local power structure is problematic. The police, tax departments, municipal committee staff etc. often do not allow unhindered functioning unless the officials are bribed. It is significant that 16.7 per cent of the extremely poor, in comparison with 6.7 per cent of the non-poor, reported to have paid bribes (see Table 29). In the rural areas, the incidence of bribe is greater than in the urban areas. The average amount of bribe in case of the extremely poor is Rs.6,833, in the case of the poor Rs.6,060 and the non-poor, Rs.9,257, respectively. If this is added to the cost already indicated earlier due to marketing problems, the poor may have been deprived of at least one-third of their earnings. Moreover, in the case of the urban areas, the extremely poor had to pay the highest rate of bribe to run the business but the pattern in the rural areas reverses.

The NHDR/PIDE Survey data provide support to the frequent allegations of corruption in obtaining loans for small businesses. In our Survey data, about 17 per cent is the rate of bribery as a percentage of the loan. Interestingly enough, the extremely poor have to pay 14 per cent, poor 16 per cent and the non-poor 19 per cent. Whereas in the urban areas the ratio is rather small, in the rural areas it is quite large.

Delay in the loan delivery also impacts on business activities and is one indicator of corruption. The households have to make frequent visits, which also involves expenditure and bribe to obtain the loan. The reasons cited for delay are, complicated procedures, lack of collateral, unacceptable lending source and non-availability of funds. As much as 41.4 per cent of the borrowers in the urban areas and 9.7 per cent in the rural areas, complained about the delay.

A significant aspect of loans received by micro enterprises is the high default rate. Only 4.9 per cent of the loans received have been repaid on time [see annexure 3 (g)]. The reasons given for delay in repayment of loans are crop failure and losses in micro enterprises. Another factor in the failure to repay loans is due to the fact that they have been used for purposes other than those for which they were borrowed.

VIII. CREDIT FOR THE POOR: WHERE DOES IT COME FROM, WHERE DOES IT GO?

Since credit has been one of the major factors constraining the growth of the micro-enterprises, as well as the productivity of the small farm sector, the issue of credit availability needs to be analyzed. In this section, we will examine the following

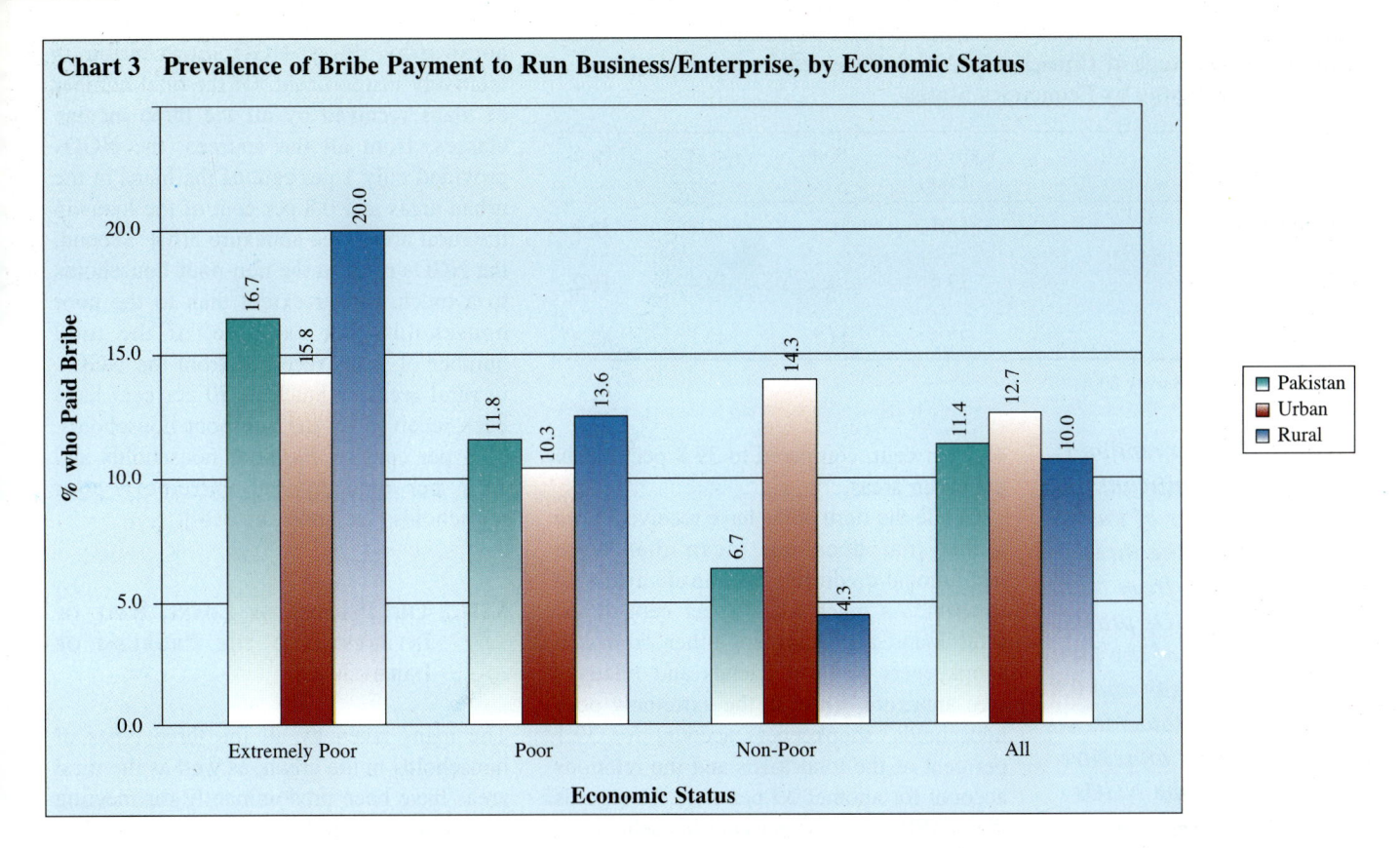

Chart 3   Prevalence of Bribe Payment to Run Business/Enterprise, by Economic Status

Economic Status	Pakistan	Urban	Rural
Extremely Poor	16.7	15.8	20.0
Poor	11.8	10.3	13.6
Non-Poor	6.7	14.3	4.3
All	11.4	12.7	10.0

questions: to what extent do poor households in various categories receive loans? for what purpose are they used? how are the total loans provided to them distributed amongst various loan giving sources? and what is the average size of loan disbursed by various sources to different categories of the poor? In this context, we will also examine the relative importance of the NGOs as a credit source for the poor, and their relative effectiveness in targeting their claimed beneficiaries.

VIII.1 Extent of Borrowing and Sources of Loans

According to our survey (see Table 30), only 35.6 per cent of households have had access to loans and the proportion does not vary substantially across the categories of extremely poor and poor households. However, the proportion is significantly lower in the urban areas, where only 16 per cent of the households have been able to receive loans. However, the proportion is similar across all the income categories. For the rural areas the proportion of households receiving loans is lowest in the case of the extremely poor, i.e., 37.3 per cent compared to 44.7 per cent and 47.7 per cent for the poor and the non-poor households, respectively.

The amount borrowed not surprisingly rises with the income level. It rises from Rs.12,925 for the extremely poor to Rs.18,152 for the poor and Rs.36,642 for the non poor categories (see Table 31). The credit as percentage of the income is 82.1, 46.4, and 36.4 in the extremely poor, the poor and the non-poor categories, respectively. The percentage of households receiving loans amongst the non-poor is lower in the urban areas than in the rural areas. Overall, the reliance of the rural households on credit has been higher,

Only 35.6 per cent of households have had access to loans

Table 29 Bribe Payment to Run Business/Enterprise by Economic Status

	Extremely Poor	Poor	Non-Poor	Total
Proportion who paid bribe				
Pakistan	16.7	11.8	6.7	11.4
Urban	15.8	10.3	14.3	12.7
Rural	20.0	13.6	4.3	10.0
Amount of bribe (Rs.)				
Pakistan	6833	6060	9257	6879
Urban	8700	5664	1200	5594
Rural	3100	6544	15300	8420

Source: NHDR/PIDE Survey 2001.

Table 30 Percentage of Households Which Received Loans during Last 12 Months by Economics Status

	Extremely Poor	Poor	Non-Poor	Total
All Pakistan	32.1	36.4	41.9	35.6
Urban	17.6	14.5	18.4	16.2
Rural	37.3	44.7	47.7	42.3

Source: NHDR/PIDE Survey 2001.

First, NGO intervention is relatively insignificant. Of the total number of loans received by all the three income classes, from all the sources, the NGOs provided only 1 per cent of the loans in the urban areas and 0.8 per cent of the loans in the rural areas [see annexure 3(h)]. Second, the NGOs cater to the non-poor households to a much greater extent than to the poor households

48.7 per cent, compared to 39.8 per cent in the urban areas.

While the rural areas have received more loans, that does not mean that more institutional credit has been made available to them. As much as 80.3 per cent of the total loans are obtained either from the shopkeepers or from friends and relatives [see annexure 3(h)]. In the extremely poor households, shopkeepers account for 39.1 per cent of the total loans and the relations account for another 39 per cent. As regards the ADBP, only 1.0 per cent households of extremely poor have received a loan from the ADBP. The proportion rises slightly to 5.1 per cent in the case of the non-poor. Moreover, whatever the loan provided by ADBP, the extremely poor who are 40 per cent of the total rural households constitute only 13.6 per cent of the total ADBP recipients, the poor 50.0 per cent. The non-poor, by contrast, who are less than 20 per cent of total households, have received as much as 36.4 per cent of the ADBP loans. This suggests that the institutional credit tends to flow to relatively richer sections of society. In the urban areas, the commercial banks do not provide any loans to the extremely poor.

Whereas much is being made about NGOs providing credit, two aspects of empirical evidence in this regard are noteworthy. First, NGO intervention is relatively insignificant. Of the total number of loans received by all the three income classes, from all the sources, the NGOs provided only 1 per cent of the loans in the urban areas and 0.8 per cent of the loans in the rural areas [see annexure 3(h)]. Second, the NGOs cater to the non-poor households to a much greater extent than to the poor households. For example, of the total number of loans received from the NGOs, in rural areas as much as 50 per cent have been received by the non-poor households, 33.3 per cent by the poor households and 16.7 per cent by the extremely poor households [see annexure 3(h)].

VIII.2 THE PURPOSE OF LOANS, RATE OF INTEREST AND THE PROBLEM OF INDEBTEDNESS

The loans taken by all the three types of households in the urban, as well as the rural areas have been predominantly for meeting consumption needs (see Table 32). The proportion of loans used for consumption purposes is 56.8 per cent in case of the extremely poor and 65.1 per cent in case of the poor, in the urban areas, and 69.0 and 57.5 per cent, respectively, in the rural areas. Since institutional creditors would not officially provide loans for consumption purposes, friends and relatives are the major lenders.

Data on the annual mark ups provide interesting insights: average mark-up is only 2.1 per cent and even lower for the poor and the extremely poor (see Table 33). However, this is because they receive loans from relatives which are interest free. By contrast, the average mark-up by the money lender is around 48 per cent. It rises to 58.8 per cent in the case of the extremely poor and 60 per cent in the case of the poor, but falls sharply to just 17 per cent for the non-poor. In the very few cases where NGOs are providing loans to the extremely poor, they are interest free. The interest rate rises to 19 per cent for the non-poor. The same pattern is observed in the case of ADBP. Here the rate of interest for the extremely poor is 8 per cent, which rises to 17 per cent for the non-poor. However, access to a public sector development bank such as the ADBP or even NGOs is rather limited. The commercial banks on the other hand do not

Table 31 Credit Received During Last 12 Months by Economic Status

	Extremely Poor	Poor	Non-Poor	Total
All Pakistan	12,925	18,152	36,642	19,591
Urban	14,045	25,084	26,870	20,281
Rural	12,699	17,096	37,496	19,483

Source: NHDR/PIDE Survey 2001.

provide any loan to the extremely poor. The rate for the poor is 19 per cent and for the non-poor only 10 per cent. The mark-up charged by factory/mill owners is 13.0 per cent for the extremely poor, but it falls to 3.0 and 5.1 per cent in the case of the poor and the non-poor (see Table 33).

That 70 per cent of the rural households never applied for any loan is significant and may be mainly the result of a lack of collateral. While 75.0 per cent could not provide the collateral, the lack of awareness relating to the procedure of obtaining loans has been another problem. At least one-quarter of the extremely poor households reported that their loan application was rejected because they did not pay any bribe. [see annexure 3(i)]. In some cases, however, the loan application has been rejected because the household has not returned the previous loan.

As was noted earlier, the loans have been a high percentage of their incomes especially for the poor. Since the loans have been used to meet the consumption needs by an overwhelming proportion, there is little likelihood that they will be repaid. Therefore, the indebtedness in both the rural and urban areas has increased sharply. The extremely poor persons on average (all Pakistan) are indebted to the extent of Rs.28,137 and the figure rises to Rs.57,780 in the case of the non-poor. Indebtedness as a proportion of income shows the acuteness of the problem. The indebtedness of the extremely poor is 276.1 per cent which declines to 75.8 per cent for the poor and 53.2 per cent for the non-poor (see Table 34). The high indebtedness is a major hurdle in poverty alleviation programmes based on credit alone.

CONCLUSIONS

In this chapter we have attempted to examine essentially two questions on the basis of the NHDR/PIDE 2001 Survey data: (1) Who are the poor? (2) What pushes them into poverty and what are the mechanisms which keep them poor? In this context we have analyzed the processes of poverty generation by showing how asymmetric access of the poor to local markets and the functioning of local power structures deprives the poor of a large proportion of their actual and potential income. We have

Table 32 Purpose of Loan by Economic Status

	Extremely Poor	Poor	Non-Poor	Total
All Pakistan				
Agricultural inputs	4.9	6.5	11.9	7.0
Purchase of any other property	4.6	7.8	7.0	6.5
Shop/Hotel/Other Non-Farm Activity	5.6	5.5	6.9	5.8
Consumption Purposes including Ceremonies	67.2	58.3	51.6	60.2
Others	17.7	21.9	22.6	20.5
Urban				
Consumption Purposes including Ceremonies	56.8	65.1	35.7	57.4
Shop/Hotel/Other Non-Farm Activity	4.5	4.7	—	4.0
Purchase of any other Property	4.5	2.3	—	3.0
Others	34.1	28.0	64.3	35.6
Rural				
Agricultural inputs	5.7	7.3	13.1	7.9
Purchase of any other property	4.6	8.0	7.6	6.7
Shop/Hotel/Other Non-Farm Activity	5.7	5.6	7.6	6.0
Consumption Purposes	69.0	57.5	53.1	60.6
Others	15.0	21.6	18.6	18.8

Source: NHDR/PIDE Survey 2001.

Table 33 Average Annual Interest/Mark-up Rate by Source of Loan and Economic Status

	Extremely Poor	Poor	Non-Poor	Total
ADBP	8.17	13.47	17.44	14.19
Commercial Bank	—	19.00	10.44	13.03
NGO	0.00	8.33	19.00	11.71
Input Supplier	8.33	4.55	30.00	8.42
Landlord	0.06	0.84	0.00	0.32
Profit Money Lender	58.83	60.50	16.67	47.64
Shopkeeper	0.53	0.10	0.25	0.30
Factory/Mill	13.00	3.00	5.08	5.25
Commission Agent	1.67	25.00	0.00	6.88
Friends/Relatives	0.55	0.73	2.93	1.07
Total	1.93	1.52	4.09	2.12

Source: NHDR/PIDE Survey 2001.

Table 34 Total Indebtedness (Mean) of the Sample Households by Economic Status

	Extremely Poor	Poor	Non-Poor	Total
Indebtedness				
All Pakistan (Rs.)	28137.24	29170.99	57780.83	34057.67
Urban (Rs.)	55825.00	33527.03	30350.00	43413.79
Rural (Rs.)	21785.28	28843.65	60800.00	32594.09
As a percentage of Income				
All Pakistan	276.09	75.84	53.17	142.82
Urban	166.10	58.71	33.61	104.49
Rural	298.55	78.28	54.95	148.70

Source: NHDR/PIDE Survey 2001.

also identified some of the major economic and social features of the poor population. This was specifically with respect to the sources of income of the poor, the sources of their loans and level of indebtedness, their major occupations, their health status, the types and costs of health facilities they use and finally the types of disputes they face and the costs of resolution.

Some of the major conclusions that emerge from our empirical analysis are as follows:

1. Poverty and Modes of Financing Consumption

(i) The basic difference between the extremely poor and the poor categories is that in the former category, the total annual household income (Rs.15,350) is substantially less than the food consumption requirement (Rs.18,497), while in the latter, the annual total household income (Rs.40,566) is sufficient to fulfill the food consumption requirement. Consequently, the extremely poor are obliged to use loans to buy food. Since availability of loans to the poor is extremely limited, they suffer from acute nutritional deficiencies.

(ii) Various forms of charity provide a significant source for financing the consumption requirements of both the extremely poor and the poor households. Two features emerge from the data in this regard: (a) Charity from the private sector is three times as large as that from the public sector. (b) The non poor are also significant recipients of the government's *Zakat* funds which are supposed to go exclusively to the poor. This indicates inefficient targeting of beneficiaries in the disbursement of *Zakat* funds.

(iii) Remittances constitute a major source of supplementary income for poor households. An improvement in the education level and hence increase in the incomes of the migrants could significantly increase the remittances component of household consumption. The data clearly show that the reason why the income of poor migrants is low is because 73.9 per cent of the migrants are illiterate or just have primary education. The income of non-poor migrants was higher because of their better educational status.

Clearly improved education and skill training of the poor can play a role in poverty alleviation by improving the incomes of migrant workers who send remittances to their families.

Policy Implications: Given the fact that the average total household receipts of the extremely poor are only 80 per cent of their minimum food consumption requirements, an increase in the volume of *Zakat* funds, improved targeting of beneficiaries and greater efficiency in the administration of *Zakat* funds is required.

2. Moving into and Out of Poverty

(i) The data show that the employment status and income level of the second earner of a household is the key determinant of the probability of moving out or falling into poverty. Here again the income level of the second earner is influenced by her/his education level.

(ii) A predominant proportion of the major earners in both rural and urban areas in poor households are unskilled workers engaged in low productivity and low income occupations. The mobility of such unskilled workers across occupations is also low.

Policy Implications: Vocational Training and apprenticeship programmes to impart technical skills after primary education to workers from poor households could contribute to poverty alleviation.

3. Local Power Structures and the Poverty Process

(i) Our data show that due to the landlord's power over small tenants, the extremely poor tenant farmers are obliged to pay as crop share a larger proportion of their farm produce compared to the non-poor tenant farmers. For example, the extremely poor have to pay 28.21 per cent of their production value to the landlord compared 8.1 per cent by the non-poor tenant farmers.

(ii) Consequently, the extremely poor households can keep only about 40 per cent of their crop output for household consumption, compared to 48 per cent by poor households and 54 per cent by non-poor households. This evidence suggests that the extremely poor and poor households are likely to run out of their household stock of food grain and be obliged to purchase grain in the market at the end of the production cycle when market prices are high. Such households are forced to borrow for food consumption or face starvation. This is also suggested by our evidence that poor households borrow for food consumption.

(iii) Given their food budget deficit many poor tenant households are obliged to supplement their incomes by working part time on the landlord's owner cultivated piece of the landholding. Given their power, the landlords, are able to pay a lower than market wage rate to their dependent tenants. The data show that a substantial proportion of poor tenant households work as wage labourers for the landlords and the wage rates of the poor are almost half the wage rates at which the non-poor households are able to sell their labour in the market.

(iv) Due to inadequate access of the poor over institutionalized credit markets as many as 50.8 per cent of extremely poor households borrow from the landlord. The resultant increase in leverage and additional social control by the landlord, obliges many poor households to work for the landlord without any wage at all (57.4 per cent of extremely poor households worked for the landlord without wages).

(v) The data show that the tenancy contracts of poor tenant households were not only more adverse than non-poor ones, but also during the last decade the tenancy arrangements for the poor have worsened. Since the majority of the extremely poor (52.5 per cent) are tenants, any deterioration in tenancy arrangements would therefore increase poverty. The data show that the financial contribution of tenants to input costs of production have increased substantially and have become a significant factor in poverty generation. For example in the case of wheat, the contribution of the tenants in the financing of tractor hiring costs has increased from 63 to 74 per cent, the labour cost contribution of poor tenants has increased over the period from 47 to 60 per cent, seeds from 51 to 67 per cent and fertilizer from 47 to 57 per cent.

Policy Implications: (i) NGOs engaged in human rights advocacy, Lawyers Associations, and apex organizations of development NGOs could form a consortium facilitated by the government to enable the poor tenants and farm labourers to form a Small Tenant and Farm Labourers Union, at the district, provincial and national levels. The purpose would be to negotiate within the existing legal framework to achieve fair wage and tenancy contracts for the farm sector. (ii) Facilitating the emergence of autonomous organizations of the poor and their institutional linkage with each tier of local government, could enable the poor to break out of the nexus of the local power structures and unequal access over markets, and thereby reduce their income losses (see chapter 5).

4. Income Loss Resulting from Unequal Access over Input Markets

As many as 28.2 per cent of the extremely poor peasants have to buy their inputs from the landlord. The data show that on average the poor have to pay 11.8 per cent more than the actual amount which they would have to pay in case these inputs were procured from least cost sources.

Human Services, Washington, USA and the Federal Bureau of Statistics, Islamabad), p. 129, Figure 57.
10. Ibid., p. 109, Figure 48.
11. Only 1.4 per cent of the extremely poor are engaged in large scale industries or financial institutions, or are public servants, and even there, they are doing low paid jobs. The plight of the poor is little better where 42.7 per cent work in the farm sector, 33.4 per cent in household establishments, 7.8 as servants and menial workers, 5.8 per cent are engaged in large scale enterprises, and 8.2 per cent in the public sector.

CHAPTER 4

POVERTY ALLEVIATION THROUGH NGOS

Photograph by Akmal Hussain

The human mind is not a vessel to be filled
But a fire to be kindled

– PLUTARCH

CHAPTER 4

Poverty Alleviation Through NGOs

Over the last two decades the tightening financial constraints on the government and growing awareness of the limitations of top down development programmes to alleviate poverty,[1] have created the space for non-governmental organizations (NGOs) and alternative approaches to development actions. During this period a variety of NGOs have established programmes at the community level. The question that arises is whether these alternative institutional forms of public action for overcoming poverty, can achieve sufficient coverage of the poor population and cost effectiveness for a significant impact on the overall poverty problem in the country. In addressing this question we will examine the institutional dynamics and management issues involved in achieving rapid coverage and efficacy of NGOs. In this context as part of this NHDR Study a small sample spot survey was conducted to investigate the impact of various types of NGOs on their beneficiaries with respect to nutrition, health and sustainable income increases. (The results are presented in section-V). Due to time and resource constraints the sample size for the survey was too small (277) for the impact assessment to be representative at the national level, even for the seven NGOs covered by the spot survey. However, the results do provide illustrative insights with respect to the relative efficacy of different types of NGOs.

In section-I, we will briefly indicate the different categories of development NGOs functioning in Pakistan. Since many of them characterize their approach as 'participatory' we will attempt to provide a paradigmatic outline of the participatory development approach in this section. In the next section-II, we will identify some of the general issues related with micro credit, independently of the differing approaches and structure of organizations providing it. In section-III, we will present brief individual profiles of NGOs in each category, to illustrate the variety of organizational approaches in the NGO sector and draw brief policy conclusions in this context. In section-IV, the results of the spot survey on impact assessment of NGOs will be presented. In section-V, we will examine the strategic issues in taking development NGOs to scale. Here we will also indicate some of the features of management and organizational structure which could help achieve efficacy and rapid growth. In section-VI, we will indicate the elements of an enabling institutional structure at the national level which can facilitate public action at the grassroots level for poverty alleviation.

I. TYPES OF NGOS AND THE PARTICIPATORY DEVELOPMENT APPROACH

I.1 THE NATURE OF POVERTY, EMPOWERMENT AND TYPES OF PARTICIPATORY DEVELOPMENT NGOS

As we have analyzed in chapter 3 of this report, the poor face a structure of markets, State and institutions, which discriminate against access of the poor over resources, public services and the process of government decision-making.[2] The poor are often locked into a system of dependence at the local level which deprives them of as much as one third of their actual income. (see chapter 3 for evidence). The dependence of individual members of poor communities originates in the fact that they are fragmented and alone. They have neither the skills nor the resources to increase their productivity, nor the organizational strength through which to acquire resources from governments, donors and the market. The participatory development approach aims to empower the poor by enabling them to organize, acquire new skills, increase productivity, achieve savings, and develop the ability to access training, technical support and credit from a variety of institutional sources.[3] The approach is based on the principle of social mobilization which was first used in its rudimentary form in Comilla (Bangladesh) during the 1960s and

The dependence of individual members of poor communities originates in the fact that they are fragmented and alone. They have neither the skills nor the resources to increase their productivity, nor the organizational strength through which to acquire resources from governments, donors and the market

Most participatory bodies include working with women in their range of activities to a greater rather than lesser degree although the range of opportunity provided to women is still not equal to that provided to men

later developed in the Saemul Dong Movement (South Korea) and the Aga Khan Rural Support Programme (AKRSP) Pakistan. The social mobilization approach was formulated into a rigorous methodology of participatory development under the auspices of the United Nations University, South Asian Perspectives Project during the 1980s.[4] Since the early 1980s a large number of development NGOs of different sizes and organizational forms have emerged across the country, most of them using the participatory development approach to varying degrees.

These include the following broad categories which may not be mutually exclusive at the margin.[5]

At present there is a wide variety of NGOs and participatory organizations in the development field. These include:[6]

(i) The RSPs which do not describe themselves as NGOs and are multi-functional in that they provide a range of services and aim to achieve a provincial and national coverage.
(ii) Urban NGOs for Participatory Development
(iii) Single-function NGOs such as those focusing on micro-credit. These often engage in supplementary functions, similar to those of (i) above.
(iv) CO Clusters and independent COs some of which are partners of support organizations and in many cases use the Participatory Development approach.

These participatory bodies are not only diverse in type, they operate in urban or rural areas and sometimes both. The scale of operation varies from a village or neighbourhood association to a nation-wide organization covering tens of thousands of households. The geographical spread too is now nation-wide. Where participatory NGOs were once spots on a map, concentrated in a few regions where the enabling environment was considered favourable, they now span all four provinces although Balochistan lags behind the other three provinces even now.

Intensity of coverage of operating area is very much a question of policy choice. To take two relatively long-lived and large-scale NGOs from our own sample, OPP/ OCT has concentrated on covering its 'home' area of Orangi[7] and a few areas in and around Karachi. Its formidable influence in the rest of Pakistan has to do more with the personality and prestige of its late founder, its own very real achievements in Orangi and the alliances it has forged elsewhere rather than a far-flung physical presence.

NRSP on the other hand spreads its approximately 13,500 COs, each with an average of 21.6 members over twenty-seven districts throughout the country. Coverage intensity is therefore necessarily low.

Women's activities are no longer a kind of appendix to NGO or CO work as they were a decade ago. Most participatory bodies include working with women in their range of activities to a greater rather than lesser degree although the range of opportunity provided to women is still not equal to that provided to men. However, there are now a number of participatory organizations that are either women-focused or which target households through women. Two such organizations, Kashf and Khwendo Kor are part of the group examined in this study.

Lastly, there is now a significant number and range of NGOs that practice advocacy on a number of issues affecting poor and disadvantaged groups as well as citizens rights. Some are exclusively advocacy oriented but many combine advocacy with other development work.

I.2 The Participatory Development Approach[8]

Participatory Development is a process which involves the participation of the poor at the village level to build their human, natural and economic resource base for breaking out of the poverty nexus. It is specifically aims at achieving a localized capital accumulation process based on the progressive development of group identity, skills development and local resources generation. The essential feature of Participatory Development is social mobilization or the formation of group identity. This is done by initiating a series of dialogues with rural communities, which can result in the formation of community organizations. The beginning of the process is therefore the emergence of a nascent form

Participatory Development is a process which involves the participation of the poor at the village level to build their human, natural and economic resource base for breaking out of the poverty nexus

of community consciousness. This is then deepened as the community identifies and implements projects for increasing income, acquiring new skills and begins to engage in collective savings.

As the sense of group identity is deepened it gives a new self-confidence through which the community can engage in more ambitious projects involving collective action and management.

I.2.1 *The Concept*: The concept of Participatory Development has three key elements:

(i) Process: It is a process whose moving forces are the growth of *consciousness* and group *identity*, and the realization, in practice, of the creative potential of the poor.

(ii) Empowerment: The process of reconstructing a group identity, of raising consciousness, of acquiring new skills and of upgrading their knowledge base, progressively imparts to the poor a new *power* over the economic and social forces that fashion their daily lives.

It is through this power that the poor shift out of the perception of being passive victims of the process that perpetuates their poverty. They become the active forces in initiating interventions that progressively improve their economic and social condition, and help overcome poverty.

(iii) Participation: The acquisition of the power to break the vicious circle of poverty is based on *participation* within an organization, in a *series* of projects. This participation is not through 'representatives' who act on their behalf but rather, the actual involvement of each member of the organization in project identification, formulation, implementation and evaluation. It is in open meetings of ordinary members at the village/mohalla level organization that decisions are collectively taken, and work responsibilities assigned on issues such as income generation projects, savings funds, conservation practices in land use, infrastructure construction and asset creation.

I.2.2 *The Dynamics of Participatory Development*: The process of participatory development proceeds through a dynamic interaction between the achievement of specific objectives for improving the resource position of the local community and the inculcation of a sense of community identity. Collective actions for specific objectives such as a small irrigation project, building a school, clean drinking water provision, or agricultural production activities can be an entry point for a localized capital accumulation process. This is associated with group savings schemes, reinvestment and asset creation. The dynamics of participatory development are based on the possibility that with the achievement of such specific objectives for an improved resource position, the community would acquire greater self-confidence and strengthen its group identity.

II. SELECTED ISSUES IN MICRO-CREDIT

Since most development NGOs whatever their organizational structure, use micro credit as an important element in their intervention, it may be useful in this sub-section to briefly examine some of the issues in micro credit.[9]

II.1 MICRO-CREDIT IN THE URBAN CONTEXT

In the urban context in Pakistan, it has been recognized that small scale, informal enterprises whether manufacturing, cottage industry, trading or services have in many cases provided higher returns on capital invested than large scale or medium scale enterprises in the formal sector. Employment coefficients with respect to output in the small-scale manufacturing sector and micro-enterprises are also high. Paradoxically, this is the very sector that is starved for capital because the poor and even large sections of the middle class in Pakistan have very little access to institutionalized credit.

The case for provision of micro-credit is clear, the impact of micro-credit has been proven in urban and peri-urban settings. A number of studies conducted by development professionals, NGO's

The process of participatory development proceeds through a dynamic interaction between the achievement of specific objectives for improving the resource position of the local community and the inculcation of a sense of community identity

themselves and donors show a highly positive impact on income as a result of utilization of micro-credit.[10]

OCT's experience shows that as families of successful users of micro-credit register sustainable income increases, the impact is not confined to greater consumption or investment in the micro-enterprise. These households also show significant improvement in such social indicators as children's education, family nutrition and improved hygiene.

On the other hand access of the urban poor to micro-credit has always been low to non-existent. The formal banking sector in Pakistan has usually avoided lending to the poor on grounds of supposed difficulties in collection and lack of collateral.

II.2 MICRO-CREDIT IN THE RURAL CONTEXT

(i) Rural use of micro-credit is important both for agricultural and non agricultural use. The need for credit is particularly important for poorer farmers. Their requirement for agricultural inputs, seeds, fertilizer, pesticide, etc. tends to be cyclical as does their income. However the two cycles do not always coincide.

The poorer the farmer the greater the proportion of his produce that has to be diverted towards household consumption. In the case of the poorest, those with the smallest or least productive land holdings, their consumption requirements will exceed their production of basic food items.

It is common practice therefore for the farmer to have to purchase seeds and other inputs at the time of sowing from shopkeepers/traders (arhtis) on credit at inflated rates (see discussion and evidence in chapter 3). The requirements to pay back these amounts along with the price of food also purchased from the Arhtis on credit puts great pressure on the small farmer. He is obliged to dispose off his crop together which any dairy or poultry produce in order to pay of these debts immediately after the harvest in the market when prices for his crop are low.[11] In a lean crop year the pressure on the farmer to buy food and inputs on credit is all the greater.

In such situations production loans for crop inputs ease the pressure on the farmer considerably. He is able to purchase better quality inputs more cheaply and independently of the local power structure.

The recent practice of combining such loans for inputs with crop insurance provides significant protection to both the farmer and the lending agencies. This policy is now being introduced by a number of NGOs.

(ii) When a farmer is living at subsistence level, he seldom has the disposable income to make improvements in his land that would improve productivity such as land levelling, lining of water channels or the practice of several farmers joining to construct a tube-well. Loans given for such improvements can be used to purchase materials, tractor time or small machinery. The impact of these loans could be highly positive.

(iii) Rural loans for non agricultural purposes include such things as village shops which provide basic consumption goods, clothing, and some inputs. Services of micro-credit users show that this is the commonest non agricultural rural use of micro-credit.

II.3 SOME CONDITIONS FOR SUCCESSFUL MICRO-CREDIT USE

In this sub-section some of the issues related with the provision of micro-credit are briefly outlined.

II.3.1 *Group Formation*: In rural particularly agricultural environments, there is a clear advantage in the formation of a CO, whether comprising the bulk of households in a village or a group within a village of broadly similar economic level. This is because of the relatively isolated and self contained nature of small rural communities and also to the nature of social cohesion in these societies.

Not only are occupations much more diverse in urban and peri-urban areas but the tight social cohesion of rural societies is greatly diffused. In urban areas/peri-urban areas, biraderi ties are replaced with broader ethnic identities and there are street or mohalla level communities or associations of persons in a particular trade or profession. Therefore, group association has been found to be beneficial for purposes of successful use and repayment of micro-credit.[12]

It is possible to provide micro-credit through groups formed specifically for the purpose or through groups formed for such other purposes as sanitation, health, and productive infrastructure. What is necessary in each case is that certain rules and conditions specific to the successful use of micro-credit be applied in every case. These include:

(i) Some form of credit discipline needs to be transferred to the group. This is often done through a process of saving whether it is a process of collective bank savings or internal savings aimed at internal lending within the group.

(ii) The group acts as a guarantor of its members who are the individual borrowers. This is more useful in rural than in urban conditions since greater social pressure can be brought to bear in village society than in urban situations.

(iii) Loans given to a first time borrower should always progress from relatively small amounts to larger amounts. Larger loans given to first time borrowers do not have a good record of success in OCT, PIEDAR and NRSP in the group studied in this exercise as well as a number of other NGOs providing micro-credit.

(iv) The business plan of the borrower must be carefully scrutinized by the lender.

- Too many individuals granted loan for the same trade or shop in one area will result in over supply of that service.

- The borrower must show clearly what his or her market is and how that market will be accessed.
- Rudimentary business managements skills should be transferred such as elementary bookkeeping, cost control, planning and not diverting capital from the business to social, consumption or other uses.

(v) Default where deliberate should always be pursued with all the means of the lending organization.

(vi) Where there is default whether deliberate or through force majeure such as through death or incapacitation of the borrower or through natural disaster, the amount should be written off, through provision made in the budget and the result reflected in the lenders books.

(vii) Delay or failure owing to bad management or poor business planning reflects badly on both the ability of the borrower and the capability of the lending agency.

(viii) There are two major issues in targeting borrowers. Firstly, smaller sized loans (<Rs.10,000) are generally better suited to the needs and repayment capacities of the poor; secondly, they also contribute to better targeting of the poor and offer less temptation to the better-off to compete for loans. Organizations that have offered relatively high loans (Rs.15-20,000 plus) report greater difficulties in repayment. Those organizations in this category visited by the NHDR research team were moving towards a smaller average size of loan and highlighted the need for better scrutiny of borrowers business plans.

II.3.2 Provision of micro-credit is a necessary but often not a sufficient condition for inducing a sustainable increase in income of the borrower. Additionally provision of technical skill, better access over input markets, and marketing support may be necessary.

Provision of micro-credit is a necessary but often not a sufficient condition for inducing a sustainable increase in income of the borrower. Additionally provision of technical skill, better access over input markets, and marketing support may be necessary

II.3.3 *The Role of Savings*: In early micro-credit practice the role of savings was central. Regular savings by CO members was linked proportionately to disbursement of loans. Not all other practitioners agree.

There is wide divergence amongst the NGOs on the role of savings and the link between credit and savings; this question links in with the question of whether loans should be made to groups or to individuals. At one pole, the RSPs have always stressed savings both as a means of strengthening COs and as a means of strengthening credit discipline.

OPP/OCT's modus operandi is radically different. It places no stress on savings. Dr Khan held that encouraging small entrepreneurs to hold savings in banks at declining real rates of interest rather than investing in their own businesses with inflation-adjusted rates of return of over 30 per cent typically makes no sense. He pointed to the ultimate absurdity of AKRSP beneficiaries holding tens of millions of rupees in bank savings where inflation erodes their holdings while the banks still refuse to extend credit to small entrepreneurs like them, choosing instead to lend to their usual rich clients elsewhere in Pakistan. Thus, the curious phenomenon of thrifty small savers in a deprived region providing funds for those engaged in conspicuous consumption in better-off regions.

Thus, while there is little doubt that regular savings and processes like internal lending help to instill financial discipline, large savings are not by themselves necessary to successful micro-credit operations.

II.3.4 *The Question of Interest*: The issue of interest apart from its economic aspects, takes on an added dimension in Pakistan where interest poses a particular cultural/religious problem. There are also factors other than cultural/religious relating to interest that warrant close attention.

(i) The philosophy of subsidized credit has always had a following in government, if not in banking and financial circles. ADBP long continued to dispense credit at lower than market rates (often to well-off clients), and there are a host of small government programmes supposedly for disadvantaged groups such as women and unemployed youth, that follow similar policies. A number of donors have in the past accepted subsidized credit in practice.

(ii) Some NGOs see their beneficiaries as a disadvantaged group that needs to be introduced to the use of credit by initial use of 'soft' terms. There is an underlying feeling that if the rural rich and politically well-connected can take advantage of subsidized credit, their own clients are surely more deserving. However, it is pertinent to note that there is a direct link between programme sustainability and interest rates and other user charges. Without this perspective there can be little understanding of either the real cost of capital or the costs of running a credit programme. In times of high growth when returns on micro-enterprise can be as high as 40 to 50 per cent, it may is possible for a successful micro-enterprise to afford market based interest rates. However, this may not be the case in periods of economic stagnation.

(iii) The prolonged economic recession in the 1990s and particularly since 1998 has affected the poor severely with marginal/disadvantaged groups generally worst off. Typically, credit used by micro-enterprises has had high rates of return in times of moderate to high economic growth. Successful use of credit in micro-enterprises has become more problematic during the present prolonged slump. The principal reasons for this are shrinking markets and pressures on borrowers to divert micro-credit to urgent consumption or emergency (for example, health) needs. There is therefore a tendency in NGOs and institutions such as the ADBP to lend money meant for the poor to the non-poor. (This is substantiated by evidence from the NHDR/PIDE Survey 2001 analyzed in chapter 3).

III. PROFILES OF PARTICIPATORY NGOS[13]

In this section profiles of NGOs in each category are presented, to indicate the different organizational structures and approaches to poverty alleviation.

III.1 NRSP AND THE RURAL SUPPORT PROGRAMMES

The Rural Support Programmes in Pakistan consist of the National Rural Support Programme (NRSP), Balochistan Rural Support Programme (BRSP), and Sarhad Rural Support Corporation (SRSC) and the Aga Khan Rural Support Programme (AKRSP).

The RSPs were originally seen as a group of Government assisted NGOs with a mandate to promote rural development. They were set up on the premise that the Federal and Provincial Governments have neither the resources nor the organizational reach to bring a range of development activities to the majority of the nation's rural population and that even if this were possible, the recurring budget for the development activities would be beyond the capacity of government. The RSPs now no longer see themselves as NGOs but as something intermediate between a government body and an NGO.

The RSPs are incorporated under the Companies Act and include both serving and retired government officers on their Boards, in their personal and in an ex-officio capacity.

III.2 ACHIEVEMENTS OF THE RSP MODEL

1. There is no doubt that the RSPs have played a central role in introducing and popularizing the participatory approach in Pakistan.
2. The RSPs have also shown that rural communities hitherto unevenly affected by a growth process external to themselves can successfully take charge of their own development.
3. They have been at the forefront of NGO/Government agency models of co-operation (despite claiming not to be NGOs).
4. The RSPs and in particular NRSP have the largest member base of any NGO in Pakistan. (It now has 293,000 members in its COs.)
5. The RSPs have set up training facilities for various aspects of participatory development which have also been used by other organizations.

III.3 WEAKNESSES OF THE RSP MODEL

Critics of the RSP model contend that:

1. The approach is expensive to implement; despite considerable individual variation the RSP method is capital-intensive compared with other, 'non-GONGO' organizations. Operating costs are also high, owing to high levels of staffing and high salary levels compared with other NGOs.[14]
2. The NHDR/A.I. Hamid Spot Survey data show that neither NRSP's loan sizes nor its selection of borrowers in the area surveyed target the poor. With one household owning two hundred irrigated acres, 13 per cent owning over thirty and a further 20 per cent owning over ten irrigated acres, targeting can at best be characterized as imprecise.
3. NRSP is by far the largest NGO with a presence in twenty-seven districts. It has also spent the greatest amount of resources compared to any other NGO in the country. Yet over a decade it has reached only 293,000 beneficiaries. This is 0.7 per cent of the forty million of rural poor. For an NGO whose raison d'etre is to overcome poverty on a national scale, this cannot be called rapid progress. Nor, going by the results of our spot survey, can it be assumed that their methodology ensures that all beneficiaries are poor.
4. Sustainability can be a serious problem. It is still not clear how much time must lapse before a community organization set up by an RSP could achieve a level of maturity that would enable it in concert with other COs, to interact directly with government and private sector agencies providing services. To date there is no example of a RSP having wound up its infrastructure even in an area where it has operated for seven or eight years.

5. Criticism has emerged even from within the RSPs that heavy reliance on RSP staff, especially social organizers in mobilizing communities and building community organizations is costly and counter-productive. This is contrasted with relying on a process of identifying, training and supporting village activists to perform these services for their own communities with long-term recurring costs borne by the communities themselves. This internal dynamic within communities reduces dependence and is more likely to produce a self-sustaining community organization capable of taking charge of its own development. To date however the new approach has not been developed and put into practice.
6. A problem not unique to the RSP's but exaggerated by their scale of operations, is the role of their credit operations. As large multi-sectoral development NGOs, the RSPs find it difficult to view credit as anything other than a supporting leg of a larger, integrated programme. Equally, they find it difficult to separate costs specific to the credit programme. This not only alters their perception of the credit programme at the policy level by allowing subsidized credit to be seen as a means of facilitating the overall multi-sectoral programme, it makes it difficult to calculate cost recovery and break-even points for the credit operation.

III.4 OPP/OCT

How is OPP/OCT different from say, the RSPs besides the obvious point that it operates in an urban, not rural area?

- Its infrastructure and overheads are far less and it lives within its means.
- It does not form COs although it will collaborate with them.
- It does not attempt to use programme staff to micro manage of communities and operates with a light touch.
- It does not expand beyond its original area or 'replicate' itself elsewhere although it has many sincere imitators and organizations to which it provides advice and sometimes material help.
- It believes in dedicated workers with salaries much lower than with other large NGOs.

OPP began with sanitation and the process involved the recognition of the different levels of sanitation.

'There are four levels of modern sanitation system:

- Inside the house—the sanitary latrine.
- In the lane—underground sewerage lines with manholes and house connections.
- Secondary or collector drains.
- Main drains and treatment plants.

OPP found the house-owners willing and competent to assume the responsibility of constructing and maintaining all sanitary arrangements at the first three levels with their own resources and under their own management, like the small farmers. These three levels constitute 80 to 90 per cent of the system. The main drains and the treatment plant must remain, like main roads and water lines, the responsibility of a central authority.'[15]

OPP also found that several barriers needed to be tackled:

- Reducing the Cost through research and extension
- Removing the Economic Barrier
- Removing the Psychological Barrier i.e., 'the mistaken belief that they should get sewerage and sanitation as free gifts.'

On micro-credit too, OPP/OCT's modus operandi is radically different:
- OCT considers the family enterprise to be the basic productive unit in the areas in which it operates. OCT's stated objective is to provide capital to emerging family enterprises, not to alleviate poverty, by giving small loans to the poorest of the poor. OCT relies on the undoubted multiplier effect on incomes and employment amongst the poorest when it invests in the micro-enterprises one rung up the economic ladder.
- Its groups are much larger in size than the five-member Grameen style group. The average number of open accounts

in each group in Orangi is twenty-one although in individual cases the number can be much higher. Loans are made to individuals who are backed by two guarantors.

- The key figure in these groups is the 'agent', analogous to the activist in some rural NGOs. The agent initially identifies and investigates potential borrowers, OCT verifies the information and carries out a business analysis. It then tracks each loan through to full repayment, delay or the occasional default.
- OCT does not accept claims of 98 or 99 per cent repayments by some NGOs. It holds that this is statistically impossible in large groups where adverse local conditions, deaths, business or family disasters and the occasional cheat will make their appearance. OCT increasingly forms groups on the basis of trades or occupations and tracks their performance. Accordingly it will not only expand or reduce the portfolio in a region or of a group according to performance, it has begun to track the viability of businesses by type and region.
- As mentioned above OCT places no stress on savings.
- OPP has established partnerships with other NGOs, such as OPD and YCHR in Punjab. In this arrangement, affiliate NGOs act as an agent for OPP by identifying, vetting and supporting qualified borrowers who receive credit from OPP which also provides training on credit operation to the NGOs as well as other support. Some of these arrangements were a success, others less so.

OPP has also experimented by giving larger sized loans to agriculturists and a fishermens cooperative. These were not a success.

III.5 KASHF

The Kashf Foundation was established to serve two main objectives: (i) Alleviate poverty; and (ii) Economically empower women from poor households.

Kashf operates in the districts of Lahore and Sheikhupura with five branches. The Ravi Rayon Branch is located in Sheikhupura District and the Yakki Gate, Sukh Nehr, Bedian and Kahna Branches are located in Lahore District. Bedian, Kahna and Ravi Rayon are peri-urban areas. Sukh Nehr and Yakee Gate are located within the Lahore City area.

Kashf insists that it is not the usual poverty alleviation oriented NGO with 'beneficiaries'. It is a service provider with 'clients'. That said, the spot survey shows that in the areas sampled at least, Kashf's targeting of the poor was one of the best in the sample of NGOs surveyed. Its target clients are working women. While women in these areas are relatively less restricted by gender and society compared with rural women since feudal and tribal mores have less of a hold, theirs is a hard lot.

In the words of Kashf's management: 'Kashf's approach in improving the economic choices of the poor focuses on supporting those within the poverty bracket who have existing economic opportunities. These households earn slightly more than one US dollar a day, but certainly less than two dollars'.

Kashf's targeting is precise, loans sizes completely appropriate to its clientele and its MIS and monitoring systems amongst the best in the NGO sector in Pakistan. Its staff is keen and efficient.

III.6 COMMUNITY ORGANIZATIONS (COs)

There is now considerable variation in working approaches practised by participatory development organizations, some borrowed, imitated or modified, others home-grown. This is particularly true of the new breed of COs now coming into prominence.

A particularly marked and interesting stage in the development process is the emergence of a wide variety of COs. Where previously local community based organizations tended to be of a charitable nature or narrowly focused on particular interests, the new ones are clearly development oriented and have absorbed and apply many of the principles of participatory development originally fostered by a few larger support organizations.

Not having the access to funds that larger support organizations have developed, independent COs have to live within their means. This implies greater reliance on activists and on networking, limited scope of operation and in the case of successful organizations, a highly focused approach.

IV. COMPARATIVE IMPACT ASSESSMENT OF NGOS

A small sample field survey was conducted for the NHDR to investigate the impact of various NGOs on the economic life of the beneficiaries. Data was collected on how well the respondents ate, before and after the NGO intervention, their health status, their household income and the issue of whether or not a sustainable increase in income occurred followed the provision of loans. The size of irrigated land owned is the single most important indicator of the economic status of rural households. Accordingly data on canal irrigated land owned by beneficiaries of various NGOs was also collected to assess their relative effectiveness in targeting of the poor.

It may be important to reiterate that given the resource and time constraints of the study the sample size was too small for the results to be representative for the country as a whole or even for the entire geographic scope of operations of the NGOs covered.

The beneficiaries of a total of seven organizations of varying sizes were interviewed. The NGOs were selected for both geographical and functional diversity. No presumption could be made in advance as to whether they represented 'best practices' or were 'best in class'. However, in many cases their methodologies could be representative of a much broader group of similar NGOs. Both urban and rural NGOs were represented in this sample. A total of 277 respondents were interviewed with an average of forty for each NGO. Since land ownership is an important indicator of economic status it is interesting that 60 per cent of the beneficiaries of NRSP, 35 per cent of PIEDAR, 20 per cent of Khwendo Kor (KK) and 10 per cent of KASHF respondents owned land. For all respondents covered across NGOs a surprising 18 per cent of total land owners owned over twenty-six acres, mostly irrigated. Another 25 per cent fell in the ten to twenty-five acres category.

IV.1 Land Ownership

If ownership of canal irrigated land is an indicator of rural wealth, NRSP has relatively the wealthiest clients. Sixty per cent of the NRSP sample beneficiaries owned irrigated land compared to 18.8 per cent in the case of PIEDAR, 17.1 per cent in the case of KK and 9.5 per cent in the case of KASHF. In terms of the size distribution of land owners NRSP once again stands out with 50 per cent of its land owning beneficiaries owning over eleven acres of irrigated land (see Table 6). The percentage of land owners with holdings above eleven acres is 11.1 per cent in the case of PIEDAR and 83 per cent in the case of KK. However, it may be noted that only 17 per cent of KK respondents owned any land at all. In the case of KASHF none of the land owning beneficiaries have more than ten acres and also only 9.5 per cent of its total beneficiaries owned any land at all (see Table 6).

IV.2 Health and Nutrition

The apparently cut and dried answer to the health and nutrition questions were obtained by the surveyors after some discussions and cross questioning. As many as 59 per cent of the respondents ate their fill daily and 27 per cent responded with 'mostly'. However faced with the question as to whether they ate better now or in earlier times, as many as 40 per cent said 'earlier' citing loss of work, reduction in business, static or declining incomes and expanding

Table 1 Household Nutrition Status by NGO

NGOs	Daily (%)	Mostly (%)	Sometimes (%)	Seldom (%)	Total (%)
KK	42.90	31.40	17.10	8.60	100.00
OPP	72.10	24.60	3.30	—	100.00
PIEDAR	66.70	12.50	14.60	6.30	100.00
NRSP	67.50	27.50	5.00	—	100.00
KASHF	45.20	40.50	9.50	4.80	100.00
OWP	73.70	21.10	—	5.30	100.00
ASB	40.60	37.50	21.90	—	100.00

Source: NHDR/A.I. Hamid Spot Survey 2001.

families as the causes of the deterioration in their diet.

In terms of the comparative picture of NGOs 68 per cent of NRSP respondents ate their fill daily (see Table 1) and 65 per cent ate better now than earlier (see Table 2). In the case of OPP 72 per cent of the beneficiaries ate their fill daily (Table 1), while 27 per cent ate more now than earlier (Table 2). As many as 43 per cent had more to eat in earlier times in the case of OPP compared to 40 per cent in the case of KK, 48 per cent in the case of PIEDAR, 18 per cent in the case of NRSP, 31 per cent in the case of KASHF, 47 per cent in the case of OWP and 56 per cent in the case of ASB (see Table 2). In their comments a number of respondents spoke of the declining quality rather than quantity of diet, pointing to declining consumption of already scarce meat, loss of household animals or access to pure dairy products, and fewer and less fresh vegetables, being obliged to buy them in the market occasionally. (These comments refer to those who are operating land below the minimum subsistence acreage).

As table 3 shows for a substantial proportion of respondents related with each NGO there has been a deterioration in health status. This is consistent with the NHDR/PIDE data set both quantitative and qualitative which shows wide spread illness amongst the poor with sickness being an important factor in pushing people into poverty (see chapter 3). In the spot survey for NGOs as table 3 shows as many as 60 per cent of the respondents in KK reported a deterioration in their health, 39 per cent in the case of OPP, 41.7 per cent in the case of PIEDAR, 40.5 per cent in the case of KASHF, 42.1 per cent in the case of OWP and 40.6 per cent in the case of ASB. However, NRSP stands out with only 12.5 per cent of its beneficiaries reporting a deterioration in their health and as many as 50 per cent reporting an improvement in their health. NRSP respondents pointed to greater agricultural productivity, higher yields, better supply of inputs and adoption of new techniques as the factors which had improved their income, consumption and health. Some of this credit should certainly go to NRSP and some to the government. However it must be remembered that in terms of both income and assets NRSP respondents were the best off in the sample.

Table 2 Nutrition History by NGO

NGOs	Have more to eat now (%)	Have more to eat in earlier times (%)	Equal (%)	Total (%)
KK	28.60	40.00	31.40	100.00
OPP	27.90	42.60	29.50	100.00
PIEDAR	35.40	47.90	16.70	100.00
NRSP	65.00	17.50	17.50	100.00
KASHF	42.90	31.00	26.20	100.00
OWP	31.60	47.40	21.10	100.00
ASB	31.30	56.30	12.50	100.00

Source: NHDR/A.I. Hamid Spot Survey 2001.

For other NGOs where between 40 to 60 per cent had reported a deterioration in their health, their comments in this context were interesting. The respondents linked declining health not only with economic conditions (declining real incomes and rising costs of medical care) but interestingly with increased mental stress (most used the urdu word *pareshani*).

IV.3 MONTHLY HOUSEHOLD INCOME

Table 4 shows the distribution of beneficiaries in each NGO by various classes of monthly household income. PIEDAR has the largest proportion of respondents in the extremely poor category, with 22.9 per cent having monthly incomes of Rs.1,000 or less, 43.8 per cent with incomes between Rs.1,000 and 5,000 per month and only 6.3 per cent with incomes above Rs.15,000 per month. In the case of KK 17.1 per cent of the beneficiaries have a monthly household income upto Rs.1,000 and 42.9 per cent between 1,000 to 5,000 rupees. In the case of

Table 3 Health History by NGO

NGOs	Health is better now (%)	Health was better earlier (%)	Equal (%)	No information (%)	Total (%)
KK	20.00	60.00	17.10	2.90	100.00
OPP	19.70	39.30	41.00	—	100.00
PIEDAR	25.00	41.70	31.30	2.10	100.00
NRSP	50.00	12.50	37.50	—	100.00
KASHF	31.00	40.50	28.60	—	100.00
OWP	21.10	42.10	36.80	—	100.00
ASB	15.60	40.60	43.80	—	100.00

Source: NHDR/A.I. Hamid Spot Survey 2001.

Table 4	Monthly Household Income by NGO				
	Total Monthly Household Income from all sources				
	Upto Rs. 1000 (%)	1000 to 5000 (%)	5000 to 15000 (%)	15000 plus (%)	Total (%)
KK	17.10	42.90	31.40	8.60	100.00
OPP	9.80	21.30	59.00	9.80	100.00
PIEDAR	22.90	43.80	27.10	6.30	100.00
NRSP	2.50	25.00	45.00	27.50	100.00
KASHF	2.40	42.90	52.40	2.40	100.00
OWP	5.30	36.80	52.60	5.30	100.00
ASB	6.30	62.50	31.30	—	100.00

Source: NHDR/A.I. Hamid Spot Survey 2001.

OPP the comparable figures are for OPP 9.8 per cent and 21.3 per cent respectively. In the case of NRSP 2.5 per cent and 25.0 per cent respectively. In the case of KASHF 2.4 per cent and 42.9 per cent respectively. In the case of OWP 5.3 per cent and 36.8 per cent respectively and in the case of ASB 6.3 per cent and 62.5 per cent respectively. Table 4 shows the largest proportion of respondents in the Rs.15,000 plus per month category are in NRSP (27.5 per cent) and the lowest in KASHF with 2.4 per cent. For the other NGOs the percentage of respondents in this relatively affluent category range between 5.3 and 8.6 per cent. It appears therefore that as far as targeting the poor is concerned KASHF and PIEDAR come out on top. As NRSP with 27.5 per cent of its beneficiaries with over Rs.15,000 monthly household income and 72 per cent of its beneficiaries with an income of Rs.5,000 to over Rs.15,000 per month, has the most imprecise targeting of the poor compared to other NGOs in the sample.

IV.4 Sustainable Income Increase

As table 5 shows for all NGOs in the sample except for KK more than 50 per cent of the beneficiaries achieved a sustainable increase in income following the receipt of a loan. The top performer is NRSP with 81.6 per cent of its beneficiaries experiencing a sustainable increase in their income after receipt of a loan. However this must be qualified by the fact that NRSP also has the highest proportion of well off beneficiaries. The proportion of beneficiaries with a sustainable increase in income following loan receipt, is 71.1 per cent in the case of OPP, 66.7 per cent in the case of KASHF, 56.5 per cent in the case of PIEDAR and 42.9 per cent in the case of KK.

V. STRATEGIC ISSUES OF UP-SCALING

V.1. Participatory Development NGOs: Consciousness, Organization and Work Procedures[16]

The defining feature of a programme for empowering the poor, is the passion, which

Table 5	Sustainable Income Increase After Loan			
	Did Loan Result in Sustainable Increase in Income			
NGOs	Yes (%)	No (%)	Equal (%)	Total (%)
KK	42.90	47.60	9.50	100.00
OPP	71.10	17.80	11.10	100.00
PIEDAR	56.50	21.70	21.70	100.00
NRSP	81.60	7.90	10.50	100.00
KASHF	66.70	33.30	—	100.00
OWP	—	—	100.00	100.00
ASB	53.30	46.70	—	100.00

Source: NHDR/A.I. Hamid Spot Survey 2001.

Table 6	Canal Irrigated Land Owned by Size of Holding of Beneficiaries, by NGO							
	NRSP		PIEDAR		KK		KASHF	
Acres	Number	%	Number	%	Number	%	Number	%
1 to 5	7	29.17	1	11.11	1	16.67	3	75.00
6 to 10	5	20.83	7	77.78	0	0.00	1	25.00
11 to 25	7	29.17	1	11.11	2	33.33	0	0.00
26 to 50	4	16.67	0	0.00	0	0.00	0	0.00
51 to 100	0	0.00	0	0.00	3	50.00	0	0.00
101 to 200	1	4.17	0	0.00	0	0.00	0	0.00
Total	24	100.00	9	100.00	6	100.00	4	100.00
Total 40 Respondents			48		35		42	

Source: NHDR/PIDE Survey 2001.

impels those who work in it and those for whom they work. It is not just an emotion but a form of consciousness. It comes from transcending the ego and relating with the community through love. Thus, passionate consciousness is both a cohering force of the community and also the synergy through which the NGO team can engage in a process of action and reflection. This principle can be the basis of its management culture and work procedures. It would be manifested in the quality of dialogues that occur between NGO personnel and rural communities, on the one hand and between members of the NGO team on the other. The dialogues are designed to identify and actualize the creative potential of individuals.

This form of learning and creative growth if pursued by an NGO through its dialogues may be called *Faqiraana* as, opposed to *Messianic*. The messianic leader/teacher/manager is one who claims to embody the truth and if his followers want to become something they can only be his shadows. By contrast, the faqiraana leader/teacher/manager is one who abnegates his own exceptionality and recognizes each individual as the unique origin of change. The participants in the dialogues whether between the NGO and a community or within the NGO itself, are essentially co-equals in a journey of actualizing each other's creative potential in the context of social change.

The organizational structure reflecting the *Messianic* approach is hierarchic and restricts the space for independent thinking. Its work procedures involve issuing instructions or blindly implementing them. By contrast the organizational structure associated with the *Faqiraana* approach is non-hierarchic, designed to provide space for thought and action by autonomous individuals in collegial interaction. Its work procedures instead of being a simple dichotomy between instructions and compliance, are designed for mutually fertilizing dialogues, action and collective reflection.

V.2 Taking Small NGOs to Scale: Some Necessary Conditions for Success[17]

The aim of up scaling of small NGOs would be to reach the district level only, but with coverage of all union councils within it. This is in view of the fact that: (i) the government is decentralizing key governmental development functions to the district level. So if NGOs fostering community organizations of the poor, could go up to a district scale, they could institutionally link up with local governments. This would enable organizations of the poor to participate in government funded development projects and also in other areas of local governance. (ii) The NGO (or RSPs) which are currently operating in a number of different districts simultaneously, have very low intensity of coverage within any one district. There may therefore be a case for having district level NGOs that have full coverage of the poor population within it.

Of the large number of NGOs with small beginnings, a few have grown to a significant size and achieved national prominence. These include OPP/OCT, SUNGI, and BANH BELI. Three questions arise in the context of their success: (a) What are the common factors in their success? (b) At this stage of their growth, what are the constraints they face to further up-scaling and/or rapid replication? (c) What are the elements of an enabling environment at the national level which could let a 'hundred flowers bloom', in the sense of nurturing the rapid growth/replication of a variety of development NGOs, enable mutually catalyzing interaction and yet maintain the unique character of each of them?

V.2.1 *Success Criteria*: Perhaps the single most important factor in their success is the quality of leadership. Specifically, it is the ability to relate with humility and love with the poor. It is to build a team which while being internally coordinated, at the same time, enables each member to become a centre of thought and action. The successful NGO leader creates the team synergy to develop innovative responses to each new problem on the ground. Yet, he/she ensures that each action by the team contributes to reinforcing the process of the poor taking charge of their own development. The effective leader focuses the team to experience the potential of the poor and to grasp the specific dynamics of how they can organize, take responsibilities and initiate change. Thus, the challenge for the NGO leadership is to so relate with the poor and

The defining feature of a programme for empowering the poor, is the passion, which impels those who work in it and those for whom they work. It is not just an emotion but a form of consciousness. It comes from transcending the ego and relating with the community through love

the team, that every act, every word, every moment of silence, contributes to fertilizing the other, rather than establishing control: Liberating rather than inducing dependency.

The second factor in the success of those small NGOs which engage in social mobilisation, is the identification, training and fostering of village level activists who gradually begin to manage existing COs, thereby, enabling NGO staff to give more time to develop new COs. This process of devolution of management responsibility from NGO staff to village level activists is a crucial factor in the enlargement of NGO coverage in a situation where funds are limited and rapid expansion of staff financially infeasible. The converse of this dynamic is that if too much money becomes available too early, it undermines discipline, initiative and energy of the NGO.

The third factor in the success of small NGOs which have reached significant scale is the development of second level management and the ability of top level leadership to devolve responsibility, acknowledge their achievements and to learn from them just as much as it is necessary for the leadership to learn from the poor. An inner wakefulness that comes from transcending the ego is necessary to be always open to learning from the poor, and from each member of one's team. It is this openness to learning from others that constitutes the basis of the organization's dynamism, its innovation and its sense of being a community.

The fourth factor in the success of small NGOs in reaching significant scale is the development of credible accounting procedures, and a regular monitoring and evaluation exercise on the basis of which donor funding can be sought when it is required. In each case the successful NGO, apart from devising efficacious modes of reflection and action with the village communities, also develops formalized recording and reporting systems.

V.2.2 Key Features in the Transition from Small Sized to District Level NGOs: Those NGOs which started small and through certain specific features (discussed above) have reached a medium-size are now faced with the challenge of up-scaling to a district level size. Typically, the successful NGOs started work in one hamlet a decade ago, are now working in scores of villages. The question is what are the key changes within the organization which could enable them to reach a full coverage of a district size. In this context, seven key changes may be required:

(i) The single leader at the top (variously called Chairman, President or Chief Executive Officer) would need to build a team of at least three or four leaders who can work independently at the top level. This is necessary in a situation where programme operations become so geographically diversified within a district that overall programme management would need to get decentralized to the Union Council and Tehsil levels.

(ii) For a major up-scaling of small NGOs to successful medium-sized NGOs, it would be necessary to receive grant funding for institutional strengthening and growth. The Pakistan Poverty Alleviation Fund that has recently been established, could provide such funding after careful evaluation of the concerned NGOs and assessment of their expansion plans.

(iii) As the organizational structure of the NGO changes from a centralized to a geographically decentralized one, within a whole district, the methodology of work would also have to change to enable introduction of procedures for monitoring and strategic planning. As full autonomy is granted to Union Council and Tehsil level regional programme heads, each of them would be expected to report and evaluate on programme performance within an agreed format and in consultation with community organizations and the regional programme team. This evaluation could be done on a monthly basis and could feed into the process of developing regional programme plans on a quarterly and annual basis. These tehsil level regional programme plans prepared initially at Union Council level regional programme offices, would include issues such as the number and locations of new COs to be formed and the deepening of existing COs. It would also include facilitating the preparation of participatory village development programmes for infrastructure, social sector services, and off-farm enterprises, as and when such services are identified by COs. The deepening of existing COs in the regional programme plans would include devolution of organizational responsibilities to Union Council and then village activists for managing village level or village cluster level apex organizations of the poor. Such devolution of responsibility would, on the one hand, enable self-managed community organizations to develop, and on the other hand, enable the NGO to keep its overheads low as it enlarges its coverage within the district. The regional planning exercise could be conducted at the Tehsil level office on a quarterly basis. However, this process could also involve annual plenary planning sessions at District level Head Office where village activists, key members of regional teams and Head Office personnel in planning, monitoring and human resource development, would interact with each other.

(iv) One of the necessary conditions for successful NGOs that up-scaled to medium-sized level, was the development of a nascent middle level management in their team, although still tightly supervised by the top leadership. As small NGOs up-scale to district level size and achieve geographic diversification, such middle level management would have to be brought to maturity, allowed greater autonomy and considerably increased in number. Such middle level management would play a key role in coordinating social mobilization, training of Union Council level managers and teshil level managers and village level activists, and accessing technical support and credit. The middle management Union and Tehsil level cadre by virtue of its proximity to the field would also be important in collecting data necessary for monitoring, evaluation and planning.

(v) The challenge to NGO up-scaling is that unlike RSPs, they must keep overheads costs to a minimum level. In order to achieve this, it is necessary for the NGO to be able to withdraw from those villages where COs have achieved adequate maturity and have developed the capacity to form apex support organizations of their own. The critical factor for enabling NGOs to devolve organizational responsibilities to apex organizations of COs, is the development of a cadre of village activists with training in the following fields: (a) community management skills, (b) ability to interact with donor organizations and government line departments, (c) expertise in a range of basic skills such as, livestock management, agriculture, soils, irrigation, natural resource management and micro-enterprise development. Such a cadre could constitute a core management team in an independent apex support organization.

(vi) As the NGO up-scales to a district level size it would generate a variety of training needs for CO members at the village level, as well as career development and professional training needs of NGO personnel. Consequently, a human resource development programme within the NGO may be necessary to identify the human resource and career development needs specific to the internal dynamics of the NGO's work. The human resource development section within the NGO would need to be a lean unit which should network with diverse specialized institutions to access the required training services.

> *NGOs that enable the formation of autonomous organizations of the poor could play an important role in creating a systematic relationship between local governance and poor communities. Such a relationship would enable the poor to participate in identification and implementation of development projects as well as decisions related with access over markets and local power structures. It could also help broaden the social base of power, authority and the allocation and use of public resources*

evaluation, and impact assessment exercises for the PPAF and NGOs, on demand. Such an institute would also network national data collection and research institutions (such as the Federal Bureau of Statistics, PIDE, LUMS) to bring their expertise together for particular impact assessment exercises. The Participatory Poverty Assessment (PPA) currently initiated by DFID could be institutionalized into a permanent feature within the MEPPAI.

CONCLUSIONS

In this chapter we have examined the issue of NGOs emerging as an institutional basis, (alongside the government), for contributing to poverty alleviation. The total coverage of NGOs currently, is relatively insignificant compared to the magnitude of the poor population. The NHDR/PIDE 2001 survey for example shows that of the total loans received by all categories of the sample population, the percentage of loans received from NGOs was only 0.8 per cent in the rural areas and 1 per cent in the urban areas. Similarly the NRSP which is by far the largest NGO in the country, operating in twenty-seven districts, nevertheless has a total coverage of only 293,000 beneficiaries. Even if we assume that all of them fall in the category of the poor (the NHDR/A.I. Hamid Spot Survey shows that a significant percentage are not), even then this constitutes 0.7 per cent of the forty million rural poor. Accordingly we have examined the issue of the increase in coverage of NGOs and the effectiveness of their impact on the poor. This was done in the context of examining different types of NGOs, the comparative effectiveness of their impact on the poor, and key organizational and management issues involved in up scaling. We also identified the elements of an enabling institutional structure at the national level, which could accelerate the growth and enhance the effectiveness of NGOs.

The NHDR/A.I. Hamid Spot Survey showed that there was considerable variation with respect to the effectiveness of targeting of the poor between various NGOs. There was also considerable variation with respect to the impact of NGO intervention on incomes, nutrition and health of the poor. This has implications for organizational forms and work procedures.

Under the devolution programme a new structure of local governments at the district level is emerging, within which elected representatives will be expected to undertake (amongst other functions) poverty alleviation at different tiers of local government (district, tehsil, union council and village levels). Within this structure NGOs that enable the formation of autonomous organizations of the poor could play an important role in creating a systematic relationship between local governance and poor communities. Such a relationship would enable the poor to participate in identification and implementation of development projects as well as decisions related with access over markets and local power structures. It could also help broaden the social base of power, authority and the allocation and use of public resources.

If NGOs are to play this role they would need to function at the district level rather than across districts. This would be necessary if only to prevent centralized trans district and un-elected organizations to impinge upon an elected decentralized system. Equally important, the emphasis perhaps may need to shift from building centralized NGOs in a large number of districts with low intensity of coverage (and high overheads) in each, towards district specific NGOs which achieve full coverage of the poor population in the villages, union councils and tehsils of that district. The question therefore becomes how small NGOs operating at the village or union council level can grow rapidly and cost effectively to achieve full coverage of the poor population of that district. A related issue is how can organizations of the poor be enabled to become genuinely autonomous on the one hand and link up with local governments on the other? We have discussed some of the organizational and management issues that would need to be addressed in this context. These involve building multiple tiers of professional management, MIS, accounting and project management systems to enable decentralization of district NGOs to tehsil and union council levels. Hierarchic, centralized structures of management may need to be replaced with decentralized ones which can provide space for thought and action by autonomous individuals in collegial interactions (this is the distinction between messianic and *faqiraana* management systems) The work procedures instead of being a simple dichotomy between instructions and compliance could be designed for mutually fertilizing dialogues, actions and collective reflection. The purpose is to build a team that enables the poor to grasp the specific dynamics of how they can organize, take responsibilities and initiate change.

In terms of the national level institutional structures which could enable rapid growth of coverage from village level to district level NGOs and also for more effective impact, the following policy proposals emerge from the analysis:

(i) To enable the Pakistan Poverty Alleviation Fund (PPAF) to foster the rapid growth and replication of partner organizations engaged in poverty alleviation. The capacity building in the PPAF could address the following dimensions: (a) to develop the ability to coordinate an independent and more rigorous evaluation and impact assessment of partner organizations; (b) providing management support for local government and NGOs (example MIS, project management and accounting systems).

(ii) Establish a national facility for large scale training of village activists, social mobilizers and management professionals.

(iii) Establish a national monitoring and participatory poverty assessment institute in the private sector supported by donors and government. It should have the expertise to undertake rigorous monitoring and impact assessment exercises for the PPAF and NGOs when required.

(iv) A large increase in the scale of credit being disbursed by PPAF and Khushali Bank is required if they are to supply a significant proportion of the microcredit currently being demanded. So far the total amount of credit disbursed by the PPAF covers only 50,000 beneficiaries which is an insignificant proportion of the total number of poor in need of microcredit.

NOTES

1. For a more detailed discussion on the limitations of top-down development programmes, See, Akmal Hussain, *Poverty Alleviation in Pakistan*, Vanguard Books, Lahore, 1994, pp. 23-36.
2. For a detailed discussion of this perspective on poverty see, Akmal Hussain, 'Pro-Poor Growth, Participatory Development and Decentralization: Paradigms and Praxis', chapter in, Wignaraja, Sirivardana (ed.), *Pro-Poor Growth and Governance in South Asia—Case Profiles of Participatory Development and Decentralization Reforms*, Zed Press London (Forthcoming).
3. For a more detailed discussion of this approach, See, Akmal Hussain, *Poverty Alleviation in Pakistan*, op. cit., pp. 23-39.
4. See, Ponna Wignaraja, Akmal Hussain, Harsh Sethi and Ganeshan Wignaraja, *Participatory Development, Learning from South Asia*, United Nations University, Oxford University Press, 1991.
5. For example, NRSP, easily the biggest RSP concentrates its work in the rural areas but also manages the Urban Poverty Alleviation Project in Rawalpindi.

    Similarly PIEDAR primarily offers micro-credit in its urban/peri-urban Kabirwala operating area, but supports community based irrigation management and primary education for rural girls (but not micro-credit) in its other, rural, operating area in Darkhana. It also supports urban waste management in low-income wards of Quetta, Balochistan, conservation of lakes in Upper Swat, NWFP, and an environmental education network that spreads across Urdu-medium schools in low income areas of Rawalpindi-Islamabad and Lahore.

    Again, Kashf for example is single function in the sense that its primary and most important service is provision of micro-credit but it has ancillary activities in elementary business management to assist its clients as well as an enterprise development initiative for the poorest women who cannot yet afford to run a business. Its Enterprise Development Section designs products, and explores markets for clients products. Kashf also works with clients on such social issues as prevention of violence against women and promotion of sanitation, etc. A new initiative, Shaafi Project, is looking at ways to improve the health of Kashf's clients. Taken together, these ancillary activities will clearly move Kashf in a multifunctional direction.
6. The discussion on types of Participatory Development NGOs is drawn from the research input of Agha Imran Hamid.
7. The agglomeration of *kachi abadis* known as Orangi has an estimated population of about a million. OPP points out that there is therefore, a

8. This sub-section is drawn from Akmal Hussain, *Poverty Alleviation in Pakistan*, op. cit., pp. 26-28.
9. This sub-section is based on the research input of Mr Agha Imran Hamid.
10. See, also impact assessment data of the Spot Survey, Section-IV.
11. For a more detailed analysis of this double squeeze on the poor peasant, see, Akmal Hussain, 'Squeezed Out by Progress,' in *Development: Seeds of Change*, 1985, p. 3.
12. OCT which does not form borrowers groups nevertheless relies on guarantees from two previous successful borrowers.
13. This section is based on the research input of Mr Agha Imran Hamid.
14. See, for example *Government/Donor/NGO Collaboration: Lessons Learnt And The Action For The Future*, a report prepared for UNDP Pakistan, 1986, pp. ii, 7-8.
15. Dr Akhtar Hameed Khan in his *Orangi Pilot Project: Reminiscences and Reflections*, op. cit.
16. The formulations about management principles in this sub-section are drawn from field experience of Akmal Hussain as the first CEO (honorary) of the Punjab Rural Support Programme. See, Akmal Hussain, *The First Four Months, CEO's Report to the Board of Directors*, PRSP, 1998.
17. This sub-section is based on Akmal Hussain, *Employment Generation, Poverty Alleviation and Growth in Pakistan's Rural Sector: Policies for Institutional Change*, Report prepared for the ILO (CEPR), Pakistan, March 1999.

CHAPTER 5

A STRATEGY OF ECONOMIC GROWTH AND EMPOWERING THE POOR

Photograph by Mansoor Zaidi

What has been said,
Has entered our consciousness,
So now we must actualize it

Whatever colour I weave
I weave deep

– SHAH HUSSAIN
17th Century Punjabi Sufi Poet
(Translation)

CHAPTER 5

A Strategy of Economic Growth and Empowering the Poor

INTRODUCTION

In chapters 1 and 2 we have identified the structural features of the economy that during the 1990s not only slowed GDP growth, but also accentuated its adverse effects on poverty and unemployment. Therefore a strategy of economic revival would need to have two inter-related dimensions: First, a restructured growth process so as to achieve not only a higher GDP growth rate but also an enhanced ability of given GDP growth rates to reduce poverty. Second, a direct attack on poverty which enables the poor to achieve a sustainable increase in productivity and incomes, and thereby contribute to a faster and more equitable economic growth.

In chapter 1, we examined the major elements of the multifaceted crisis of finance, economy and the human condition. We also identified some of the structural and institutional features that need to be addressed in a strategy to overcome the crisis. In chapter 2, we traced the historical inter-play between the deterioration in institutions of governance, economic policy and the structure of economic growth which induced rising unemployment and poverty. In chapter 3, we analyzed the processes through which poverty is perpetuated at the local level to draw attention to the points at which efficacious policy interventions can be made. Based on our analysis of the processes of poverty and the structure of the economy we will in this chapter articulate a broad strategy of pro poor growth. In section-I, we will indicate in summary form some of the major structural features of the economy and the poverty process that need to be addressed in such a strategy. We will also briefly indicate the adverse implications of environmental degradation in Pakistan on growth and poverty. In section-II, we will give an outline of a strategy that can achieve both faster growth and faster poverty alleviation. Many of the proposals contained in this strategy have already been adopted by the government. Nevertheless, this section may be helpful in providing a conceptually integrated perspective on a revival strategy that can be pursued. In section-III, we will present the outline of an approach for a direct attack on poverty through Participatory Development at the local level. In this context, we will discuss the role of women's NGOs and the dangers being faced by them from local power structures. We will also examine the challenge and opportunity of the induction of a large number of women councillors in local government institutions. Finally, we will draw some of the lessons from the experience of decentralization reforms from South Asian countries in the context of the pitfalls of implementation. In section-IV, we will briefly review some of the economic policy measures that have already been initiated by the government.

I. STRUCTURAL FACTORS IN SLOW GROWTH AND RISING POVERTY

Let us begin by identifying the major features of the crisis in the real economy that need to be addressed. These are:

I.1 GOVERNANCE, POVERTY AND UNEMPLOYMENT

Poverty and unemployment have increased rapidly during the 1990s. This is due to the fact that while GDP growth declined during the 1990s, there has also been a decline in employment elasticities, labour productivity and real wages in both agriculture and industry (see chapter 2). At the same time three aspects of governance during the 1990s intensified the economic burden on the poor (see chapter 2):

(i) Due to poor financial management of successive governments in the past both the level of development expenditure and efficiency of its use declined. This contributed to the decay in the already inadequate social infrastructure and also to a slow down in GDP growth and falling employment elasticities.

(ii) The failure to control budget deficits combined with the attempt to finance them through indirect taxation also contributed to increasing poverty, since the adverse impact of such taxation has a relatively greater impact on the poor.

(iii) Widespread corruption in government may have contributed to increasing poverty in three ways: (a) The changing magnitude of corruption over time and at different levels of decision making in government was a major factor in the uncertain policy environment and a constraint to estimating accurate project feasibilities. This could be expected to slow down investment growth and employment. (b) The transfer of some of the domestic savings of the private sector to corrupt politicians and government officials rather than into investment could be a factor in slowing down GDP growth. (c) The financial cost of individual projects increased, thereby simultaneously slowing down GDP growth for given levels of investment and also reducing the employment elasticities with respect to investment (see chapter 2 for a more detailed analysis).

I.1.1 *Policy Implications*: (a) Induce higher investment, reduce incremental capital output ratios, and increase employment elasticities with respect to both output and capital in order to increase employment. (b) Increase the level and efficiency of government development expenditure to increase employment. (c) Increase transparency of governance and reduce corruption to alleviate poverty. (d) Improve the efficiency of institutions responsible for delivering public services to alleviate poverty.

I.2 Asymmetric Markets, Local Power Structures and Poverty

As the analysis in chapter 3, based on NHDR/PIDE survey data shows, that poor peasants face input and output markets where they have to pay a relatively higher price for their inputs and get a relatively lower price for their outputs compared to large farmers. At the same time, due to lack of access over the formal credit markets the poor peasant often has to borrow from the landlord and as a consequence is obliged to work on the landlord's farm at less than market wage rates. The poor peasants could be losing one-third of their income due to asymmetric markets for inputs and outputs (see chapter 3).

In the urban and semi urban areas where the poor households are predominantly involved in micro-enterprises an important factor in low incomes is the low productivity and profitability of their micro-enterprises (see chapter 3).

I.2.1 *Policy Implications*: Better access for the poor over the markets for labour, land, agricultural inputs and outputs, means changing the balance of power in favour of the poor at the local level. This requires facilitating emergence of autonomous organizations of the poor, particularly poor women at the village, Union Council, Tehsil and district levels. It also means enabling the poor to access credit, training and technical support for increased employment, productivity and incomes.

I.3 Institutional Factors in Slow and Unstable Crop Sector Growth[1]

In agriculture, the average annual growth rate of major crops has declined from 3.34 per cent during 1980s to 2.38 per cent in 1990s. At the same time, the frequency of negative growth years in some of the major crops has increased. The slow down in growth and increased instability of output in major crops has resulted in sharply increased rural poverty on the one hand and a slow down in the export growth on the other. Underlying this phenomenon are five major institutional constraints (see chapter 1 for details).

I.4 Some Constraints to the Growth of the Large Scale Manufacturing Sector

The large scale manufacturing sector which historically was growing at 7 to 11 per cent per annum is now growing less than 3 per cent. The factors underlying this dramatic decline include the following:

(a) A fundamental structural constraint to industrial growth as indeed the underlying factor in slow export growth, is the failure to diversify exports. The large scale manufacturing sector, particularly exports are concentrated in the traditional low value added end of textiles. (b) A changed pattern of global demand for industrial products with a shift towards higher value added and knowledge intensive products. Pakistan's industrial structure was not positioned to respond quickly to these changed market conditions. (c) An erosion of the domestic framework within which investment and growth is sustained. This includes: (i) A continued threat to the life and property of citizens due to a continued poor law and order situation. (ii) High electricity tariffs, relatively high interest rates (though these have fallen this year), (iii) Lack of trained professionals especially in the high skill sector, (iv) An inadequate technological base through which industry can respond in a flexible way to changing patterns of demand, (v) An adverse policy environment in the past within which tariff and export incentives were distorted against those entrepreneurs who were seeking to improve quality and productivity for export growth, (vi) Dumping of smuggled, poor quality and extremely low priced imported goods which are often counterfeit copies of branded Pakistani manufactured goods.

I.5 Environmental Degradation, GDP Growth and Poverty[2]

The available studies on the quantitative impact of environmental degradation on GDP indicate the substantial adverse consequences of air and water pollution on public health (and hence on GDP via labour productivity) and the impact of deforestation and soil degradation on productivity in the agriculture sector. For example the study by C. Brandon (World Bank) includes public health impact of air and water pollution, and productivity impact of soil and rangeland degradation, deforestation and reduction in tourism.[3] However, this study does not include the impact of water pollution on fisheries, nor the impact of loss of bio-diversity, loss of cultural heritage, and long-term effects on hazardous wastes due to lack of data. The study by M.W. Addison[4] includes destruction of mangrove forests but not losses of tourism revenue. These studies on the basis of considering six sectors alone estimate income losses from environmental degradation of between 3.5 to 4.2 per cent of GDP.

Both the above mentioned studies suggest that the greatest loss to national income is with respect to the health impact of water pollution, especially diarrhea and other water borne diseases. It appears that implicit national income losses of between US$380 million to US$883 million could be avoided by providing safe drinking water and sanitation. Similarly primary health impacts attributed to urban air pollution are estimated at between US$174 to US$369 million while losses of agricultural output attributable to soil degradation are estimated to be between US$221 to 357 million.[5]

II. RESTRUCTURING GROWTH FOR FASTER POVERTY REDUCTION[6]

Having examined some of the main factors underlying the crisis in the real economy, let us outline a possible economic strategy that could be undertaken, to lay the basis for a sustainable pro poor growth. Such a strategy could be designed to optimize four parameters: (a) Achieve higher GDP growth with a relatively low investment (i.e. have a low incremental capital output ratio). (b) Generate higher employment for given growth rates of GDP (c) Generate higher exports (d) Achieve greater equity and poverty alleviation.

A four pronged revival strategy needs to be undertaken in the light of the structural constraints to growth and poverty alleviation specified in section-I of this chapter.

II.1 Improving the Supply of Irrigation Water

The first prong of the growth strategy should be a national campaign on a war footing to rehabilitate Pakistan's irrigation system which is currently in a state of acute disrepair due to decades of poor maintenance. Such a campaign would involve organizing semi-skilled labour for

The economic growth strategy should aim to optimize four parameters: (a) Achieve higher GDP growth with a relatively low investment (i.e. have a low incremental capital output ratio). (b) Generate higher employment for given growth rates of GDP (c) Generate higher exports (d) Achieve greater equity and poverty alleviation

the desilting of canals, strengthening the banks, organizing villagers for making 'Pucca Khaalas' (concrete lined water courses) and to improve the gradient of water courses and farmlands in order to improve both the delivery and application efficiencies of irrigation. Such a campaign being inherently labour intensive would not only generate employment rapidly but also help to improve water availability and yields per acre at the farm level. If the campaign is professionally designed and managed, the funding for financing wage payments to the newly employed labour force could be sought from multilateral agencies, some of which have poverty alleviation and sustainable agricultural growth as their priority concerns. The district level development institutions in the local government system could coordinate with union councils, village development councils and autonomous farmers associations to implement such a campaign.

II.2 INFRASTRUCTURE DEVELOPMENT

In addition to the campaign for improved maintenance of the irrigation system other labour intensive infrastructure projects should also be undertaken to simultaneously generate employment and stimulate aggregate demand in the economy. Such projects could be the building of farm to market roads, national high ways and ports, upgrading the railway system and enlarging its transport capacity for bulk cargo together with an improved communication system and increased production of cheaper energy through domestically available coal rather than imported furnace oil.[7]

Such infrastructure projects would need to be undertaken through joint venture arrangements between domestic construction outfits such as the Frontier Works Organization and specialized foreign firms. The joint ventures would have to be pro-actively facilitated by the government.

II.3 MILK, MARINE FISHERIES AND HIGH VALUE ADDED AGRICULTURE PRODUCTS

The third prong of the revival strategy is to rapidly develop export led production capacity for milk, fisheries and high value added agricultural products such as fruits, vegetables and flowers. Let us illustrate this initiative by using the example of milk. At the moment Pakistan is producing approximately 177 billion rupees worth of milk annually for domestic consumption. This makes milk the largest agricultural product. By comparison, wheat, Pakistan's largest crop has an annual production value of approximately 111 billion rupees. Unlike wheat however, the output of milk can be accelerated sharply within a couple of years. Currently Pakistan's milch cattle have a yield per animal which is one-fifth of the European average. Demonstrable experience in the field has shown that the milk yields per animal in Pakistan can be doubled within two years through scientific feeding, breeding and marketing. If the institutional framework could be established for training the farmers in scientific feeding and breeding and if the logistics could be set up to collect milk from the farm door by means of refrigerated transport, milk output in Pakistan could be doubled. This would have a dramatic impact not only on the incomes of poor peasants, but also on exports and overall GDP growth.

Pakistan lies at the hub of milk deficit regions such as Central Asia, West Asia and South East Asia. Hence it could be argued that if milk out put in Pakistan could be doubled, exports earnings would increase to such an extent that they would make a major contribution to overcoming the balance of trade deficit. Such an initiative therefore can lead to accelerated exports, higher GDP growth and improved income distribution in Pakistan. A possible institutional framework for such an initiative could be the establishment of dairy development boards at the provincial level linked up with development institutions at the district and union council levels in the local government structure.

Marine Fisheries, also provide a significant potential for improving foreign exchange earnings although not as large as the potential for milk. Here again what is required is improved institutional support and better management rather than huge investments by the Government. In the case of marine fisheries currently there are large losses and failure to achieve significant exports due to the fact that the storage conditions of fish during transportation are both unscientific and unhygienic by international quality standards. Currently alternate layers of fish and hard, sharp edged ice are placed in containers on the boats. Under the weight of upper layers of fish and the sharp edged ice, fish at the lower layers are crushed, and the resultant bleeding causes putrefaction. To avoid this, it is necessary to provide shelves for layered storage of fish in boats, topped by dry ice, with fiberglass covers. Through such measures it would be possible to bring back the fish at the European Union standards of minus 7°C and thereby make it exportable. An export potential of 300 million dollars exists over the next three years if such improved management of the marine fisheries industry could be achieved.

The third element in increasing high value added production and export in the agricultural sector would be to facilitate the production of fruits, vegetables and flowers for exports. This would require institutional support for improved quality of output, improved grading, packaging, and refrigerated transport right up to the cargo terminals for air freight to the export market.

II.4 Rapid Growth of Small Scale Enterprises (SSEs)

The fourth prong of the strategy would be to provide the institutional support necessary for the rapid growth of small scale enterprises. These SSEs include high value added units in light engineering automotive parts, moulds, dyes, machine tools and electronics and computer software.

Training of a large number of software experts with requisite support in credit and marketing could quickly induce a significant increase in software exports from Pakistan. Pakistan could build a pool of software experts for a large increase in export earnings. This would of course require a proactive government to establish joint ventures between large software companies such as Microsoft and Pakistan's private sector institutions such as LUMS and INFORMATICS. The Ministry of Science and Technology is already moving rapidly ahead in facilitating the growth of information technology in Pakistan. In this sub-section however we will focus on small scale manufacturing enterprises.

Small scale industries have a low gestation period, are labour intensive, and can generate a larger output per unit of investment compared to the large scale manufacturing sector. Therefore the rapid growth of small scale enterprises would not only accelerate economic growth in the medium term at relatively low levels of investment, but would also increase employment and exports for given levels of GDP growth. The key strategic issue in accelerating the growth of SSEs is to enable them to shift to the high value added, high growth end of the product market.

Field visits to a large number of small scale enterprises in the Punjab and Frontier province have revealed that they have considerable potential for growth and high value added production such as components for engineering goods or components of high quality farm implements for the large scale manufacturing sector.[8] Yet they are in many cases producing low value added items like steel shutters or car exhaust pipes. This results in low profitability, low savings and slow growth.

II.4.1 *Constraints to the Rapid Growth of SSEs*: Small scale enterprises in small towns of Pakistan face the following major constraints:

(i) Inability of small units to get vending contracts for the manufacture of components from the LSM sector.
(ii) Due to lack of expertise in production management, the frequent inability to achieve quality control, and to meet tight delivery schedules.
(iii) Lack of specific skills like advanced mill work, metal fabrication, precision welding, all of which are needed for producing quality products with low tolerances and precise dimensional control. In other cases accounting and management skills may be inadequate.
(iv) Difficulty faced by small units in getting good quality raw materials, which often can only be ordered in bulk (for which the small entrepreneurs do not have the working capital), and from distant large cities.
(v) Lack of specialized equipment.
(vi) Absence of fabrication facilities such as forging, heat treatment and surface treatment which are required for manufacture of high value added

products, but are too expensive for any one small unit to set up.

(vii) Lack of capital for investment and absence of credit facilities.

II.4.2 *Overcoming the Constraints to the Growth of SSEs*: Overcoming the aforementioned constraints would involve providing institutional support in terms of credit, quality control management, skill training and marketing. This could be done by facilitating the establishment of industrial support centers (ISCs) located in the specified growth nodes in selected towns where the entrepreneurial and technical potential as well as markets already exist. (For details of the growth nodes see Annexure I). Such support institutions (ISCs) while being facilitated by the government and autonomous organizations such as SMEDA can and should be in the private sector and market driven.

The concept of the Industrial Support Centres is based on the fact that small scale industrialists in Pakistan have already demonstrated a high degree of entrepreneurship, innovation and efficient utilization of capital. The ISCs would provide an opportunity for rapid growth to SSEs through local participation in extension services, prototype development, and diffusion of improved technologies, equipment and management procedures. The ISC would constitute a decentralized system which ensures continuous easy access to a comprehensive package of support services such as credit, skill training, managerial advice and technical assistance. The ISCs could also be linked up with national research centres, and donor agencies for drawing upon technical expertise and financial resources of these agencies in the service of SSI.

The Industrial Support Centres could have the following functional dimensions:

(i) Marketing

Provision of orders from the large scale manufacturing sector for components, and from farmers for farm implements. These orders would then be subcontracted to the cluster of SSI units that the ISC is supposed to serve. The individual order would be sub-contracted to the SSI on the basis of the skills and potential strengths of the unit concerned.

(ii) Monitoring and Quality Control

Having given the sub-contract, the ISC would then monitor the units closely and help pinpoint and overcome unit specific bottlenecks to the timely delivery and quality control of the manufactured products. These bottlenecks may be specialized skills, equipment, good quality raw material or credit.

(iii) Skill Training and Product Development

Skill training for technicians could be provided by the new good quality vocational training institutes (VTIs) that have emerged since the late 1990s. in the Punjab under the auspices of the Vocational Training Council and similar VTIs could be established in other provinces. The ISC would provide specialized supplementary skill training on its premises to workers in the satellite SSI units when required. At the same time, it would provide advice on jigs, fixtures, special tools and product development where required.

(iv) Forging and Heat Treatment Facilities

The ISC's would establish at their premises plants for forging, heat treatment and surface treatment. The SSI units could come to the ISC to get such fabrication done on the products they are manufacturing on sub-contract, and pay a mutually agreed price for this job to the ISC.

(v) Credit

The ISC would provide credit to the SSI's for purchase of new equipment and raw materials. In cases where raw materials are available in bulk supply, the ISC could buy it from the source, stock it on its premises and sell at a reasonable price to units as and when they need the raw materials.

III. DIRECT ATTACK ON POVERTY

Establishing the institutional basis for enabling the poor to increase their incomes, savings and investment, would not only constitute a direct attack on poverty but would also contribute to a faster and more equitable economic growth process. In this section we will examine the issue of empowerment of the poor with special reference to women. In this context we will explore the institutional imperatives of making the newly emerging local government structures more effective in achieving the empowerment of poor women.

III.1 AUTONOMOUS ORGANIZATIONS OF THE POOR, WOMEN AND EMPOWERMENT

A vital dimension of the economic strategy would be a national campaign to empower the poor at the levels of Village/Mohalla, Union Council, Tehsil and District. The idea is to facilitate the growth of community organizations of the poor at the village/mohallah level. In view of the fact that poor women in Pakistan suffer from a double burden that of being poor and being women, it is essential to enable poor women to form their own autonomous community organizations to be able to break out of both the poverty nexus and gender based discrimination. Through these COs the poor can identify income generating projects, initially at the household level, acquire skill training from a variety of sources such as government line departments, autonomous institutions, private sector firms, NGOs and donors; and access credit for micro-enterprise projects through apex organizations such as the PPAF, Khushali Bank, Small Business Finance Corporation (SBFC) and commercial banks. Special organizational arrangements would need to be made in these apex institutions to take credit to poor women and women's COs, since poor women have even lesser access over institutional credit compared to poor men.

It is important that such village level community based organizations (CBOs) be autonomous and be permitted to form cluster apex organizations with other CBOs (As shown in chapter 4, large cross district and centralized, government created NGOs are slow, have high overheads and are imprecise in their targeting of the poor). Autonomous CBOs by means of social mobilisation, increased productivity through skill training, increased income, savings and investment would begin a process of localised capital accumulation. Such a process (which we can call Participatory Development) would be integrally linked with the emergence of a new consciousness of empowerment. The poor can begin to take autonomous initiatives to improve their material conditions of life. They would thus break out of the poverty nexus and shift from being victims to active subjects of social and economic change. Such a process of village level increases in productivity, incomes and savings would not only constitute a direct attack on the poverty problem but would also contribute to a faster and more equitable macro economic growth. (For a more detailed discussion of these issues see chapter 4).

Such autonomous organizations of the poor could become not only a framework for grassroots economic growth, but would also constitute countervailing power to that of the power structures of local elites. At the same time, these autonomous organizations of the poor would enable the individual poor household to get better access over input and output markets. (In chapter 3 we have seen how local power structures and asymmetric markets systematically deprive the isolated individual households of the poor of their actual and potential income).

Facilitating the emergence of autonomous organizations of the poor particularly organizations of poor women, could enable the newly established local government institutions to function in a more equitable and effective manner. The equity would be with respect to class as well as gender. This would require establishing institutionalized links between autonomous organizations of the poor and local government bodies at the Village, Union Council, Tehsil and District levels. These institutional links between organizations of the poor and elected local bodies would enable more participatory and equitable processes of project identification, design and implementation for local level development.

Establishing the institutional basis for enabling the poor to increase their incomes, savings and investment, would not only constitute a direct attack on poverty but would also contribute to a faster and more equitable economic growth process

III.2 Government, Society and the Threat to Women's Community Organizations

Governments in Pakistan in practice have failed to provide the minimum necessary protection and security to women's NGOs even though they are included as 'policy implementers' in their policy documents on development

As indicated in the preceding sub-section an essential feature of the proposed direct attack on poverty is to facilitate and enable the formation of women's community organizations. Yet, governments in Pakistan in practice have failed to provide the minimum necessary protection and security to women's NGOs even though they are included as 'policy implementers' in their policy documents on development.[9] The antagonism of local vested interests against women's NGOs has been particularly intense in the NWFP. These vested interests include extremist religious groups and forest contractors. For example women's NGOs engaged in literacy and education programmes and others providing credit and health facilities to women in Dir, Malakand, Swabi, Karak, Takhtbai and Batagram areas have been threatened, stoned and physically attacked. Scattered incidents of attacks against women's NGOs in the NWFP began initially with the opposition to the enfranchisement of women in the Federally Administered Tribal Areas (FATA) in 1997. The momentum of persecution by local power interests gradually built up and reached a climax on 8 October 2001. On this date the offices, and health and education facilities of a women led CBO in Takhtbai (a small town in NWFP), were looted, set on fire and raised to the ground. Later eight women's organizations in Takhtbai Tehsil, two in Bajaur, and one in Batagram were attacked and looted.[10] Earlier in July 2001 the office of a leading women's organization in Karak was bombed. The objection from religious extremists in the area was against the running of home schools for girls and providing health and education facilities for women. The beneficiary households in the area of course did not see the provision of these services to be in violation of local cultural values. However, the religious extremists had the backing of local political leaders. The local administration rather than restrain these elements advised the NGOs. to shift from the area.[11]

III.2.1 *Policy Challenge*: Clearly an important element in the enabling environment for poverty alleviation of women in particular, and economic growth in general, is the re-establishment of the writ of the State.

III.3 Local Government, Poverty Alleviation and Women

The recent formation of local government structures involving a decentralization of administrative responsibilities with respect to the government's development effort has opened up new possibilities of empowering the poor and giving greater gender balance to both governance and poverty alleviation. However, a number of measures would need to be taken to transform decentralization of administration into a process of devolution of power. This issue will be discussed in the ensuing sub-section. In this sub-section we will examine the prospects and pitfalls involved in the actual functioning of local government institutions with respect to the participation of women.

There is potential in the new local government structures to bring the voice of poor women into the process of local level governance and development. As many as 40,000 seats (33 per cent of the total) have been provided for women in various tiers of local government. Contrary to received wisdom there was an unprecedented mobilization of women with an unexpectedly large number of poor women from amongst the peasantry, workers and middle income groups being elected to local government structures.

Given the experience of the relatively small number of women who entered the national legislature, women have not only participated actively in various debates but the quality of their interventions in the national legislature has in some instances been higher than that of their male colleagues. Therefore, the emergence of a much larger number of elected women in local government institutions combined with the ensured representation of women from workers and peasants, provides promise of better prospects for women in governance in the future. However, recent reports of the bias against women councillors in the actual functioning of local bodies gives cause for concern.

III.3.1 *Problems of Gender Bias in Local Governance*: At this stage there are three problems in this regard: (i) The role and authority of the various tiers of local government have neither been clearly defined so far, nor are the women councillors aware of their domain of authority. According to field reports the official orientation session for the elected women has caused more confusion than clarity, even though women members of local bodies are eager to start work.[12] Clearly the government needs to specify the authority and functioning procedures of various tiers of local government and also undertake a major programme of training both elected members and administrative officials of local government bodies, with respect to design and implementation, finance and accounting for local level development projects. (ii) There is confusion about the relationship and functional coordination between the new structure of local government and the existing administrative system. As a result Nazims have not been given information in many districts about the schemes already approved by the previous administration (in health, public works and education) nor adequate budgets provided for their implementation. Planning for new projects at the local level has not even begun nor is there the provision of trained personnel and procedures for doing so. Despite these problems such is the enthusiasm of local councillors that according to field reports, a number of them have taken independent initiatives on a voluntary and self-help basis, for small local level projects such as schools, health facilities and road repair.[13] (iii) In the functioning of local government institutions at the Union Council, Tehsil and District levels, women councillors in many cases are not being treated in a collegial fashion by the male councillors. According to some of the female councillors from Sindh and Punjab in the few meetings that have been held so far, male councillors have been indifferent towards their female counterparts in the process of local level governance. For example women are relegated to the back seats. They are neither given an opportunity to speak during the discussions, nor is the agenda of the meeting shared with them before hand.

III.3.2 *Measures for More Effective Functioning of Women Councillors*: To rectify the above-mentioned problems, three measures may be helpful: (a) Familiarize and train councillors about the procedures and rights in the process of local government decision making. (b) Establish women Ombudsmen at the district level to which women councillors working at various tiers can take their complaints with respect to discriminatory behaviour by male councillors. (c) Establish institutional links between autonomous COs of poor women at the local level and women councillors. This could enable the latter to design and implement development projects on the basis of the participation of women in the community.

III.3.3 *Capacity Building Programme for Women in Local Government*: In the recent local government elections it appears that 79 per cent of the women councillors had been elected for the first time and 53 per cent were illiterate.[14] This reinforces our argument in the preceding sub-section that training and capacity building would be important to make the increased presence of women in local government more effective. In this regard a new initiative has been taken recently in bringing together Government, NGOs, private training institutions and donors to undertake such capacity building. The project is called 'Women's Political Participation Project' and is being conducted under the auspices of the Ministry of Women and Development (MOWD). It is being funded by the UNDP through its Gender Equality Umbrella Project (GEUP) and the Norwegian Agency for Development (NORAD). Its most important specific objectives are: (i) To enable the women councillors (30 per cent) in district, tehsil and union council to become a critical mass that would substantially change the gender balance in the conduct of governance at the local level. This is to be achieved by enhancing their participation in the advocacy and implementation of an integrated gender sensitive poverty alleviation strategy at the local level. (ii) To build and develop the 'mentoring and nurturing' approach which is based on the principle of 'women learning from women'. Mentoring means enabling the women councillors not only to perform the responsibilities of their existing job more effectively but also to advance their political career through learning new skills and sharing experiences. (iii) To strengthen the

The role and authority of the various tiers of local government have neither been clearly defined so far, nor are the women councillors aware of their domain of authority

links between women councillors and their constituencies through civic participation and public accountability.

It is anticipated that this project will lead to the establishment of a Women's Political School which is run by women and for women and where women can support each other in learning and action to achieve higher levels of decision making responsibilities. Such a school would help to foster solidarity, cooperation and the building of a policy consensus amongst women from different local councils.

III.4 Gender Budgeting for Women's Development[15]

In the preceding sub-section we have discussed the institutional changes required to enable a systematic involvement of autonomous organizations of poor women as well as elected women's councillors in local government. In this sub-section we will indicate the concept of gender budgeting and how this can provide support at the national, provincial and local government levels to the process of achieving greater gender equality.

The concept of gender budgeting involves not an 'add on' budget for women, but a gender analysis of the entire government budget (whether at the national, provincial or local levels) of the differential gender impact of the allocation of government's budgetary resources. In pursuing the strategic aim of gender equality in poverty, growth and governance, cross sectoral programmes as well as sector specific projects would be identified to promote gender equity and women's development. Gender budgeting would constitute the financial basis of implementing such programmes and projects. For example, gender specific projects would include the establishment of girls schools, women's vocational centers and institutions for provision of micro credit and technical support for poverty alleviation projects initiated by women at the village or mohallah level. Similarly projects for providing high quality pre-natal and post natal care for women to reduce morbidity rates of mothers, infant mortality rates and fertility rates. Gender specific programmes for greater gender equality would include programmes for gender sensitization of government's officials at the national, provincial and local levels; programmes for training women in NGOs, clusters of NGOs and apex women organizations in governance and management skills, and the design, implementation and monitoring of development projects for women. Apart from financing women specific projects and programmes, gender budgeting could also include the financing of efforts to achieve gender equity within various government departments. This would include financing efforts at equal representation within management and decision making positions of government and equitable pay and conditions of service. An equally important aspect of gender budgeting would be to examine the taxation system to determine the differential impact of direct and indirect taxes on women. Just as taxes impact on the disposable income between the rich and the poor, in the same way such taxes also affect the distribution of disposable income, employment opportunities, savings and investment of women and men respectively within various income groups.

The efficacy of gender budgeting would also depend on its impact evaluation with respect to the strategic aim of gender equality. Such an evaluation would involve identifying: (i) The impact of gender specific projects, programmes, budgetary allocations for affirmative action amongst government's officials and also changes in the tax regime. (ii) Outputs of various projects, programmes and government policies would be examined to see whether they are adequately distributed between women and men to achieve gender equality. (iii) Examine the activities associated with the design and implementation of projects, programmes and policies to assess whether they are appropriate and adequate for achieving gender equality.

Essential to the initiative of gender budgeting would be the establishment of a gender specific data base of GDP estimates, labour force statistics, household incomes and expenditures surveys, as well as impact assessment surveys of the work of NGOs and autonomous and semi-autonomous organizations. There is no data base available to determine the gender distribution of income and expenditure within different income groups of the population. Equally important there is no data base available for the more sensitive issue of intra household distribution of income between various income groups of the population. Such data would be important to generate on a systematic basis at the district, provincial and national levels in order to undertake gender budgeting.

III.5 DEVOLUTION VERSUS DECENTRALIZATION: THE LESSONS FROM SOUTH ASIA

Almost every country in South Asia has undertaken decentralization reforms with the stated purpose of empowering the poor and thereby achieving good governance. Yet there are a number of pitfalls in the implementation of these reforms. As Pakistan embarks on its own programme of devolution, it may be useful to point out that devolution cannot simply be seen in terms of a decentralization of administrative functions within existing government structures. Rather decentralization has to create the space within which an institutionalized relationship can begin between autonomous organizations of the poor and various tiers of local government.

A number of pitfalls can emerge in the implementation of devolution reforms. Unless they are addressed at an early stage these reforms may not achieve the desired objectives. The following four lessons may be drawn on the basis of case studies of decentralization reforms in South Asian countries:[16]

(i) Formal decentralization of administrative power in itself does not necessarily help the poor as S.K. Upadhyay[17] points out in the context of the Nepal case study. Empowerment of the poor, he argues, requires that formal decentralization be accompanied by a rigorous process of social mobilization. This involves consciousness raising, conscientisation and building organizations of the poor. It is only such a process that will enable the poor to acquire countervailing power. Without this dimension of countervailing power, decentralization will merely result in the appropriation by elites of the 'fruits of decentralization for their own narrow benefit'. In this context the Bangladesh case study by Dr Shaikh Maqsood Ali[18] makes an important distinction between decentralization of administrative power in favour of its regional/local offices as opposed to decentralization in favour of the local people. Apart from this it could be argued that in areas where asymmetric structures of power prevail (for example, coalitions of rich peasants/landlords, local influentials such as traders, revenue and police officials) mere decentralization of administrative power could intensify the oppression of the poor.

(ii) The second lesson emerging from the case studies is that if decentralization is to enable empowerment of the poor, it must be holistic, i.e., incorporate political power, enhanced confidence, emergence of social consciousness and administrative and fiscal devolution. At the same time it must reach down to the grass roots level through various intermediate levels, with institutionalized participation of the poor in governance at every level. Upadhyay refers to this holism and multi layered devolution in the Nepal case study.

(iii) The political dimension of decentralization must be inclusive and capable of absorbing what Upadhyay calls 'diverse ethnic and other identity groups as equal partners occupying spaces in the polity'. He argues that the centralized polity excludes such identities which may be a factor in ethnic strife and social polarization. While the poor once organized are able to generate new resources at the local level yet, as participatory development is scaled up, internally generated resources may be insufficient. Therefore externally generated resources become necessary but these have to be carefully applied through a sensitive support system that strengthens rather than weakens the autonomy of

Formal decentralization of administrative power in itself does not necessarily help the poor

the organizations of the poor. Such a support system could be provided by a combination of apex NGOs, state institutions, banks and local governments. Upadhyay emphasizes the importance of such support organizations being sensitized by a pro poor perspective.

(iv) In the case of urban areas it appears that communities who have developed their own funds and managed development themselves are able to establish a more equitable relationship with local government institutions.[19] It can be argued that to enable urban communities to manage their own development it is necessary to provide technical advice and managerial guidance. At the same time an institutionalized process of consultation and coordination may be necessary between urban community organizations and local government institutions to prevent them from working at cross purposes.

IV. THE GOVERNMENT'S POLICY MEASURES

The government of President Musharraf had attempted to deal with the multifaceted crisis (analyzed in chapters 1 and 2) by formulating the most comprehensive set of reforms in Pakistan's history. The strategic objective was to establish the institutional basis for good governance and a policy framework for achieving both economic revival and poverty reduction. The reform programme (which the newly elected government is expected to pursue), consists of two main dimensions: (1) Improved governance. The elements in this context include financial management reforms, tax reforms, civil services reforms and devolution. (2) Economic Revival and Poverty Reduction.

In this section on the basis of information contained in the government's Interim Poverty Reduction Strategy Paper (I-PRSP) we will describe some of the main features of each type of reform. We will also briefly indicate what has been done and what remains to be done.

IV.1 INSTITUTIONAL REFORMS FOR BETTER GOVERNANCE

IV.1.1 *Financial Management Reforms*: An important contributory though not necessarily causative factor in corruption and inefficient use of the government's financial resources have been obsolete and malfunctioning systems of financial management. The Financial Management Reforms aim to modernize financial procedures and introduce management information systems to improve budget decision making, achieve greater transparency and avoid misuse of funds.

The specific policy actions taken by the government in this regard include: (i) Establishment of a Fiscal Monitoring Committee (FMC) to provide quarterly data on consolidated expenditure verified by the Accountant General. (ii) Expenditure controls at the federal level have been enhanced through a new system of budgeting. (iii) Provincial Fiscal Reconciliation Committees have also been established to improve the quality and timely availability of expenditure data at the provincial level. (iv) Public Accounts Committees have been established at the federal and provincial levels, which it is thought will promote transparency and rigour in public expenditure management. (v) The Public Accounts Committees and the Pakistan Public Procurement Authority have also been established to achieve transparency and greater efficiency in public expenditure. (vi) The Medium Term Budget Framework (MTBF), which could significantly improve expenditure control and fiscal management has been prepared but is yet to be put in place.

•*What is to be done*: (i) It may be pertinent to mention here that while improvement in management systems and procedures are necessary, they are not sufficient to improve efficiency in the use of the government's financial resources. What is also important is the professional skill, team work and commitment of the personnel who implement such procedures and improve them in the light of experience. (ii) At the same time, the envisaged Financial Management Act would need to be promulgated if the Financial Management Reforms are to be sustainable. (iii) The fiscal responsibility law which the government is considering needs to be enacted since it could play a crucial role in constraining government borrowing and thereby help achieve fiscal stability. (iv) The concept of gender budgeting needs to be introduced into the process of budget allocations to identify and finance projects, which specifically aim to overcome the gender bias in development.

IV.1.2 *Tax Reform*: Pakistan has a narrow tax base, a grossly inadequate tax to GDP ratio of 13 per cent, and a low elasticity of tax revenue with respect to the GDP growth rate. Consequently even when GDP growth rates were over 5 per cent, fiscal pressures had forced governments in the past into increasing loan dependence (see chapter 1). The problem intensified during the 1990s when GDP growth rates declined and current expenditures remained high (see chapter 2). If the government is to increase its development expenditures, provide basic services to the people and finance necessary current expenditures without increasing indebtedness, then clearly increasing the tax GDP ratio and elasticity of tax revenue is essential. This would require: (i) Broadening the tax base (ii) Simplifying the tax structure so as to have a small number of buoyant taxes, and eliminating distortions that created unintended disincentives to investment and exports (iii) Increasing the share of direct taxes in total tax revenues so as to reduce the adverse impact of taxation on the poor. (iv) Drastic improvement in the tax administration to reduce leakage and tax evasion.

The government has addressed these imperatives in its tax reforms which envisage the following: (i) Reduction in the multiplicity of taxes, (the wealth tax has already been eliminated). (ii) To encourage domestic manufacturing industries and reduce the bias against exports the government has reduced the maximum rate of duty on imported inputs from 35 per cent to 30 per cent and has reduced the number of duty slabs from 5 to 4. (iii) Broadening the scope of the generalized sales tax and placing a tax on agriculture incomes just as there is in other sectors of the economy. (iv) Making the process of tax collection simpler and more transparent. The enabling legislation for the achievement of this objective is the new Income Tax Ordinance (ITO) 2001 which allows for 'universal self assessment, uniform tax rates…, elimination of exemptions and detailed audit of companies through a parametric process'.[20] However these planned measures are yet to be undertaken. Similarly the proposals of the Task Force on Reforms in Tax Administration, which claim to 'virtually eliminate contact between tax payer and collector…and to create a fair and accountable tax system'[21] remain to be implemented. The government also intends to re-organize the Central Board of Revenue (CBR) to improve tax collection by making it more professional, transparent and accountable.

The government's policy measures with respect to improving the tax collection system is beginning to bear at least modest fruit. For example tax collection improved by over 10 per cent during 1999-2000; the number of income tax payers increased by 7.4 per cent and sales tax payers by 40 per cent. Perhaps a potentially far-reaching achievement is success in completing the tax survey and registration campaign, which has provided data profiles of 600,000 taxpayers. This data now needs to be collated, analyzed and translated into administrative action to widen the tax base and substantially increase tax revenues.

IV.I.3 *Civil Services Reforms*: Pakistan's civil service which in its earlier form was the 'steel frame' of the British Raj has over the last three decades undergone a process of institutional decay. Repeated political intrusions, since the Z.A. Bhutto regime into both decision making procedures and individual careers, have served to weaken the internal integrity of its decision making process, its esprit de corps, and individual motivation.[22] At the same time, the centralized structure of the civil service, skill composition, over staffing and low salaries may be incongruent with its contemporary tasks of delivering public services and managing public policy of a country in crisis.

The government aims to bring to the civil service, enhanced professionalism, reduced corruption and improved motivation and performance. In the pursuit of these objectives the government has taken the following policy measures:[23] (i) The Federal Public Service Commission (FPSC) Ordinance has been amended to give greater independence to the FPSC and enlarge its

In order to improve the delivery efficiency of public services (in the context of civil service reforms), what is required is to have a smaller number of highly professional and highly paid staff members working with precisely specified and time bound tasks, and systematic performance monitoring and evaluation

responsibilities for recruiting professionals. It is thought that this will enable merit based appointments and hiring of senior professional staff. (ii) Legal provisions have been put into place to enable corrupt civil servants to be dismissed and inefficient civil servants to be retired. (iii) Additionally the National Accountability Bureau (NAB) has been given powers to investigate and prosecute corrupt civil servants in addition to other officials and politicians engaging in corruption and misuse of power. (iv) To improve accountability and the incentives to perform, the decision making powers on career management and promotions upto grade 19 have been delegated to line managers. (v) The civil service educational institutions (Civil Services Academy, National Institute of Public Administration, and the Pakistan Administrative Staff College) are being restructured to enhance their capacity for skill training. (vi) In pursuance of the civil service reforms objective to reduce over staffing, the Pakistan Railways have cut down 30,000 positions.

•*What is to be done*: In order to improve the delivery efficiency of public services (in the context of civil service reforms), what is required is to have a smaller number of highly professional and highly paid staff members working with precisely specified and time bound tasks, and systematic performance monitoring and evaluation. In this regard the recommendations of the Committee on Right Sizing and Restructuring need to be implemented quickly.

IV.1.4 *Devolution of Power*: The National Reconstruction Board has announced a devolution plan under which powers and responsibilities for a variety of administrative functions, including those related to social services, will be devolved from the federal and provincial levels to elected district level authorities and local councils. At a formal level the devolution programme was put into place in August 2001. The government hopes that it will enable greater participation of the people at the grassroots level in development and also improve the delivery efficiency of social services such as health, education, family planning, sanitation and clean drinking water. The government plans to introduce grassroots organizations such as Village Councils and Citizens Community Boards to involve local communities in development. The government expects that these institutions would enable the citizens at the local level to monitor the functioning and effectiveness of the delivery of basic services.

•*What is to be done*: The devolution of power plan by the government and the recent elections of local government institutions in which 33 per cent of the councillors are women, opens up new possibilities of people centered development, and a more participatory democracy. However, as discussed in section III.2, III.3 and III.4 of this chapter the implementation of the programme is faced with a number of problems and pitfalls. Crucial to achieving the objectives of the devolution programme are the following imperatives: (i) Enabling the emergence of autonomous community organizations of the poor particularly of poor women at the local level. (ii) The provisions of the devolution programme should be modified to enable an institutionalized relationship between these autonomous organizations of the poor and each tier of the local government structure. (iii) The relationship and functional coordination between the new structure of local government and the existing administrative systems need to be clearly specified and relevant personnel informed. (iv) A large-scale gender sensitization programme for local government councillors needs to be undertaken to familiarize them with the procedures of involving women councillors into decision making, and to inform local government representatives at each tier about the domain of their authority. (v) Local government representatives and officials need to be trained to systematically interface with and involve local communities in the process of design and implementation of development projects. (vi) A large-scale programme of training, needs to be undertaken to equip local government officials and elected representatives at various tiers, in a variety of skills required in the practice of development: These include feasibility preparation; design and management of development projects; financial management; and accounting skills.

IV.2 ECONOMIC REVIVAL AND POVERTY REDUCTION

IV.2.1 *Addressing the Water Crisis*: As discussed in chapter 1, section II.2 shortage of water at the farm level is one of the most important constraints to a higher and more stable agricultural growth. We also pointed out that slow and unstable agriculture growth was a major factor in increasing rural poverty since the increased frequency of bad harvests has a relatively greater adverse effect on the poor. Therefore increasing the storage capacity in the irrigation system and at the same time improving its delivery and application efficiencies is an urgent policy imperative. The government has indeed addressed this issue and has developed a major new water sector plan with a budget of Rs.86.1 billion, for dealing with the water crisis. It has the following elements: (i) Creation of an additional storage capacity of 4.5 million acre feet (MAF). This will be done through a number of new medium sized dams such as Gomalzam and Mirani dams and new irrigation schemes such as Rainee, Thar and Katchi canals. (ii) Improvement of the delivery efficiency of irrigation by lining and renovating 90,000 water courses which are expected to save about 8 MAF. (iii) To deal with the issue of water logging and salinity under the water sector plan, it is envisaged that in the existing and new Salinity Control and Reclamation Projects (SCARPs), an additional area of 2.7 million hectares will be reclaimed for agricultural production. (iv) The problem of salt deposits on the top soil is being addressed through a master plan that is being prepared to identify various spines for disposal of drainage effluent. Additionally the rehabilitation of the Left Bank Outfall Drain and the construction of a new Right Bank Outfall Drain are important initiatives planned for completion by the year 2004.

IV.2.2 *Infrastructure Development:* The government has undertaken a number of development initiatives in some of the main sub-sectors of infrastructure in order to improve the environment for private sector investment and also to stimulate aggregate demand. The major features of some of these initiatives are briefly discussed in this section based on information provided in the I-PRSP of the government.

(i) Communications

The Pakistan Railways which had been generating large deficits and was also undergoing a deterioration in its service, is now being re-organized. A number of measures have been taken (including reduction in staff strength by 30,000 workers, reducing pilferage of gas and electricity and rationalizing operation) which are expected to provide rupees one billion financial benefit to the Railways. Additionally an allocation of Rs.6.3 billion has been made in the development plan 2001-02 for purchasing new locomotives, increasing rolling stocks and track rehabilitation.

To improve road transport, some of remote areas are being linked with the National Highway Network for improving rural access to markets. Additionally some of the major projects being undertaken include the Kohat Tunnel Project, Jacobabad-Sibi-Quetta Highway, Islamabad-Muzaffarabad Highway, D.I. Khan-Qilla Saifullah-Quetta Highway, Bund Road Lahore, Multan-D.G. Khan-Qilla Saifullah Road, upgrading into a dual highway the Karachi-Thatta-Hyderabad Road and the Mansehra-Naran-Jhalkat road.

(ii) Energy Sector

A comprehensive restructuring plan for WAPDA and KESC is underway which is expected to reduce systems losses. In this regard work is in progress to transform WAPDA's distribution, transmission and generation companies into financially viable entities. In the case of oil and gas there is a policy shift away from expensive thermal and furnace oil towards cheaper hydel gas and coal. After commissioning of PARCO refinery, the country is now self sufficient in refining petrol and LPG. As the Chashma Power Project comes on line it will add another 300 megawatt of electricity to the country's power supply.

(iii) Telecommunications and Information Technology

IT usage in Pakistan is low because the country has one of the lowest tele densities in the world (2.5 per cent). However, while one year ago only twenty-nine cities had access to the Internet facility now 400 cities, towns and villages have internet access. Another 300 are expected to be provided with the facility by next year. There has been a 110 per cent increase in Internet usage during the last six months alone.

In order to rapidly increase the number of IT Professionals eighteen projects have been launched for training IT professionals from blue collar IT workers to professional degree holders. The COMSATS, institute of information technology is now ready to award masters and bachelors degrees in computer sciences.

IV.2.3 *Stimulating the Growth of Small and Medium Enterprises*: The government has re-organized the Small and Medium Enterprise Development Authority (SMEDA) and provided increased resources to it in the hope that it will lead the process of stimulating the development of the SME Sector. The kind of support for the SME sector by SMEDA includes facilitating documentation with financial institutions, free technical managerial and marketing advice, information on sector briefs, pre-feasibility reports, and access to trade information with respect to export demand for Pakistani products. Apart from this a number of regulatory changes proposed by SMEDA are being undertaken to allow greater freedom of enterprise to the SME sector.

•*Comment*: These measures are likely to improve the regulatory environment and access over information for primarily medium sized enterprises. However they are designed neither to give SMEDA the necessary outreach to actual clusters of existing small-scale enterprises, nor to establish the institutional basis of identifying and overcoming unit specific bottlenecks to their efficiency and growth (see the discussion in section II.4 of this chapter).

The Small Business Finance Corporation (SBFC), is being re-vitalized and given the mandate to provide financial support to the SME sector and the financial limit of individual loans is being increased from Rs.1.5 million to Rs.30 million (This measure however is likely to benefit medium as opposed to small enterprises). Additionally the SBFC and the Regional Development Finance Corporation (RDFC) are being merged to form a bank catering to the needs of the SME sector.

IV.2.4 *The Government's Direct Poverty Reduction Policy—An Assessment*: There are four basic weaknesses of the government's poverty reduction strategy: (a) It makes no attempt at changing the structure of power at the local level in favour of the poor. It is this power structure which (as we have analyzed in chapter 3) lies at the heart of the problem of poverty: It systematically deprives the poor of at least one-third of their income through distortions in the markets for inputs, outputs and services. (b) The funds allocated for poverty reduction are aimed at being spent within a top down process through local governments. Consequently it is likely that funds will be both leaked and also mis-targeted. (c) There is no systematic attempt in the government's strategy for facilitating the building of organizations of the poor that can enable them to participate in identifying, designing and implementing the projects for poverty reduction. At the same time there is no institutional linkage between autonomous organizations of the poor that do exist, and local governments. (d) The scale of funds as well as micro-credit directed at the poor is insignificant compared to the large scale of the problem, as we shall indicate in this section. According to the I-PRSP one of the core principles of the Government's Poverty Reduction Strategy is to improve access of the poor to 'productive assets, mainly housing, land and credit'.[24] We shall discuss the housing for the poor programme at the end of this section. Let us start by examining the nature and scale of the government's planned programme of providing land and credit as a means of directly attacking the poverty problem.

(i) Land for Poor Farmers

The government quite rightly thinks that access to cultivable land would have a positive effect on poor households. However the instrument through which land is to be provided to poor households is rather limited in terms of the scale of its impact. The objective is to distribute three million acres of land available with the government to poor rural households. This is to be followed up with the provision of a range of services such as infrastructure and micro-credit for purchase of inputs. Of course if this objective could be achieved it would have a significant positive impact on the poor. The question is what is the scale of the impact relative to the scale of the poverty problem in Pakistan. The government has not made it clear what proportion of the three million acres it plans to give to the poor, are cultivable and what proportion is irrigated. Let us suppose that all three million acres are both cultivable and irrigated. If each poor recipient gets on average five acres of this irrigated land, then together with the financial and technical support for its utilization, it can be supposed that the entire household of the recipient could pull out of poverty. Even with these optimistic assumptions the government's strategy of 'land for the poor' will alleviate poverty for 0.6 million rural households which is only 9.6 per cent of the 6.2 million rural households that are currently below the poverty line. Thus, while the government's strategy of land for the poor is a laudable one, it can at best have only a modest impact in terms of the scale of the problem of rural poverty.

(ii) The Government's Micro-credit Initiatives

Let us consider now the government's plan to provide the poor access over micro-credit. The I-PRSP Document proposes that 'access to credit is the shortest way of empowering the poor and improving their income generating opportunities'. While provision of credit is certainly one of the necessary conditions for empowering the poor it is not sufficient. Empowerment as we have argued in chapter 4, implies organization, consciousness and a sustainable increase in their incomes. Only then can the poor break out of the nexus of local structures of power and have better access over markets as well as the local institutions of governance. Nevertheless provision of micro-credit can be a vital instrument for increasing the incomes of the poor.

Let us briefly consider the existing scale of the government's efforts at providing micro-credit to the poor. The Pakistan Poverty Alleviation Fund (PPAF) and the micro finance bank (The Khushali Bank) are the two main, relatively new government sponsored apex institutions for microcredit. According to the I-PRSP, the PPAF has so far disbursed Rs.507 million to 50,000 borrowers. Considering that there are about 45 million people in Pakistan living below the poverty line the coverage of PPAF is only 0.1 per cent. The Khushali Bank which is more recent than the PPAF is functioning on an even smaller scale at the moment. (As the NHDR/PIDE Survey shows, chapter 3, only 0.4 per cent of the extremely poor and 0.6 per cent of the poor receive loans from NGOs while 1.1 per cent of the extremely poor and 3.1 per cent of the poor in rural areas receive loans from the ADBP). Therefore even though both the PPAF and the Khushali Bank would need to operate on a much larger scale together with ADBP and other commercial banks with special windows for micro-credit, if a significant proportion of the poor in need of micro-credit are to actually receive it.

(iii) Housing for the Poor

The government's policy of housing for the poor is focused on measures to provide proprietary rights and improved service delivery to Katchi Abadis (unserviced localities predominantly inhabited by the poor in urban and peri-urban areas). The government intends to grant proprietary rights to residents of Katchi Abadis established before 23 March 1985. Moreover, occupants in urban areas who are able to pay in lump sum the development charges within a period of three months would get 50 per cent concession on these charges.

The government is also developing a strategy for improving service delivery systems in Katchi Abadis. At the same time, the Ministry of Housing and Works in collaboration with provincial governments is expected to develop a programme for improving the living conditions in slums and Katchi Abadis. It is estimated that between 35 to 50 per cent of the urban population is living in Katchi Abadis. Therefore if the government's planned measures to provide proprietary rights to residents of Katchi Abadis and improve service delivery in them are actually implemented, then it would have a major impact on the living conditions of the urban poor.

V. SUMMARY POLICY PROPOSALS

V.1 *The Political and Social Framework for Overcoming the Crisis*: The emergence of an Islamic Pakistan that is modern, tolerant and democratic as envisioned by the Quaid-i-Azam, Mohammad Ali Jinnah, could provide the political and social framework for overcoming the crisis of poverty, growth and governance.

An essential element in the enabling environment for investment, economic growth and poverty alleviation is to re-establish the writ of the state, specifically in the context of violent extremist tendencies. This is particularly necessary for the poverty alleviation of poor women.

V.2 *Restructured GDP Growth*: To enable a faster growth with an enhanced capacity for employment generation and poverty alleviation a four-pronged growth strategy is proposed: (i) Rehabilitation of the canal irrigation system so as to reduce transportation losses of irrigation water and provide more water at the root zone of the crops. This would not only generate faster employment but also help farmers to increase their yield per acre. (ii) Develop the ability to produce and export more milk, marine fisheries and high value added agriculture products such as fruits, vegetables and flowers. Increased production and export of these products would not only put more income into the hands of the small agricultural producers and fishermen, but also accelerate export growth. (iii) Develop infrastructure such as dams (for both increased reservoir capacity and cheap energy production), ports, national highways, railways, farms to market roads, and cheaper coal based rather than furnace oil based energy production.

(iv) Accelerate the growth of small-scale enterprises (SSEs) which generate both higher output, employment and exports for given levels of investment. This could be done by facilitating the establishment in the private sector of Industrial Support Centres (ISCs). These would constitute the institutional basis for providing unit specific support to SSEs, to enable them to shift to higher value added products and accelerate their growth.

V.3 *Poverty Alleviation through Countervailing Power*: Due to inadequate access of the poor over institutionalized credit markets as many as 50.8 per cent of extremely poor households borrow from the landlord. The resultant increase in leverage and additional social control by the landlord, obliges many poor households to work for the landlord without any wage at all (57.4 per cent of extremely poor households worked for the landlord without wages). To create countervailing power for enabling the poor to break out of this nexus two initiatives could be undertaken:

- NGOs engaged in human rights advocacy, Lawyers Associations, and apex organizations of development NGOs could form a consortium facilitated by the government to enable the poor tenants and farm labourers to form a Small Tenant and Farm Labourers Union, at the district, provincial and national levels. The purpose would be to negotiate within the existing legal framework to achieve fair wage and tenancy contracts for the farm sector.

- Facilitating the emergence of autonomous organizations of the poor and their institutional linkage with each tier of local government, could enable the poor to break out of the nexus of the local power structures and unequal access over markets, and thereby reduce their income losses

V.4 *Poverty Alleviation by Increasing the Profitability of Micro-enterprises*: The NHDR/PIDE Survey shows that over 52 per cent of the urban poor are engaged in micro enterprises which predominantly have low profitability. Enabling the poor to improve the productivity, sales and net profits would contribute significantly to poverty reduction. An overwhelming proportion reported that enhanced availability of credit, better location and transport facilities would help to increase their incomes from micro-enterprises.

V.5 *Increasing Incomes of the Poor by Increasing Productivity*: A predominant proportion of the major earners in both rural and urban areas in poor households are unskilled workers engaged in low productivity and low income occupations. The mobility of such unskilled workers across occupations is also low.

Vocational Training and apprenticeship programmes to impart technical skills after primary education of workers from poor households could contribute to poverty alleviation.

V.6 *Increasing the Supplementary Income of the Poor:*

- Remittances constitute a major source of supplementary income for poor households. The data show that the reason why the income of poor migrants is low is because 73.9 per cent of the migrants are illiterate or just have primary education. The income of non-poor migrants was higher because of their better educational status.

    Clearly improved education and skill training of the poor can play a role in poverty alleviation by improving the incomes of migrant workers who send remittances to their families.

- Given the fact that the average total household receipts of the extremely poor are only 80 per cent of their minimum food consumption requirements, an increase in the volume of Zakat funds, improved targeting of beneficiaries and greater efficiency in the administration of Zakat funds is required.

V.7 *Health and Poverty*: Our analysis has shown that health is a major factor that pushes people into poverty. Therefore improving nutrition and health conditions are important for poverty alleviation. Improving the nutrition, preventive hygiene, provision of safe drinking water, improving the service delivery of basic health units, public transport, and improved diagnostic and treatment capabilities of Tehsil and District Hospitals are urgent imperatives to deal with the crisis of health and poverty.

V.8 *Women, Poverty and Governance*:

- In making a direct attack on poverty it is essential to facilitate the growth of autonomous organizations of the poor, especially of women at the local level to enable the poor to achieve better access over input and output markets and increase their productivity and incomes on a sustainable basis. An essential aspect of the emergence of autonomous organizations of the poor, particularly of women is to enable an institutionalized relationship with different tiers of local government. To the extent that this is achieved, it would not only enhance the ability of local governments to work for the poor but also broaden the basis of power and decisions related to resource allocation and resource use.

- The current government programme of devolution appears to have considerable potential in terms of enabling greater participation of women and the poor in governance. However, if it is to succeed in this objective four policy issues may be relevant: (a) There is a distinction between decentralization of administrative function and devolution of power to the people. To enable the latter, specific norms have to be created in the local government structure for an institutionalized relationship with autonomous organizations of the poor with respect to selection, design and implementation of development projects. (b) Putting into place specific and verifiable procedures to ensure that women councillors are in practice involved in decisions within local government structures. In this context it may be worth considering the institution of women ombudsmen at the tehsil level to whom women councillors can take their complaints in case they are discriminated against in the process of governance decisions. (c) Specifying clearly the domains of authority of local government representatives in each tier, their relationship with the existing administrative structure and also ensuring that local government personnel at each tier are aware of the scope of their authority and obligatory operational procedures. (d) A large scale programme of training local government representatives and officials in specific skills related with local level governance and development. (These include project feasibility, design, and project management, as well as skills in financial management and accounting).

V.9 *NGOs, Governance and Poverty Alleviation*:

- Under the devolution programme a new structure of local governments at the district level is emerging, within which elected representatives will be expected to undertake (amongst other functions) poverty alleviation at different tiers of local government (district, tehsil, union council and village levels). Within this structure NGOs that enable the formation of autonomous organizations of the poor could play an important role in creating a systematic relationship between local governance and poor communities. Such a relationship would enable the poor to participate in the identification and implementation of development projects as well as decisions related with access over markets and local power structures. It could also help broaden the social base of power, authority and the allocation and use of public resources.

- If NGOs are to play this role they would need to function at the district level rather than across districts and achieve full coverage of the poor population within the district.

- The total coverage of NGOs currently, is relatively insignificant compared to the magnitude of the poor population. As the NHDR/PIDE 2001 Survey shows that of the total loans received by all categories of the poor the percentage of loans received from NGOs was only 0.8 per cent in the rural areas and 1 per cent in the urban areas. A quantum increase in the scale of credit being disbursed by PPAF and Khushali Bank will need to be undertaken and measures put into place for impact assessment (see chapter 4 for details).

V.10 *Saving Children Engaged in Hazardous Industries*:

- A large number of children from poor families are working in hazardous occupations which are causing repeated injuries, chronic diseases, physical and mental deformities and in some cases, death. Clearly, the task is to withdraw them from such occupations and enable them to go to school. However, the experience of Pakistan and other South Asian countries is that mere legislation is not enough to protect these children. (After all, there has been a law against employment of children in precisely such occupations since 1938 and a much more rigorous law since 1991). Action is needed as follows:

- An administrative mechanism targeted towards the ending of child labour in hazardous occupations over the next five years needs to be urgently put in place. This mechanism can consist of specifying the number of children, location of hazardous work units, the details of the hazards in each work unit and the names of the employers in the area under the jurisdiction of each District Nazim in the country. This data should be available to the local government institutions in each district, whose task should be to indicate specific achievement targets for the District Co-ordination Officer (DCOs), (in terms of which their salaries, promotion and benefits should be decided). The achievement targets would consist of withdrawing children from hazardous occupations in each locality; to arrange for an adult member of their family to start work;

and to enable the concerned employer to hire adults, improve work safety and increase productivity.

V.11 *Environmental Management, Health, Productivity and Poverty*: The available studies on the quantitative impact of environmental degradation on GDP growth, indicate the substantial adverse consequences of air and water pollution on public health (and hence on GDP via labour productivity) and the adverse impact of deforestation and soil degradation on productivity in the agriculture sector.

The capacity to implement environmental management programmes is yet to be developed. The effort must start from the strengthening of local government institutions, autonomous organizations of the poor and civil society associations at all levels. Particularly important for the coming decades will be: (i) Implementing the National Environmental Quality Standards (NEQS) that are already in place and strengthening the professional capabilities of Environmental Protection Agencies (EPAs) (ii) Farmers' organizations for irrigation and drainage management in the irrigated croplands. (iii) Community organizations for protecting sub-watersheds and sustaining livelihoods in the Indus uplands. (iv) Associations of the poor, empowered for example by grazing licenses, for self-regulated access to natural resources in the relevant ecological units, such as the rangelands of Cholistan, Tharparkar, and Balochistan and (v) Mohalla and lane organizations for sanitation and solid waste management in the low-income wards of cities and towns.

CONCLUSIONS

In this chapter we have presented an outline of an economic strategy to achieve growth with greater poverty alleviation. It has two broad thrusts: (1) A restructured economic growth process that would not only enable a faster GDP growth but enhanced poverty alleviation for given GDP growth rates. (2) Direct attack on poverty which would empower the poor by enabling them to organize themselves at the local level, to increase their productivity, incomes, savings and investment. Thus the poor could achieve not only a sustainable increase in their incomes but in so doing also contribute to a faster and more equitable GDP growth rate.

The strategy of a faster and restructured growth is a four-pronged one which addresses the main structural features of the economy. These features have been identified in our analysis in chapters 1, 2 and 3 as being the major factors underlying both the slow down in GDP growth during the 1990s as well as its reduced ability to alleviate poverty. Therefore the growth strategy would aim to: (a) change the composition of investment so as to generate faster GDP growth for given levels of investment. (b) Change the composition of GDP to increase employment elasticity with respect to output and thereby enhance the employment generation capability of economic growth. (c) Accelerate the growth rate of exports and (d) Enable a shift of the labour force from low skill, low productivity sectors to higher skilled and higher productivity sectors in order to achieve a faster increase in incomes of the lower income groups. In consideration of these strategic parameters the proposed four-pronged growth strategy focuses on: (1) Rehabilitation of the canal irrigation system so as to reduce transportation losses of irrigation water and provide more water at the root zone of the crops. This would not only generate faster employment but also help farmers to increase their yield per acre. (2) Develop the ability to produce and export milk, marine fisheries and high value added agriculture products such as fruits, vegetables and flowers. Increased production and export of these products would not only put more income into the hands of the small agricultural producers and fishermen, but also accelerate export growth. (3) Develop infrastructure such as dams (for both increased reservoir capacity and cheap energy production), ports, national highways, railways, farm to market roads, and cheaper coal based rather than furnace oil based energy production. This would not only create a facilitating environment for private sector investment but also generate employment and stimulate aggregate demand. (4) Accelerate the growth of small scale enterprises (SSEs) which generate both higher output, employment and exports for given levels of investment. This could be done by facilitating the establishment in the private sector of Industrial Support Centres (ISCs).

The capacity to implement environmental management programmes is yet to be developed. The effort must start from the strengthening of local government institutions, autonomous organizations of the poor and civil society associations at all levels

12. The newly elected councillors in some cases are turning to civil society organizations for help. However existing civil society organizations may not necessarily have the capacity for the major effort required to familiarize, train and actively involve women in the process of identification, design and implementation of development projects. Nevertheless, six national level resource organizations in the non-governmental sector have reportedly started work to promote political education and enhanced participation of women in the election process. (Khawar Mumtaz, op. cit. p. 21).
13. Ibid., p. 22.
14. This sub-section is based on a project note (Gender, Equality Umbrella Project) provided by the UNDP Office, Islamabad. The Principal author is grateful to the UNDP Staff for providing this project note.
15. This sub-section is based on a concept note provided by Dr Socorro L. Reyes, titled: *Gender Budgeting: A Concept Note*. The Principal Author would like to thank her for providing him this input.
16. See, Akmal Hussain, 'Pro-Poor Growth, Participatory Development and Decentralization: Paradigms and Praxis,' Part-III of the forthcoming book, P. Wignaraja and S. Sirivardana (eds.) *Pro-Poor Growth and Governance in South Asia— Case Profiles of Participatory Development and Decentralization Reforms*, Zed Press, London (Forthcoming).
17. See, S.K. Upadhyay, 'The Nepal Case Study,' in P. Wignaraja and S. Sirivardana (eds.) *Pro-Poor Growth and Governance in South Asia*, op. cit., Annexure to Part-III.
18. See, Dr Shaikh Maqsood Ali, 'The Bangladesh Case Study,' in P. Wignaraja and S. Sirivardana (eds.), op. cit., Annexure to Part-III.
19. See, Arif Hassan, 'The Pakistan Case Study,' in P. Wignaraja and S. Sirivardana (eds.), op. cit., Annexure to Part-III.
20. Pakistan Interim Poverty Reduction Strategy Paper (I-PRSP), Government of Pakistan, November 2001, p. 15.
21. Ibid., p. 15
22. For a more detailed discussion on the relationship between the politics of successive regimes and institutional decay of the civil service, see, Akmal Hussain, 'The Dynamics of Power, Military, Bureaucracy and the People,' in K. Rupasinghe and K. Mumtaz, *Internal Conflicts in South Asia*, Sage, London, 1995.
23. Pakistan's Reform Programme: Progress and Prospects Report, The World Bank Group, March 2001.
24. Pakistan, Interim Poverty Reduction Strategy Paper (I-PRSP), Government of Pakistan, November 2001, p. 36.

References

Addison, M.W., 1996. 'Setting Environmental Priorities'. (Mimeo) Draft.

Asian Development Bank, July 2002. 'Poverty in Pakistan'.

Brandon, C., 1995. 'Valuing Environmental Costs in Pakistan: The Economy-Wide Impact of Environmental Degradation'. Asia Environment Division, World Bank.

Burki, Shahid Javed, 1999. *Pakistan: Fifty Years of Nationhood*. Vanguard, Lahore.

———, 1998. 'Governance, Corruption and Development: Some Major Obstacles to Growth and Development'. *The Banker*, Lahore.

Canfield, Catherine, 1984. 'Pesticides Exporting Death'. New Scientist, 16 August 1984.

Ghaus, Aisha, Pasha, Hafiz A. and Ghaus, Rafia. 'Social Development Ranking of Districts of Pakistan'. *The Pakistan Development Review* (Winter 1996), Volume 35, No. 4, Islamabad.

Government of Pakistan, 2001. 'A Debt Reduction and Management Strategy—Summary Report'.

———, 2001. Interim Poverty Reduction Strategy Paper.

———, February 2002. 'Interim Population Sector Perspective Plan 2012'.

———, Finance Division. Economic Survey. Islamabad

———, Planning Commission, 2001. Ten Year Perspective Plan and Three Year Development Programme. Islamabad.

———, Planning Commission. The Third Five Year Plan, 1965-70. Karachi.

Griffin, K. and Khan, A.R. 'Growth and Inequality in Pakistan'. Macmillan, London.

Hamid, N. 'The Burden of Capitalist Growth, A Study of Real Wages in Pakistan'. *Pakistan Economic and Social Review*, Spring 1974.

Hamid, Naved and Hussain, Akmal. 'Regional Inequalities and Capitalist Development'. *Pakistan Economic and Social Review*, Autumn 1974.

Herald, Monthly. Karachi.

Hussain, Akmal, 1980. 'Impact of Agricultural Growth on Changes in the Agrarian Structure of Pakistan with Special Reference to the Punjab Province'. D. Phil Thesis, University of Sussex.

———, 1985. 'Squeezed Out by Progress', Development, Seeds of Change.

———, 1986. 'Economic Growth, Poverty and the Child'. Paper presented at the Harvard Conference on Who Speaks for the Child, Harvard University, Cambridge, Mass., 11-12 August 1986.

———, 1988. *Strategic Issues in Pakistan's Economic Policy*. Progressive Publishers.

———, 1989. 'Labour Absorption in Pakistan's Rural Sector'. ILO/ARTEP.

———, 1992. 'Child Workers in Construction and Related Industries in Pakistan'. ILO/ARTEP, Geneva, 1 October 1992 (Mimeo).

———, 1994. *Poverty Alleviation in Pakistan*. Vanguard Books.

———, 1999. 'A Medium Term Strategy of Economic Revival'. Paper presented to the Federal Finance Minister of Pakistan.

———, 1999. 'Employment Generation, Poverty Alleviation and Growth in Pakistan's Rural Sector: Policies for Institutional Change'. Report prepared for the International Labour Organization, Country Employment Policy Review, Pakistan, ILO/CEPR.

———, February 1991. 'Women, Environment and Development'. Paper presented to the Centre for Research and Management, Islamabad.

Jillani et al. 'Labour Migration'. PIDE Research Report No. 126.

Kemal, A.R., 1999. 'Patterns and Growth of Pakistan's Industrial Sector'. Included in Khan, Shahrukh Rafi, *Fifty Years of Pakistan's Economy*. Oxford University Press, Karachi.

Khan, Akhtar Hameed. *Orangi Pilot Project: Reminiscences and Reflections*.

Khan, Shahrukh Rafi, 1999. *Fifty Years of Pakistan's Economy*. Oxford University Press, Karachi.

Majid, Nomaan. 'Pakistan: An Employment Strategy'. ILO/SAAT, December 1997.

Mian, Alim and Mirza, Yasin, 1993. 'Pakistan Soil Resources, National Conservation Strategy'. Sector Paper IV, Environment and Urban Areas Division, with IUCN.

Naqvi and Zareen. 'Poverty in Pakistan: Review of Recent Literature'. South Asia Poverty Reduction and Economic Management Unit, The World Bank, Islamabad.

Naseem, S.M., 1977. 'Rural Poverty and Landlessness in Asia'. ILO Report, Geneva.

National Health Survey of Pakistan, Pakistan Medical Research Council, Federal Bureau of Statistics, Pakistan and the Department of Health and Human Services, USA, 1998.

Newsline, Monthly. Karachi.

Nishtar Medical College, Multan, 1990. 'Discover the Working Child'. UNICEF, Islamabad.

Noman, Omar, 1988. *The Political Economy of Pakistan, 1947-85*. Routledge, Kegan and Paul, London.

Overcoming Poverty: The Report of the Task Force on Poverty Eradication, May 1997.

Pasha, Hafiz, 1999. 'Fifty Years of Finance in Pakistan: A Trend Analysis' in Khan, Shahrukh Rafi (ed.) *Fifty Years of Pakistan's Economy*.

Postel, Sandra, July 1999. 'Pillars of Sand: Can the Irrigation Miracle Last?' W.W. Norton & Company, New York.

Punjab Rural Support Programme. Summary Field Report.

Qureshi, Ata and Iglesias, 1992. 'Implications of Global Climate Change for Pakistan Agriculture: Impacts on Simulated Wheat Production'. Climate Institute, Washington, DC USA.

Rahim, Sikander, February 2001. 'Myths of Economic Development'. Lahore School of Economics, Occasional Paper No. 10.

Reyes, Socorro L. 2002. 'Gender Budgeting: A Concept Note', UNDP, Mimeo

Roos, D. (ed.), 1980. *Nicomachean Ethics*. Oxford University Press.

Rosegrant, Mark W. and Evenson, Robert, 1993. 'Agricultural Productivity Growth in Pakistan and India: A Comparative Analysis'. Paper presented at Pakistan Institute of Development Economics, Ninth General Meeting, Islamabad.

Rupasinghe, K. and Mumtaz, K. (ed.), 1996. *Internal Conflicts in South Asia*. Zed Books, London.

Sathar, Zeba A. and Kazi, Shahnaz, 1997. 'Women's Autonomy, Livelihood and Fertility'. PIDE.

Social Policy and Development Centre, 2002. *Social Development in Pakistan, Annual Review 2002*. Oxford University Press, Karachi.

Soligo and Stern, J.J., 1965. 'Tariff Protection, Imports Substitution and Investment Efficiency, The Pakistan Development'.

Streeten, Paul et al., 1981: *First Things First: Meeting Basic Needs in Developing Countries*. Oxford University Press, New York.

Syed, Najam Hosain, 1986. *Recurrent Patterns in Punjabi Poetry* Second Edition. Punjab Adbi Markaz, Lahore.

The Economist, Weekly. London

The World Bank Group, March 2001. 'Pakistan's Reform Programme: Progress and Prospects Report'.

Tinker, Anne G., 1998. 'Improving Women's Health in Pakistan'. Human Development Network, The World Bank.

UNDP, Human Development Report 2002, Deepening democracy in a fragmented world, OUP, 2002.

UNDP, Pakistan, 1986. 'Government/Donor/ NGO Collaboration: Lessons Learnt and the Action for the Future'.

UNICEF, 1992. 'Situation Analysis of Children and Women in Pakistan'.

White, L.J. 'Industrial Concentration and Economic Power in Pakistan'. Princeton University Press.

Wignaraja, P. and Sirivardana, S. (Forthcoming). *Pro-Poor Growth and Governance in South Asia*. Zed Press, London.

Wignaraja, Ponna, Hussain, Akmal, Sethi, Harsh and Wignaraja, Ganeshan, 1991. *Participatory Development, Learning from South Asia*. United Nations University, Oxford University Press.

World Bank, 1990. 'Women in Pakistan: An Economic and Social Strategy'.

———, March 1994. 'Pakistan Irrigation and Drainage: Issues and Options'. World Bank Report No. 11884-PAK.

———, May 2002. 'Poverty in Pakistan: Vulnerabilities, Social Gaps, and Rural Dynamics'.

———, November 1994. 'Pakistan: A Strategy for Sustainable Agricultural Growth'. World Bank Report No. 13092.

———. 'Governance and Development' Washington DC.

CHAPTER 1

Annexure I

I (a) Disaggregated Human Development
   Indices, by Provinces and Districts
I (b) Method of Calculation

ANNEXURE I (a)

TABLE 1
DISAGGREGATED HUMAN DEVELOPMENT INDEX FOR PAKISTAN, PROVINCE-WISE AND RURAL/URBAN

Name	Literacy Ratio % 1998	Enrolment Ratio % 1998	Infant Survival Ratio % (per 1000)	Immunization Ratio % 1998	Real GDP per capita (PPP$) 1998	Educational Attainment Index	Health Index	Adjusted real GDP per capita (PPP$) Index	HDI
Urban	65	94	93.5	64	2319	0.747	0.85	0.374	0.656
Punjab	64	94	93.6	64	2380	0.740	0.85	0.384	0.657
Sindh	69	94	93.1	60	2308	0.773	0.83	0.372	0.659
NWFP	53	90	94.7	77	2074	0.653	0.89	0.332	0.627
Balochistan	56	88	94.4	51	1837	0.667	0.81	0.292	0.591
Rural	36	63	96.4	45	1464	0.450	0.81	0.230	0.496
Punjab	38	69	96.2	52	1523	0.483	0.83	0.239	0.517
Sindh	35	47	96.5	27	1418	0.390	0.76	0.222	0.456
NWFP	34	66	96.6	51	1241	0.447	0.83	0.192	0.489
Balochistan	33	61	96.7	32	1653	0.423	0.77	0.261	0.486
Overall	45	71	95.5	49	1715	0.537	0.82	0.272	0.541
Punjab	46	75	95.4	55	1770	0.557	0.83	0.281	0.557
Sindh	51	64	94.9	38	1804	0.553	0.78	0.287	0.540
NWFP	37	70	96.3	54	1364	0.480	0.84	0.213	0.510
Balochistan	36	64	96.4	34	1677	0.453	0.78	0.265	0.499
Islamabad	72	58	95.9	72	1743	0.673	0.89	0.277	0.612

Note: Estimates by Wasay Majid and Akmal Hussain.
1. GDP per capita and Infant Survival Rates for Islamabad are calculated as an average of Punjab and Pakistan.
2. Enrolment rate is for primary level only.
3. Immunization refers to fully immunized children based on record and recall having received BCG, DPT1, DPT2, DPT3, Polio1, Polio2, Polio3, and Measles.
4. Province-wise per capita income has been estimated from the Household Integrated Economic Survey: 1998-99. Real GDP per capita in 1998 PPP$ for provinces has been calculated by multiplying the ratio of the province per capita income to the national per capita income of Pakistan by Pakistan's GDP per capita in PPP$ of $1715 (1998) reported in the HDR 2000, UNDP.

Source: Pakistan Integrated Household Survey: Round 3, 1998-1999, Federal Bureau of Statistics, Government of Pakistan, Islamabad.

ANNEXURE I (a)

TABLE 2 (c)
HUMAN DEVELOPMENT INDEX FOR NWFP DISTRICTS

District	Literacy Ratio % 1998	Enrolment Ratio % 1998	Immunization Ratio % 1998	Infant Survival Ratio %	Real GDP per capita (PPP$) 1998	Educational Attainment Index	Health Index	Income Index	HDI
Abbottabadd	56.6	48.1	76.9	96.3	2,194	0.538	0.905	0.353	0.598
Bannu	32.1	24.1	68.8	96.3	1,399	0.294	0.881	0.219	0.465
Batgram	18.3	14.5	52.4	96.3	618	0.170	0.831	0.087	0.363
Buner	22.6	21.4	68.5	96.3	1,094	0.222	0.880	0.167	0.423
Charsadda	31.1	26.0	78.4	96.3	1,974	0.294	0.909	0.316	0.506
Chitral	40.3	42.1	86.2	96.3	660	0.409	0.933	0.094	0.479
Dera Ismail Khan	31.2	24.2	58.8	96.3	912	0.289	0.851	0.137	0.425
Hangu	30.5	26.9	66.5	96.3	297	0.293	0.874	0.033	0.400
Haripur	53.7	44.1	73.2	96.3	3,000	0.505	0.894	0.488	0.629
Karak	41.9	35.4	79.1	96.3	953	0.397	0.911	0.144	0.484
Kohat	44.0	35.8	60.7	96.3	2,141	0.413	0.856	0.344	0.537
Kohistan	11.1	6.9	44.7	96.3	640	0.097	0.808	0.091	0.332
Lakki Marwat	29.7	29.3	66.3	96.3	1,074	0.296	0.873	0.164	0.444
Lower Dir	29.9	22.5	77.4	96.3	438	0.274	0.906	0.057	0.413
Malakand	39.5	27.9	65.3	96.3	1,031	0.356	0.870	0.157	0.461
Mansehra	36.3	36.6	71.1	96.3	855	0.364	0.887	0.127	0.459
Mardan	36.5	32.6	79.1	96.3	1,835	0.352	0.911	0.292	0.519
Nowshera	42.5	32.4	78.8	96.3	1,801	0.391	0.911	0.286	0.529
Peshawar	41.8	49.6	83.0	96.3	1,450	0.444	0.923	0.227	0.531
Shangla	14.7	14.2	29.0	96.3	624	0.145	0.761	0.088	0.332
Swabi	36.0	30.6	75.0	96.3	2,046	0.342	0.899	0.328	0.523
Swat	28.7	23.9	73.4	96.3	1,062	0.271	0.894	0.162	0.442
Tank	26.3	20.6	53.9	96.3	530	0.244	0.836	0.072	0.384
Upper Dir	21.2	20.3	64.1	96.3	293	0.209	0.866	0.033	0.369

Notes:
1. HDI calculation uses Life Expectancy data for determining the Health Index. Since this was not available at the district level, the Immunization Ratio has been used as a proxy.
2. Enrolment rate is for primary level only.
3. Immunization refers to fully immunized children based on record and recall having received BCG, DPT1, DPT2, DPT3, Polio1, Polio2, Polio3 and Measles.
4. District-wise Real GDP per capita (PPP$ 1998) has been calculated by multiplying the ratio of the respective district's cash value of crop output and its manufacturing Value added to the national values, into Pakistan's GDP per capita in PPP$ (1998) of $1,715 reported in the HDR 2000, UNDP.
5. Estimation by Umar Zafar, Wasay Majid and Akmal Hussain.

Sources: Population Census Organization, Statistics Division, GoP 1998-2000; HIES: 1998-99, Federal Bureau of Statistics, GoP; Human Development Reports, UNDP, 1996 & 2000; and World Development Indicators, 2001.

ANNEXURE I (a)

TABLE 2 (d)
HUMAN DEVELOPMENT INDEX FOR BALOCHISTAN DISTRICTS

District	Literacy Ratio % 1998	Enrolment Ratio % 1998	Immunization Ratio % 1998	Infant Survival Ratio %	Real GDP per capita (PPP$) 1998	Educational Attainment Index	Health Index	Income Index	HDI
Awaran	14.8	12.2	31.3	96.4	1,490	0.139	0.769	0.234	0.381
Barkhan	15.7	18.0	52.6	96.4	1,652	0.165	0.833	0.261	0.420
Bolan	15.7	17.7	48.9	96.4	664	0.164	0.822	0.095	0.360
Chagai	26.9	27.7	63.1	96.4	1,688	0.272	0.864	0.267	0.468
Dera Bugti	11.7	7.5	27.3	96.4	78	0.103	0.757	(0.004)	0.285
Gwadar	25.5	28.8	65.5	96.4	337	0.266	0.871	0.040	0.392
Jaffarabad	18.5	17.5	49.4	96.4	2,230	0.182	0.823	0.359	0.454
Jhalmagsi	12.3	4.1	32.1	96.4	1,093	0.096	0.771	0.167	0.345
Kalat	19.8	15.3	50.8	96.4	1,437	0.183	0.827	0.225	0.412
Kech	27.5	34.2	63.2	96.4	2,321	0.297	0.864	0.374	0.512
Kharan	15.1	14.1	49.2	96.4	503	0.148	0.822	0.068	0.346
Killa Abdullah	16.1	14.9	49.9	96.4	1,159	0.157	0.825	0.178	0.387
Killa Saifullah	17.5	21.2	46.3	96.4	2,254	0.187	0.814	0.363	0.455
Kohlu	12.2	5.2	22.7	96.4	1,303	0.099	0.743	0.202	0.348
Lasbela	22.3	19.7	43.6	96.4	3,206	0.214	0.806	0.523	0.514
Loralai	20.5	18.1	58.2	96.4	3,798	0.197	0.849	0.623	0.556
Mastung	27.6	22.5	54.3	96.4	2,992	0.259	0.838	0.487	0.528
Nasirabad	12.7	8.2	52.6	96.4	3,253	0.112	0.833	0.531	0.492
Panjgur	31.4	36.8	65.9	96.4	1,783	0.332	0.873	0.283	0.496
Sibi	25.5	19.1	32.2	96.4	1,452	0.234	0.771	0.228	0.411
Zhob	16.8	14.8	53.3	96.4	1,889	0.161	0.835	0.301	0.432
Ziarat	34.3	41.6	71.6	96.4	5,046	0.367	0.890	0.833	0.697

Notes:
1. HDI calculation uses Life Expectancy data for determining the Health Index. Since this was not available at the district level, the Immunization Ratio has been used as a proxy.
2. Enrolment rate is for primary level only.
3. Immunization refers to fully immunized children based on record and recall having received BCG, DPT1, DPT2, DP3, Polio1, Polio2, Polio3 and Measles.
4. District-wise Real GDP per capita (PPP$ 1998) has been calculated by multiplying the ratio of the respective district's cash value of crop output and its manufacturing value added to the national values, into Pakistan's GDP per capita in PPP$ (1998) of $1,715 reported in the HDR 2000, UNDP.
5. Estimation by Umar Zafar, Wasay Majid and Akmal Hussain.

Sources: Population Census Organization, Statistics Division, GoP 1998-2000; HIES: 1998-99, Federal Bureau of Statistics, GoP; Human Development Reports, UNDP, 1996 & 2000; and World Development Indicators, 2001.

ANNEXURE I (b)
Calculation Procedure for HDI Estimates at the National, Provincial and District Levels

I Human Development Index (HDI) – Composition and Calculation

The HDI comprises of three main components each affecting, in one way or another, a human being's life by way of his/her access to 'means' and/or desired 'ends'.

The three main components of the HDI are:

(i) Health
(ii) Education
(iii) Income

The indicators used for measuring and consequently calculating their respective composite indices for the compilation of the HDI are:

a. Life expectancy
b. Adult literacy and combined enrolment rate; and
c. Adjusted GDP per capita in PPP$

For the construction of each index, fixed minimum and maximum values have been established.

(i) Health Index
Life expectancy is calculated by choosing a global acceptable range, which suggests a maximum of 85 years and a minimum of 25 years.

Therefore the Life Expectancy Index is calculated as:

$$= X - 25 / 85 - 25 \qquad = X - 25 / 60$$

(ii) Educational Attainment Index
This component of the HDI is calculated by using 100 per cent as a maximum and 0 per cent as a minimum for levels of educational attainment. It gives two-third weight to adult literacy and one-third weight to combined enrolment rates.

Therefore the Educational Attainment Index is calculated as:

$$= X - 0 / 100 - 0 \qquad = X / 100$$

(ii) Income Index
The construction of the income index is a bit more complicated. The fixed minimum and maximum values for the income index are US$100 and US$40,000. The average world income of PPP$5,711 is taken as the threshold level, and any income above this level is discounted using the Atkinson's formula for the utility of income.

The discounted value of the maximum income of PPP$40,000, using the Atkinson formula is PPP$6,040. As Pakistan's GDP per capita in PPP$ is $1,715 (1998), we do not need to calculate the adjusted GDP per capita PPP$.

Therefore the Income Index for Pakistan is calculated as:

$$= X - 100 / 6,040 - 100 \qquad = X - 100 / 5,940$$

Now to arrive at an HDI value, we simply calculate the arithmetic mean of the three indices.

II Data used for calculating Pakistan's HDI – at Province and District level.

As there is no data available on life expectancy either for provinces or districts of Pakistan, we constructed a Health Index using Infant Survival rates (available only at the provincial level) and Immunization rates (available at District level).

Our index gives a 70 per cent weigh to Infant Survival rates and consequently a 30 per cent weight to the Immunization rates. The range or 'goal posts' for both the indicators are a 100 per cent for a maximum level of health and 0 per cent for no level of health.

Note that as Infant Survival rates are available only at the provincial level, therefore, when constructing the HDI at district level, the component of the Health Index used the value of the respective province for each of its districts.

III Rationale for using Immunization rates for the HDI

Prior to the 1998 census, there was no data available on Health that could be used for calculating a HDI at the district level. The inclusion of Immunization rates in the latest census provided us with an opportunity, for the first time, to be able to construct a HDI at the district level.

Immunization rates used in our study are based on full immunization, which involves a child having received all of the following: 'BCG', 'DPT1', 'DPT2', 'DPT3', 'Polio1', 'Polio2', 'Polio3', and 'Measles'.

Acknowledging that it is not the conventional indicator used in the construction of the HDI, it nevertheless gives us some information on health.

Immunization rates may very well suggest future preservation from deadly diseases and ailments that may handicap a person which could lead to a deteriorated life style and consequently hardship in acquiring income and furthermore utilizing this income in its most productive and satisfactory manner. It also implicitly suggests an element of awareness towards accepting the wonders of medical science by the uneducated rural poor. This may translate into higher social returns. Furthermore, rates of immunization give us the actual number of people that have 'accessed' the health care system. It does not reflect just an average figure based on a group of people representing the region who apparently *only* have 'access' to the health care system, as is reflected in part by the life expectancy statistic.

A possible reason for the inclusion of Immunization rates in the latest national census may very well be critically analyzed as a one off policy measure of the Government at the time. It could be part of a government agenda, which required penetrating a large part of the rural population to be immunized. Such one off inconsistent policy measures do not reflect the true extent of past and future conditions. Keeping this in mind, we gave a lower weight to immunization rates in the calculation of the health index.

IV Calculation of Real GDP per Capita (PPP$) at District Level

Calculation of the Real GDP per Capita in Purchasing Power Parity in US Dollars (PPP$) requires data on GDP per capita. This data was available only at the national and provincial levels, but not at the district level in Pakistan. Therefore, for district level estimates, we used the cash value of crop output and the manufacturing value added at the district level. Its ratio to the national value of the crop output and the manufacturing value added was multiplied into Pakistan's Real GDP per Capita (PPP$ 1998), which is US$ 1,715.

The Real GDP per capita (PPP$) at the district level was aggregated at the provincial level and compared with the Province Real GDP per capita (PPP$) computed earlier by multiplying the ratio of the province income per capita to the national income per capita, into Pakistan's Real GDP per capita (PPP$ 1998). Since the GDP estimate at the provincial level was more comprehensive than at the district level, the Real GDP per capita (PPP$) at the district level was then adjusted by a factor that was the ratio of the 'actual' Province Real GDP per capita (PPP$) calculated from the income per capita data to the value obtained by aggregating the district Real GDP per capita (PPP$) in the first round.

V A Note on District, Provincial and National HDI Estimates

The all Pakistan HDI differs slightly from the figure estimated by the UNDP Human Development Report 2002. This is because the district and provincial HDI estimates in the Pakistan NHDR use a proxy for life expectancy in the health index based on immunization rates and infant survival rates (in the absence of district and provincial level life expectancy figures). To achieve consistency in the National HDI estimates so as to enable HDI comparison at district, provincial and national levels, the same proxy was used in the all Pakistan HDI estimate given in table 4(a) in the text of Chapter 1. Similarly in the absence of district level real GDP per capita, (in PPP$) figures, a proxy based on value added in agriculture and industry respectively was used. This proxy was also reflected in the NHDR estimate of the all Pakistan HDI.

The robustness of our estimation procedure using proxies at the district level, is indicated by the fact that the consequent national estimate of HDI (0.541) does not differ very much from the UNDP Human Development Report where only the directly available figures of life expectancy and real GDP per capita (in PPP$) are used.

CHAPTER 1
Annexure II

Children in Hazardous Industries

ANNEXURE II
TABLE 1
NUMBER OF CASUALTIES LAST YEAR DUE TO ANY HAZARD AND NUMBER OF WORKPLACES, BY TYPE OF INDUSTRY

Industry	(a) Reported Number* of Casualties during last year	(b) Number of Workplaces	(c) Number of Casualties per Workplace last year
Construction	677	58	12
Steel Window Manufacture	752	48	15
Electrification	60	23	3
Furnishing	125	17	7
Tiles	111	11	11
Cement	64	8	8
White Washing	160	35	5

Source: Akmal Hussain, Field Survey on Child Workers in Construction and Construction-related Industries, September 1992.
*Note: Respondents reported that an individual child worker experiences repeated injuries during the year, and returns to work after first aid or medical treatment.

ANNEXURE II
TABLE 2
LETHALITY INDEX OF HAZARDS AND DANGER INDEX OF INDUSTRIES

Hazard	(A) Standardized Index of hazards	(B) Standardized Danger Index of Industry					
		Construction	Steel Window	Electrification	Furnishing	Tiles	Cement	White Washing
Insufficient Light at Workplace	5	2.68	3.96	2.70	0.79	4.80	4.25	4.46
Workplace hazards due to incorrect location of Equipment and other Protuberances, Electricity, Wires, Switches, etc.	4	2.65	3.74	—	1.18	2.92	3.6	2.38
Lack of Protective devices while using dangerous Equipment and Material	3	2.46	2.34	1.85	2.52	2.77	—	0.16
Workplace dangers due to Proximity to Road, etc.	2	0.95	1.43	0.62	1	—	—	10.54
Unsafe Machinery without Safety devices	1	0.50	1.23	0.54	0.61	0.38	0.80	0.46
Composite Danger Index	—	9.24	12.7	5.71	6.1	11.33	9.05	8.00

Source: Akmal Hussain, Field Survey on Child Workers in Construction and Construction-related Industries, September 1992.

ANNEXURE II

TABLE 3
NUMBER OF CHILD WORKERS REPORTING CASUALTIES*
DUE TO SELECTED HAZARDS BY EDUCATION LEVEL OF EMPLOYER

Hazards	All	Illiterate	Primary	Middle	Matric	F.A.	B.A.
Inadequate light at workplace	173	1	37	37	79	17	2
Proximity to Road	16	0	0	3	8	3	2
Dangerous Building Structure	18	0	4	4	9	1	0

Source: Akmal Hussain, Field Survey on Child Workers in Construction and Construction-related Industries, September 1992.
* Casualties occurred in last year. The numbers refer not to the number of casualties, but the number of respondents in each case reporting one or more casualties.

ANNEXURE II

TABLE 4
SEX ABUSE AT WORK PLACE
Number of Children Reporting Sex Abuse Against Them as a Percentage of Respondents in the Industry by Age and Type of Industry

Industry	All Age Groups (%)	Age Group 8–10 (%)	Age Group 11–15 (%)
Construction	15	6	9
Steel Windows	4	2	2
Electrification	2	—	2
Furnishing	15	6	9
Tiles	11	5	6
Cement	13	—	13
White Washing	4	1	3

Source: Akmal Hussain, Field Survey on Child Workers in Construction and Construction-related Industries, September 1992.

ANNEXURE II

TABLE 5
EMPLOYER VIOLENCE
Number of Child Workers Reporting Employer Violence Against Them by Industry and Age of Child

	Employer Violence against Child Workers by Industry									Employer Violence by Age of Child Worker		
All Industries	Construction and Wood Work	Steel Windows	Electrification	Furnishing	Tiles	Cement	White Washing	Others		All Ages	8–10	11–15
20	7	7	1.3	5	0	0	1	0		20	7	13
(5)	(4)	(7)	(4)	(15)	(0)	(0)	(1)	(0)		(5)	(5)	(5)

Source: Akmal Hussain, Field Survey on Child Workers in Construction and Construction-related Industries, September 1992.
Note:
1. Figures in brackets refer to the number of child workers reporting employer violence against them as a percentage of the total number of respondents in that category.
2. Violence including punching with fist or use of sticks, and chains.

CHAPTER 2
Annexure

ANNEXURE
TABLE 1
GROWTH RATES OF THE MANUFACTURING SECTOR

Period	Small Scale Manufacturing	Large Scale Manufacturing	Total Manufacturing
1959/60 to 1969/70	2.85	12.43	9.24
1970/71 to 1979/80	7.21	4.84	5.50
1980/81 to 1989/90	8.40	8.16	8.21
1990/91 to 1995/96	7.88	4.40	5.59
1996/97 to 1999/2000	5.31	2.21	1.29

Source: Federal Bureau of Statistics, GOP, and Economic Survey, Economic Advisor's Wing, Ministry of Finance, GOP, 2000-2001.

ANNEXURE
TABLE 2
PERCENTAGE SECTORAL SHARE OF MANUFACTURING IN GDP (CONSTANT PRICES)

Period	Small Scale Manufacturing	Large Scale Manufacturing	Total Manufacturing
1949-50	4.56	1.83	6.39
1959-60	4.18	5.60	9.78
1969-70	2.92	10.23	13.14
1979-80	3.54	9.46	13.00
1989-90	4.36	11.32	15.68
1994-95	5.15	11.22	16.37
1998-99	4.55	11.10	15.65

Source: Federal Bureau of Statistics, GOP, and Economic Survey, Economic Advisor's Wing, Ministry of Finance, 2000-2001.

ANNEXURE
TABLE 3
SHARES OF DIFFERENT MANUFACTURING INDUSTRIES IN THE VALUE ADDED ORIGINATING IN THE MANUFACTURING SECTOR

Years	1959/60	1969/70	1980/81	1985/86	1990/91	1995/96
All Industries	100.00	100.00	100.00	100.00	100.00	100.00
Food Manufacturing	8.33	14.78	20.12	17.65	14.05	15.19
Tobacco Manufacturing	5.56	7.96	13.26	10.15	6.35	6.18
Manufacturing of Textiles	40.19	32.30	15.93	15.54	26.35	22.31
Chemicals & Chemical Products	8.42	8.92	8.00	11.82	10.41	11.51
Basic Metal Industries	3.13	2.41	3.98	3.97	5.54	4.15
Manufacturing of Metal Products	3.91	1.79	1.06	0.85	0.86	0.71
Electrical Machinery	2.43	3.33	3.47	3.36	4.11	7.67
Transport Equipment	3.30	1.39	2.47	2.50	2.59	3.50
All Others	24.74	27.13	31.71	34.16	29.74	28.77

Source: Census of Manufacturing Industries, FBS, Statistics Division, GOP, Various Issues.

ANNEXURE
TABLE 4
PERIOD AVERAGES OF EXPORTS OF VARIOUS COMMODITY GROUPS AS A PERCENTAGE OF TOTAL EXPORTS OF PAKISTAN

Years	Agricultural & Food & Live Animals Exports as a % of Total Exports	Intermediate goods as a % of Total Exports	Capital goods as a % of Total Exports	Textile & Related Goods as a % of Total Exports
1960-1970	55	8	0.87	30
1973-1977	35	7	0.73	31
1978-1987	33	6	1.14	29
1988-1999	17	4	0.33	50

Source: Federal Bureau of Statistics, Statistics Division, GOP.

ANNEXURE
TABLE 5
GOVERNMENT EXPENDITURE OF DEFENCE AND GENERAL ADMINISTRATION AS A PERCENTAGE OF TOTAL GOVERNMENT REVENUE (CONSOLIDATED FEDERAL AND PROVINCIAL)

Year	%
1980-81	35
1981-82	36
1982-83	34
1983-84	35
1984-85	37
1985-86	34
1986-87	34
1987-88	30
1988-89	32
1989-90	32
1990-91	31
1991-92	30
1992-93	32
1993-94	31
1994-95	29
1995-96	29
1996-97	30
1997-98	34
1998-99	36
1999-2000	33

Source: Economic Survey, Government of Pakistan (GOP), Economic Advisor's Wing, Finance Division, Various Issues.

ANNEXURE I
SURVEY DESIGN

The survey was designed to generate both quantitative and qualitative data sets. The quantitative component was generated through the NHDR/PIDE 2001 Survey covering eight poor communities of the country; of which two were urban while the rest of the six communities were rural. The fieldwork for the NHDR/PIDE 2001 Survey was carried out in July-August 2001. It can be said that this survey was a complete census, since it covered all households located in the sampled communities.

Two stage stratified sample design was adopted for the survey. At the first stage, seven districts of the country, Lahore and Muzaffargarh in Punjab, Badin, Mirpur Khas and Karachi in Sindh, Dir in NWFP and Khuzdar in Balochistan, were selected. In each district, a poor community was selected randomly at the second stage, except Lahore district where two communities, one rural and one urban were included in the sample. Karachi and Lahore were included in the sample because large slum areas have developed over time in these two largely urban districts of the country. There are more than 500 *Katchi Abadis* in Karachi alone. It is believed that an overwhelming majority of households situated in slum areas are poor and live in unhealthy conditions.

The rest of the five districts (Muzaffargarh, Badin, Mirpur Khas, Dir and Khuzdar) were selected for the rural sample; they are among the poorest districts of the country, as revealed by the last available ranking of districts, carried out by A.F. Aisha Ghaus, Hafiz A. Pasha and Rafia Ghaus.[1] This ranking was based on eleven indicators related primarily to education, health and water supply. While this study focuses on social indicators rather than poverty profiles as the basis of district ranking, nevertheless it provides valuable insights into differential between districts with respect to their social development.

In Punjab, the least developed districts, according to the above study, were Rajanpur, Pakpattan, Muzaffargarh, Lodharan, D.G. Khan, Vehari and Layyah. All these districts are located in South Punjab region.

In Sindh, Jacobabad, Mirpur Khas (Tharparkar), Badin, Sanghar, Thatta and Dadu were ranked as the least socially developed districts of the province. The results of a few recent studies are also in line with the above-mentioned ranking. For example, a survey done by the School of Nutrition Programme of Aga Khan University in seven districts of Sindh (including Badin, Thatta, Mirpurkhas and Dadu located in both regions of Sindh) indicates that 70-80 per cent of the rural households were poor.

In NWFP, the identified least developed districts were Kohistan, Dir and Mansehra. All districts of Balochistan except Quetta, Sibi and Ziarat were grouped in the least developed category.[2]

It appears from these regional (as well as district) differentials that poverty is concentrated in certain regions of the country. Within Punjab, based on both regional level poverty indicators and district ranking, southern Punjab appears to be a relatively poor area. In Sindh certain districts seem to be poor while in NWFP, Dir, Kohistan and Mansehra are the poor districts. The whole province of Balochistan is poor by all indicators of poverty and development. By taking into account these regional variations, five districts, Muzaffargarh, Badin, Mirpur Khas, Dir and Khuzdar, were selected for the NHDR/PIDE 2001 rural sample in order to generate data on different poverty indicators at the household as well as community level. As pointed out earlier, in each of these five districts, one community was selected randomly.

The size of villages in terms of population varied across and within the selected districts. It was therefore inappropriate to select villages which varied substantially in size. A medium-sized village comprising approximately 300 households was selected randomly from each of the above-mentioned five districts by using the village level data given in the 1998 district census reports. For the urban sample, two poor communities consisting of approximately 300 households were selected from the slum areas of Karachi and Lahore. Moreover, by way of comparison, a rural community from Lahore district was also included in the sample.

The size of the NHDR/PIDE Survey 2001 sample by community is reported in Table 1. In total, 2,240 households were covered; of which 1623 households were from rural areas, while the urban sample consisted of 617 households. The total number of households in seven communities ranged from 267 in Muzaffargarh to 344 in Lahore. In Khuzdar, however, a village with only 183 households was included in the sample. In Balochistan villages are relatively small in terms of population.

Since the NHDR/PIDE Survey 2001 is a sample survey of seven districts of Pakistan, it cannot be claimed that it is representative either for rural or for urban areas of the entire country. However,

ANNEXURE II
VARIABLES CONTAINED IN QUESTIONNAIRES

I. Household Composition

Relationship to the head of household
Sex
Age (in completed years)
Religion
Marital status
Literacy and level of education
School enrolment
Type of school and medium of instruction
Vocational/technical education

Employment and Earnings

Activity status
Employment status
Industry status
Occupational status of main job
Occupational status of secondary job
Number of hours worked on main job
Number of hours worked on secondary job
Total work experience
On the job training
Labour market earnings from first job
Labour market earnings from the second job
Earnings from other activities

II. Household Expenditure

Food
Clothing and Footwear
Fuel and Lighting
Transport
Housing
Household Effects
Personal Effects
Recreation
Medical
Education
Miscellaneous Items
Durable Goods

Ownership of Durable Items of the Household

Bicycle
Radio
Television
Video Cassette Recorder
Sewing Machine
Knitting Machine
Washing Machine
Electrical appliances
Camera

Refrigerator
Gas stove
Car / Jeep
Motorcycle/scooter
Personal Computer
Air-conditioner
Other items

Transfer Income

Zakat, Ushr, Nazrana, or Fitrana
Domestics and Foreign Remittances
Assistance from Government / other Sources
Grants / Inheritance
Pension

Ownership of Land and Property

Rent from Property and Land
Value of the Property Sold
Value of the Property Purchased
Money spent on renovations
Value of the Property or Land Received as Gift
Value of the Property or Land Lost

Financial Assets and Liabilities

Total bank Deposits
Total savings
Total Interest / Profit Received
Total Withdrawal
Total Securities, Types and Value
Profit / Interest on Securities
Total Loans to Pay
Amount Paid
Amount Remains
Time Period for payment and Interest Rate
Purpose and Institution From which Loan Received
Life Insurance
Annual Installments and Duration
Total Payment Made
Provident Fund
Annual Contribution
Balance

III. Balance Sheet

Total Income
Total Expenditure
Income / Expenditure Ratio

IV. Health Information and Housing Facilities

(i) Illness

Illness in the last two weeks
Type of illness
Consultations with health attendant
Recovery time from the illness

(ii) Housing
Present occupancy status
Number of rooms
Source of drinking water
Sanitation system
Type of toilet facilities
Garbage collection

Agricultural

Agricultural landownership
Land rented out
Land rented in
Harvesting of different crops during the last year
Livestock
Agricultural operating expenses during the last year
Persons working and labour costs

Non-Agricultural Establishment

Major activity of the business
Persons working during the last working month
General operating expenses and revenues
       Manufacturing
       Mining and quarrying
       Service related business
       Transport
       Wholesale and retail trade
       Hotels and restaurants
       Construction
Land, building, equipment and other items owned

Migration

In-migration
Out-migration

CHAPTER 3
Annexure III

(a) Micro-Enterprises and Profitability
(b) Distribution of Transfer Incomes
(c) Outmigrants by Economic Status
(d) Employment Status
(e) Percentage Distribution of Agricultural and Non-Agricultural Workers by Economic Status
(f) Type of Enterprises in Rural and Urban Areas
(g) Timely Repayment of All Loans by Economic Status
(h) Sources of Loans by Economic Status
(i) Reason for Rejection of Loan Application

ANNEXURE III (a)
MICRO-ENTERPRISES AND PROFITABILITY

CAUSES REPORTED FOR THE DECLINE IN PROFIT BY ECONOMIC STATUS

Problem Faced in Running Business	Extremely Poor	Poor	Non-Poor	Total
ALL PAKISTAN				
Less Demand	6.5	64.5	29.0	100.0
Transport Problems	—	80.0	20.0	100.0
Inflation	12.0	64.0	24.0	100.0
Police Disturbance	—	100.0	—	100.0
Change in Locality of Shop	—	100.0	—	100.0
Other Shopkeepers Disturbance	33.3	55.6	11.1	100.0
Lack of Funds	33.3	44.4	22.2	100.0
Decline in Purchasing Power	3.8	50.0	46.2	100.0
Too Old	4.3	70.0	25.7	100.0
Health Disturbance	11.1	77.8	11.1	100.0
Municipal Committee Disturbance	—	—	100.0	100.0
Input Price Increased	25.0	50.0	25.0	100.0
Business split	—	3.8	2.9	3.2
GST	—	—	100.0	100.0
Location	—	—	100.0	100.0
Increase in Petrol Prices	—	66.7	33.3	100.0
Others	8.7	56.5	34.8	100.0
Total	17.7	125.8	60.5	204.0
URBAN				
Less Demand	21.7	65.2	13.0	100.0
Transport Problems	60.0	40.0	—	100.0
Inflation	22.7	63.6	13.6	100.0
Police Disturbance	—	100.0	—	100.0
Change in Locality of Shop	—	100.0	—	100.0
Other Shopkeepers Disturbance	42.9	42.9	14.3	100.0
Lack of Funds	40.0	60.0	—	100.0
Decline in Purchasing Power	25.0	70.0	5.0	100.0
Too Old	47.7	45.5	6.8	100.0
Health Disturbance	25.0	75.0	—	100.0
Municipal Committee Disturbance	—	100.0	—	100.0
Input Price Increased	40.0	40.0	20.0	100.0
Business split	—	50.0	50.0	100.0
Increase in Petrol Prices	—	100.0	—	100.0
Others	37.0	51.9	11.1	100.0
Total	68.2	116.5	18.8	203.5
RURAL				
Less Demand	12.5	37.5	50.0	100.0
Inflation	—	66.7	33.3	100.0
Police Disturbance	—	100.0	—	100.0
Other Shopkeepers Disturbance	50.0	50.0	—	100.0
Lack of Funds	25.0	25.0	50.0	100.0
Decline in Purchasing Power	—	16.7	83.3	100.0
Too Old	7.7	42.3	50.0	100.0
Health Disturbance	100.0	—	—	100.0
Input Price Increased	—	66.7	33.3	100.0
Business split	—	100.0	—	100.0
GST	—	—	100.0	100.0
Location	—	—	100.0	100.0
Increase in Petrol Prices	—	—	100.0	100.0
Others	10.15	26.3	63.2	100.0
Total	20.5	74.4	110.3	205.1

ANNEXURE III (b)
DISTRIBUTION OF TRANSFER INCOMES

	Average Receipts of the Group				Respective Share		
	Extremely Poor	Poor	Non-Poor	Total	Extremely Poor	Poor	Non-Poor
ALL PAKISTAN							
Boarders or Lodgers	7904	18364	65000	13827	63.6	31.8	4.5
Zakat from Government	897	908	917	904	44.6	46.2	9.2
Zakat from Private Sources	2337	673	1000	1792	66.7	30.6	2.8
Ushr, Fitrana	765	1750	—	952	81.0	19.0	—
Nazrana	445	750	—	492	84.6	15.4	—
Remittances from within Pakistan	20245	30280	48882	28303	51.6	31.3	17.2
Remittances from outside Pakistan	55545	73042	181944	83864	40.0	43.6	16.4
Gifts Assistance	10608	5519	1833	8285	59.5	33.3	7.1
Pension	7950	9334	69100	24103	12.5	62.5	25.0
Total	13050	21934	72044	22235	53.7	36.2	10.1
URBAN							
Boarders or Lodgers	1533	12000	—	4150	75.0	25.0	—
Zakat from Government	300	3333	—	2575	25.0	75.0	—
Zakat from Private Sources	3971	400	1000	3244	77.8	11.1	11.1
Ushr, Fitrana	1300	—	—	1300	100.0	—	—
Nazrana	500	1000	—	667	66.7	33.3	—
Remittances from within Pakistan	1900	24000	—	5583	83.3	16.7	—
Remittances form outside Pakistan	—	10000	—	10000	—	100.0	100.0
Gifts Assistance	5875	5875	1833	5237	42.1	42.1	15.8
Pension	9900	2533	—	4375	25.0	75.0	—
Total	3397	5895	1625	4144	57.4	35.2	7.4
RURAL							
Boarders or Lodgers	8668	18854	65000	14795	62.5	32.5	5.0
Zakat from Government	919	639	917	795	45.9	44.3	9.8
Zakat from Private Sources	1665	700	—	1307	63.0	37.0	—
Ushr, Fitrana	600	1750	—	871	76.5	23.5	—
Nazrana	433	500	—	440	90.0	10.0	—
Remittances from within Pakistan	23521	30611	48882	30653	48.3	32.8	19.0
Remittances form outside Pakistan	55545	75783	181944	85231	40.7	42.6	16.7
Gifts Assistance	12835	5043	—	10803	73.9	26.1	—
Pension	6000	12249	69100	30678	8.3	58.3	33.3
Total	14920	24704	80847	25551	52.8	36.5	10.6

Source: NHDR/PIDE Survey 2001.

ANNEXURE III (c)
OUTMIGRANTS BY ECONOMIC STATUS

	Extremely Poor	Poor	Non-Poor	Total
ALL PAKISTAN				
Average age of migrants (Years)	31	25	28	28
Sex of the migrants (%)				
Male	100.0	87.1	92.2	93.2
Female	—	12.9	7.8	6.8
Marital Status				
Married	65.2	47.3	68.6	58.9
Unmarried	32.6	50.5	31.4	39.4
Others	2.2	2.2	—	1.7
Education level of outmigrant (%)				
No education	48.9	44.1	27.5	42.4
Upto Primary	25.0	17.2	15.7	19.9
Middle	7.6	11.8	7.8	9.3
Matric	10.9	15.1	17.6	14.0
Higher education	7.6	11.8	31.4	14.4
URBAN				
Average age of migrants	39	26	—	36
Sex of the migrants				
Male	100.0	66.7	—	93.8
Female	—	33.3	—	6.3
Marital Status				
Married	76.9	—	—	62.5
Unmarried	23.1	33.3	—	25.0
Others	—	66.7	—	12.5
Education level of outmigrant (%)				
No education	76.9	66.7	—	75.0
Upto Primary	23.1	—	—	18.8
Middle	—	—	—	—
Matric	—	—	—	—
Higher education	—	33.3	—	6.3
RURAL				
Average age of migrants	29	25	28	27
Sex of the migrants				
Male	100.0	87.8	92.2	93.2
Female	—	12.2	7.8	6.8
Marital Status				
Married	63.3	48.9	68.6	58.6
Unmarried	34.2	51.1	31.4	40.5
Others	2.5	—	—	0.9
Education level of outmigrant (%)				
No education	44.3	43.3	27.5	40.0
Upto Primary	25.3	17.8	15.7	20.0
Middle	8.9	12.2	7.8	10.0
Matric	12.7	15.6	17.6	15.0
Higher education	8.9	11.1	31.4	15.0

Source: NHDR/PIDE Survey 2001.

ANNEXURE III (d)
EMPLOYMENT STATUS

Average of Sample	Extremely Poor	Poor	Marginally Non-Poor	Total
ALL PAKISTAN				
Employees				
Regular paid employee with fixed wage	13.4	19.1	30.0	18.6
Casual paid employee	36.9	22.5	13.8	26.6
Paid worker by piece rate of service performed	17.4	14.4	8.9	14.7
Paid non-family enterprise	0.1	0.3	—	0.2
Total	67.8	56.3	52.7	60.1
Employers				
Employer employing less than 10 persons	0.3	0.5	1.8	0.6
Employer employing >= 10 persons	—	—	0.6	0.1
Total	0.3	0.5	2.4	0.7
Independent Workers				
Own account non-agriculture worker	12.5	17.4	19.3	15.8
Own Cultivator	6.3	15.3	19.9	12.6
Share Cropper	11.9	8.2	3.7	8.9
Contract Cultivator	0.5	0.6	0.9	0.6
Total	31.2	41.5	43.8	32.9
Unpaid Family worker	0.3	1.3	1.2	0.9
Others	0.5	0.3	—	0.3
URBAN				
Employees				
Regular paid employee with fixed wage	6.3	9.6	17.4	9.2
Casual paid employee	33.9	28.7	33.3	31.3
Paid worker by piece rate of service performed	31.8	26.3	15.9	27.3
Paid non-family enterprise	0.4	—	—	0.2
Total	72.4	64.6	66.6	68.0
Employers				
Employer employing less than 10 persons	26.4	33.4	30.4	30.3
Employer employing >= 10 persons	—	0.3	2.9	0.5
Total	26.4	33.7	33.3	30.8
Independent Workers				
Own Cultivator	0.8	1.4	—	1.0
Share Cropper	—	0.3	—	0.2
Total	0.8	1.7	—	1.2
Others	0.4	—	—	0.2
RURAL				
Employees				
Regular paid employee with fixed wage	16.4	23.3	33.3	22.5
Casual paid employee	38.3	19.9	8.5	24.8
Paid worker by piece rate of service performed	11.2	9.2	7.0	9.6
Paid non-family enterprise	—	0.4	—	0.2
Total	66.9	52.8	48.8	57.1
Employers				
Employer employing less than 10 persons	0.4	0.6	1.6	0.7
Employer employing >= 10 persons	—	—	0.8	0.1
Total	0.4	0.6	2.4	0.8
Independent Workers				
Own account non-agriculture worker	6.5	10.4	16.3	10.0
Own Cultivator	8.7	21.4	25.2	17.3
Share Cropper	17.0	11.6	4.7	12.4
Total	32.2	43.4	46.2	39.7
Contract Cultivator	0.7	0.9	1.2	0.9
Unpaid Family worker	0.4	1.9	1.6	1.3
Others	0.5	0.4	—	0.4

Source: NHDR/PIDE Survey 2001.

ANNEXURE III (e)
PERCENTAGE DISTRIBUTION OF AGRICULTURAL AND NON-AGRICULTURAL WORKERS BY ECONOMIC STATUS

	Extremely Poor		Poor		Non-Poor		Total	
	Agri.	Non-Agri	Agri.	Non-Agri	Agri.	Non-Agri	Agri.	Non-Agri
Total	62.0	38.0	59.1	40.9	48.2	50.8	57.3	42.7
Male	60.8	39.2	53.5	46.6	46.3	23.0	53.6	46.4
Female	72.1	27.9	85.5	14.5	72.9	27.1	80.2	19.8

Source: NHDR/PIDE Survey 2001.

ANNEXURE III (f)
TYPE OF ENTERPRISES IN RURAL AND URBAN AREAS

Average of Sample	Extremely Poor	Poor	Non-Poor	Total
PAKISTAN				
Farm	40.4	30.3	28.6	33.9
Non-financial, non-farm employing <10 persons	39.8	39.1	29.9	37.9
Non-farm, non-financial establishment employing >= 10 persons	3.7	8.2	11.9	7.0
Financial institutions (banks, insurance company, pension fund)	—	0.1	0.6	0.1
Federal, provincial or local government or defence forces	0.4	6.8	14.5	5.5
Non-profit institutions	0.6	0.5	0.3	0.5
Household (servants)	2.3	1.3	0.6	1.6
Others	12.8	13.8	13.5	13.4
URBAN				
Farm	1.3	1.7	1.5	1.5
Non-financial, non-farm employing <10 persons	57.0	52.1	46.3	53.4
Non-farm, non-financial establishment employing >= 10 persons	8.9	13.4	14.9	11.8
Financial institutions (banks, insurance company, pension fund)	—	0.3	—	0.2
Federal, provincial or local government or defence forces	0.4	3.1	3.0	2.0
Non-profit institutions	1.7	—	—	0.7
Household (servants)	4.6	1.7	3.0	3.0
Others	26.2	27.6	31.3	27.4
RURAL				
Farm	57.2	42.7	35.9	47.0
Non-financial, non-farm employing <10 persons	32.4	33.4	25.5	31.7
Non-farm, non-financial establishment employing >= 10 persons	1.4	5.8	11.2	5.1
Financial institutions (banks, insurance company, pension fund)	—	—	0.8	0.1
Federal, provincial or local government or defence forces	0.4	8.4	17.5	6.9
Non-profit institutions	0.2	0.7	0.4	0.5
Household (servants)	1.3	1.0	—	1.0
Others	7.1	7.8	8.8	7.7

Source: NHDR/PIDE Survey 2001.

ANNEXURE III (g)
TIMELY REPAYMENT OF ALL LOANS BY ECONOMIC STATUS

	Extremely Poor	Poor	Non-Poor	Total
Pakistan	3.3	4.4	9.2	4.9
Urban	—	—	10.0	1.1
Rural	4.0	5.0	9.1	5.4
REASONS				
Pakistan				
Crop Failure	27.6	17.3	17.8	21.1
Enterprise/Shop not making profit	13.8	7.6	4.7	9.3
Expenses on wedding, death, births, etc.	30.0	22.4	23.4	25.3
Business Expansion	5.5	4.7	7.5	5.5
Insufficient funds to repay loan	54.8	49.8	57.0	52.9
Others	15.7	12.6	8.4	13.0
No Response	152.5	185.6	181.3	172.9
Urban				
Crop Failure	5.1	—	—	2.4
Enterprise/Shop not making profit	17.9	10.8	22.2	15.3
Expenses on wedding, death, births, etc.	51.3	45.9	55.6	49.4
Business expansion	7.7	8.1	11.1	8.2
Insufficient funds to repay loan	61.5	59.5	66.7	61.2
Others	23.1	29.7	11.1	24.7
No Response	133.3	145.9	133.3	138.8
Rural				
Crop Failure	32.6	20.0	19.4	24.2
Enterprise/Shop not making profit	12.9	7.1	3.1	8.3
Expenses on wedding, death, births, etc.	25.3	18.8	20.4	21.3
Business expansion	5.1	4.2	7.1	5.0
Insufficient funds to repay loan	53.4	48.3	56.1	51.6
Others	14.0	10.0	8.2	11.0
No Response	156.7	191.7	185.7	178.5

Source: NHDR/PIDE Survey 2001.

ANNEXURE III (h)
SOURCES OF LOANS BY ECONOMIC STATUS

| | The loans obtained from various agencies |||| Distribution of loans of agencies by various categories ||||
	Extremely Poor	Poor	Marginally Non-Poor	Total	Extremely Poor	Poor	Marginally Non-Poor	Total
ALL PAKISTAN								
ADBP	1.0	2.7	5.1	2.5	13.6	50.0	36.4	100.0
Commercial Banks	—	0.2	3.2	0.7	—	16.7	83.3	100.0
NGO	0.3	0.7	1.9	0.8	14.3	42.9	42.9	100.0
Input Supplier	1.9	3.0	4.5	2.9	24.0	48.0	28.0	100.0
Landlord	10.9	4.7	5.1	7.0	55.7	31.1	13.1	100.0
Profit Money Lender	2.2	0.5	1.9	1.4	58.3	16.7	25.0	100.0
Shopkeeper	39.1	37.2	26.1	35.9	39.1	47.8	13.1	100.0
Factory/Mill	0.3	0.7	3.8	1.1	10.0	30.0	60.0	100.0
Commission Agent	1.0	0.5	1.9	0.9	37.5	25.0	37.5	100.0
Friends/Relatives	40.4	49.1	45.9	45.4	31.9	49.9	18.2	100.0
Others	2.9	0.5	0.6	1.4	75.0	16.7	8.3	100.0
Total	100.0	100.0	100.0	100.0	35.9	46.1	18.0	100.0
URBAN								
NGO	—	2.3	—	1.0	—	100.0	—	100.0
Input Supplier	2.2	2.3	—	1.9	50.0	50.0	—	100.0
Profit Money Lender	6.7	4.5	7.1	5.8	50.0	33.3	16.7	100.0
Shopkeeper	8.9	—	14.3	5.8	66.7	—	33.3	100.0
Factory/Mill	—	—	7.1	1.0	—	—	100.0	100.0
Commission Agent	—	—	7.1	1.0	—	—	100.0	100.0
Friends/Relatives	73.3	90.9	64.3	79.6	40.2	48.8	11.0	100.0
Others	8.9	—	—	3.9	100.0	—	—	100.0
Total	100.0	100.0	100.0	100.0	43.7	42.7	13.6	100.0
RURAL								
ADBP	1.1	3.1	5.6	2.9	13.6	50.0	36.4	100.0
Commercial Banks	—	0.3	3.5	0.8	—	16.7	83.3	100.0
NGO	0.4	0.6	2.1	0.8	16.7	33.3	50.0	100.0
Input Supplier	1.9	3.1	4.9	3.0	21.7	47.8	30.4	100.0
Landlord	12.7	5.3	5.6	8.0	55.7	31.1	13.1	100.0
Profit Money Lender	1.5	—	1.4	0.8	66.7	—	33.3	100.0
Shopkeeper	44.2	41.7	27.3	39.9	38.6	48.7	12.7	100.0
Factory/Mill	0.4	0.8	3.5	1.2	11.1	33.3	55.6	100.0
Commission Agent	1.1	0.6	1.4	0.9	42.9	28.6	28.6	100.0
Friends/Relatives	34.8	44.0	44.1	40.8	29.7	50.2	20.1	100.0
Others	1.9	0.6	0.7	1.0	62.5	25.0	12.5	100.0
Total	100.0	100.0	100.0	100.0	34.8	46.5	18.6	100.0

Source: NHDR/PIDE Survey 2001.

ANNEXURE III (i)
REASON FOR REJECTION OF LOAN APPLICATION

	Extremely Poor	Poor	Non-Poor	Total
Reasons for not Applying for Loan				
No need of loan (sufficient funds)	35.5	27.8	39.0	32.6
Don't want to pay interest for religious reasons	42.4	43.6	35.3	41.9
Don't know from where to get a loan form	48.2	44.4	26.6	43.5
Don't believe that people will give me loan	45.3	46.6	29.4	43.7
Service charges/interest rates too high	39.8	47.0	36.7	42.6
Others	15.2	14.3	15.6	14.9
Reasons for Rejection of loan application				
Don't have the collateral	60.0	66.7	75.0	66.7
Limited knowledge and no proper guidance	40.0	33.3	50.0	40.0
Officer/lender asking bribe	20.0	16.7	—	13.3
Previous loan was outstanding	40.0	16.7	25.0	26.7
Others	20.0	16.7	25.0	20.0
No Response	40.0	33.3	100.0	53.3
Total	220.0	233.3	300.0	246.7

Source: NHDR/PIDE Survey 2001.

CHAPTER 5
Annexure I

Growth Nodes for Small Scale Enterprises

ANNEXURE I
GROWTH NODES FOR SMALL SCALE ENTERPRISES

The proposed growth nodes for rural industrialization where the new Industrial Support Centres (ISC's) could be located are as follows:

PUNJAB

(1)	Lahore-Chunian Axis.	Centre: Bhai Pheru.
(2)	Lahore-Sheikhupura Axis.	Centre: Sheikhupura
(3)	Gujranwala-Sialkot Axis.	Centre: Sialkot.
(4)	Rawalpindi-Mianwali Axis.	Centre: Mianwali.
(5)	Bahawalpur-Bahawalnagar Axis.	Centre: Bahawalnagar.

NWFP

(1)	Haripur-Abbottabad Axis and Haripur-Havelian Axis.	Centre: Haripur.
(2)	Islamabad-Nowshera-Peshawar Axis.	Centre: Peshawar.
(3)	Peshawar-Kohat Axis.	Centre: Kohat.

BALOCHISTAN

(1)	Lesbela-Quetta Axis.	Centre: Lesbela.
(2)	Lesbela-Mekran Axis.	Centre: Mekran.

SINDH

(1)	Hyderabad-Nawabshah Axis.	Centre: Nawabshah.
(2)	Nawabshah-Sanghar Axis.	Centre: Sanghar.
(3)	Nawabshah-Larkana Axis.	Centre: Larkana.
(4)	Larkana-Sukkur Axis.	Centre: Sukkur.

ANNEXURE 1
GROWTH MODELS FOR SMALL-SCALE ENTERPRISES